THE GREAT WHITE WAY

The
Great White
Way

A RE-CREATION

OF BROADWAY'S GOLDEN ERA

OF THEATRICAL ENTERTAIN-

MENT **Allen Churchill**

ILLUSTRATED

NEW YORK

E. P. DUTTON & CO., INC. 1962

Library of Congress Catalog Card Number: 62-14717.

CONTENTS

ILLUSTRATIONS

(Following page 152)

Weber and Fields

Edna Wallace Hopper; De Wolf Hopper

Mrs. Leslie Carter

Charles Frohman

Clyde Fitch; Maude Adams

Minnie Maddern Fiske; *The Easiest Way*

Julia Marlowe and E. H. Sothern

Nora Bayes; Frank Bacon

*All photographs courtesy of the New York Public Library
except that of Charles Frohman*

THE GREAT WHITE WAY

1: THE GREAT WHITE WAY

It is the night of November 12, 1900, and a new musical comedy prepares for its opening at the Moorish-turreted Casino Theatre, on the southeast corner of Broadway and Thirty-ninth Street in New York.

Florodora is its name—though a million misspellings over years to come will try desperately to persuade the world that it is really *Floradora*. Like most musical shows of this turn-of-the-century time (and a large number of dramatic productions), *Florodora* is an import from London, where it has been a considerable success. Book and lyrics are from the accomplished pen of Owen Hall, who has previously written *The Gaiety Girl*, *The Geisha*, and *An Artist's Model*. Of these *The Geisha*, presented in this country in 1896, was the first American production ever to be labeled a musical comedy; up to that point in history musicals were either operettas or musical farces. *Florodora's* lilting melodies—they are certain to be this considering the source—come from Leslie Stuart, who has provided lightsome tunes for other musical successes. He has also composed a rousing military number called "Soldiers of the Queen," which is so popular that it has been dubbed England's new national air.

Finally, the star of *Florodora* is diminutive Edna Wallace Hopper, a sweet singer, graceful dancer, and mischievously al-

3

luring to look upon. Yet with all this, the chief claim to fame of this five-foot bundle of charm is that for a time she was Mrs. De Wolf Hopper, wife of the popular comedian-singer. De Wolf Hopper stands a well-proportioned six-foot-four, with a voice of diapason sonorousness. During their brief marriage, he and his dainty wife made a very incongruous couple indeed.

In all, *Florodora* promises exceedingly well, and members of the first-night audience are prepared to be most thoroughly entertained. Already holders of orchestra or box seats for the opening are alighting from two-wheel, high-perch hansom cabs, four-wheel closed carriages, open victorias, or other horse-drawn vehicles. One or two wealthy couples—hardly more—may chug up in new horseless carriages of a make like Pope-Hartford. Or perhaps a stick-steered Brewster electric brougham which, in addition to being totally silent, seems more dependable than a gas-driven buggy. But automobiles are not yet deemed trustworthy enough to arrive at the proper destination at the right time. Further, the frequent explosions of exhausts frighten horses, while the trusty chauffeur who dozes contentedly as his employer attends the theatre or opera has yet to make an appearance on the American scene.

Most of the people who step from the horse-drawn conveyances under the Casino marquee are in evening dress—the white silk scarfs and shiny silk hats of the gentlemen indicating that under the black overcoats are the dazzling shirt fronts of white-tie-and-tails or the more informal dinner coat. Over décolleté gowns the ladies keep out the cold with ermine and sables, faces framed by high, luxurious collars. Peeping out beneath long fur coats are the long skirts decreed by current fashion. "The proper skirt length is just showing the tip of the shoe," an oracle has just stated. On top of elaborate piled-high coiffures, some women wear hats which flaunt ostrich plumes and egret feathers. Inside the theatre these ladies will steadfastly refuse to take off the hats until requested to do so. "Madame, will you please remove your hat?" is a catchword of the era.

First-night audiences in turn-of-the-century New York invariably dress elegantly, but at the Casino there is a special reason for chic. The auditorium of this ornate theatre is on the second floor, so that ticket holders mount a wide, plush-carpeted flight of marble stairs. (Holders of second balcony—or gallery—seats are sent around the corner to another entrance.) Thus, after ascending the splendid stairway to be seated, the elegantly dressed folk descend at intermission time, while the gentleman puffs his Between the Acts. After the final curtain, they descend again—and those who have reached the lobby usually pause to look back at those on the stairway.

Though this first-night crowd is especially resplendent, succeeding audiences will be almost as much so. For playgoers of the time firmly believe that going to a theatre calls for ceremony. Orchestra and box seats may cost two dollars or a dollar-fifty and balcony seats one dollar or fifty cents, with the gallery even less, but to a world not yet exposed to the distractions of motion pictures, radio, or television, a night at the play (or vaudeville) is the only possible method of real entertainment. Hence a night in a theatre seat is to be richly cherished, and many holders of orchestra seats invariably appear in evening clothes and décolleté, no matter how long a play has been running. Some have just finished a roast beef dinner at Delmonico's or Sherry's, and after the theatre will sit down before a bird-and-bottle supper at one of the dozen or more lobster palaces along the Great White Way. It all adds up to audiences of whom one actress fondly remembers: "What a magnificent sight it was from the stage in those days! The women wore gorgeous evening gowns and the men were always in formal attire, their white shirts and waistcoats gleaming in the darkness. And I shall never forget the wave of perfume that wafted across the footlights to us on the stage. How happily we basked in it!"

Prominent among those ushered to seats at *Florodora's* Casino Theatre premiere are the inveterate first-nighters Diamond Jim Brady and his pretty companion Edna McCauley, offspring of a Brooklyn cop; Stanford White, *bon vivant* and architect-creator of the Madison Square Garden and the Washington Square Arch; Richard Harding Davis, world-famous journalist and virile inspiration to the young, recently become a playwright himself; Oscar Hammerstein, the impressive impresario whose Opera House gives strenuous competition to the Metropolitan; Harry Von Tilzer, successful composer of such popular songs as "Wait Till the Sun Shines, Nellie," "Bird in a Gilded Cage," and "Down Where the Wurzburger Flows"; millionaire Jesse Lewisohn; social titans Mrs. Stuyvesant Fish and Mrs. Herman Oelrichs; restaurateur Louis Sherry; Tammany chieftain Richard "Boss" Croker; publisher William Randolph Hearst with a pretty girl on either arm; criminal lawyer Abraham Hummel; and the millionaire James R. Keene.

Like others in the audience, these celebrated folk probably enter the Casino believing *Florodora* the name of a pretty girl— what else could it be? But the rising of the curtain shows otherwise. *Florodora*, it develops, is a mythical island somewhere in the Philippines. (In the second act a startling jump takes the locale to Wales.)

Yet there are pretty girls involved in *Florodora*, even if one of them does not bear the lovely name. The most important girl in the show is named Dolores and she is the daughter of the recently deceased owner of a factory which manufactures a perfume also known as "Florodora." On the death of Dolores' father this gentle industry has been rudely usurped by an uncouth American (England still distrusted the United States). As a result Dolores lives in unhappy poverty on a Florodora farm. The American's name is Cyrus Gilfain and he too has a daughter.

Her name is Angela and she has been accompanied to the isle of Florodora by vivacious Lady Holyrood (Edna Wallace Hopper), an English widow in antic quest of a mate.

Also in the cast, with the weighty responsibility of returning the perfume factory to rightful-owner Dolores, is a Scotland Yard detective disguised as an itinerant hypnotist and phrenologist. Back at Scotland Yard, this worthy is deferred to as Captain Arthur Donegal, but it is typical of both the times and of *Florodora* that his name-in-disguise is Arthur Tweedlepaunch. The funniest scene of the evening arrives when Tweedlepaunch, robustly interpreted by comedian Willie Edouin, performs a violin solo in which the violin gradually falls to pieces in his hands.

Florodora's premiere comes at a time when next-morning reviews by dramatic critics sometimes run to 5000 words. Most renowned of aisle-sitters is William Winter of the *New York Tribune*, who sometimes exceeds this number. After a major opening—say, of E. H. Sothern in *Hamlet*—Mr. Winter's cogent essay of evaluation may stretch to 8000 tight-packed words. In commenting on *Florodora* the day after, New York reviewers do not travel to such extremes, but they do report that solos, duets, and trios are scattered throughout in zestful abandon. Specifically, they hail such melodies as "Under the Shade of the Palms," "I've an Inkling," "Queen of the Philippine Isles," and the rip-roaring "I Want To Be a Military Man." "It is all sparkling music, with a rhythm that inspires a sort of muscular participation," one reviewer opines. Another pays left-handed tribute by objecting to the number of encores. "The management should allow fewer of these," he complains. "The practice is wearing and delays too long the hour of retiring."

In all, newspaper critics highly approve the Leslie Stuart music and the settings, which cost an unusual $20,000. The plot is called weak and farfetched. Oddly, no critic fully rises to the challenge offered by a brief scene built around a gentle tune called "Tell Me, Pretty Maiden." To the first easy strains of this, six girls trip from one side of the Casino stage. Each is identical in height and weight, attired in matching black ostrich-plume hats and frilly pink walking costumes, with parasols gracefully over shoulders. Simultaneously, six exceedingly handsome young men in gray frock coats and gray top hats saunter from the other side of the stage. Politely doffing silk toppers, the young gentlemen melodically inquire, "*Tell me, pretty maiden, are there any more at home like you?*" In charming unison, the six pretty maidens chorus back, "*There are a few, kind sir, and pretty girls and proper, too.*"

Gaily and decorously this fetching number continues, and on exiting at its end, each of the young parasol-carrying maidens tosses a nod, a smile, and a wink to the audience. This last provides the fire that provokes flame. Intimate informality of this sort has heretofore been unknown in musical comedy—usually girls of the chorus smile brightly over the heads of audiences. As the full impact of the nods and winks strikes the audience, handclaps and cheers burst from the orchestra seats, while from the depths of first and second balconies come a few whistles. Rapidly the Double Sexette appears for an encore, and before this delightful number concludes the kind-sirs and pretty-maidens are summoned back ten times. Never during any of the subsequent 505 performances of *Florodora* in New York does this number sink below six.

The *Florodora* Double Sextette seizes the imagination of New York in a manner that is still legendary. Though the six handsome gentlemen perform a necessary function in the song, it is the lovely girls who become the toasts-of-the-town. "They are goddesses, the first of their class to immortalize the chorus girl," one critic states in fulsome tribute to the damsels. The Florodora Girls are instantly hailed as the most beautiful females of all time.

Men about Manhattan like portly Diamond Jim, redheaded Stanford White, and the jaded playboy Freddie Gebhard next day send to the box office, reserving seats at the Casino on a long-term basis. Nightly these and other Good-Time-Charlies slip into aisle seats just before the "Tell Me, Pretty Maiden" number, departing immediately after the final encore. Of Stanford White it is said that he is able to sit through forty consecutive performances before growing weary of the pretty maidens. Freddie Gebhard does better. After a suitable aisle-seat apprenticeship he marries one of the six Florodora Girls.

Everything about *Florodora*—and perhaps about Broadway at this moment—pales into insignificance beside the tremendous good fortune of the Sextette beauties. On the night *Florodora* opens the six receive a sparse twenty-five dollars a week, from which is deducted money for high-heel shoes and stockings provided (but not paid for) by the management. At the end of "Tell Me, Pretty Maiden" the six have become the most sought-after girls on Broadway, rising in the space of an encore from the twenty-five-dollar-a-week class to the millionaire bracket— in the matter of companionship at least. For in time the six original girls all marry millionaires, and in several cases the millions are attached to a resounding English title. All the Florodora Girls seem beautiful, but two are applauded as surpassingly so. One is Vaughn Texsmith, who has cleverly contrived a stage name by combining her own with that of her native state. The other is Marie Wilson, who almost overnight grosses $750,000 from stock tips bestowed on her by a Morgan-partner admirer. It is this astute and winsome young lady who becomes Mrs. Freddie Gebhard.

Even so, stock tips are the least fascinating of the attentions lavished on the Florodora Girls. Ropes of pearls, fur coats, riding horses, and town houses are pressed upon them by wealthy admirers. Picking up bouquets tossed over the foot-

lights, the girls often find jewels imbedded in the flowers. At
the stage door millionaires await the girls each night. "They
came in broughams—there were few motorcars handy in those
days—and they came in tails and white ties, and it was always a
scream to go out to see which man was coming for which girl,"
Edna Wallace Hopper recalls.

No other Broadway beauties—not even those of *Ziegfeld
Follies* to come—enjoy the mad whirl bestowed on the Florodora
Girls. From the nightly crush of beseeching millionaires at the
Casino stage door, three of the original six quickly winnow hus-
bands or wealthy protectors, disappearing (as someone has said)
into the pleasant oblivion of wealth and retirement. So begins a
series of Sextette replacements. Yet Florodora Girls are not hard
to find. Nearly every good-looking girl along the Great White
Way dreams of becoming a member of the glorious group, if only
for enough nights to pick a rich admirer. In all, the turnover
among Florodora Girls is so great that in slightly over a year no
less than seventy-three Broadway beauties get a chance to live
the effervescent, champagne life of the girls who respond to the
words "Tell Me, Pretty Maiden."

At the turn-of-the-century moment of the *Florodora* Sextette,
New York was a picturesque metropolis.

By day, its wide, tree-lined avenues were filled with a stream
of hansom cabs, drivers perched high on the rear seats of these
curious vertical vehicles. Open victorias (gravy-boat shaped),
closed carriages (funereal), horseless chuggers, or electrics completed the traffic on New York's stately thoroughfares. On streets
leading off the main avenues traffic was usually desultory, permitting children to play. Those who walked seemed—by later
standards—to stroll. The city's vast army of newsboys may have
shouted "Wuxtra!" through all hours of the day and night, and
cruelty may have been a frequent sight on streets as drivers of

wagons harshly whipped horses across quivering flanks. In East Side slums and West Side Hell's Kitchen children may have gone hungry, unschooled, and uncared for. But on the surface New York seemed an altogether pleasant city.

It was not always a quiet city, except along Fifth, Madison, Park, and Lexington Avenues, or the better residential streets. The town's centers of activity were loud with the tumult of now-forgotten sounds. The shattering rumble of Elevated trains was heard from tracks above Sixth, Third, and other utilitarian avenues. Major street intersections were a bewildering criss-cross of trolley tracks, and often the trolleys ran directly under the El, adding their own individual clamor to the roar from above. On Broadway, Twenty-third Street, Forty-second, Fifty-ninth, Canal—almost every important artery—the insistent clang of the trolley bell mingled with the shouts of the drivers of delivery wagons, to create vast confusion and din.

Of course, the rich had it best. To the social Four Hundred, life-in-the-season offered a succession of splendid dinners at Delmonico's, cotillions at Sherry's, costume balls with *tableaux vivants* at the Waldorf Astoria (newly opened at Fifth Avenue and Thirty-fourth Street), and dances in Fifth Avenue mansions which resembled French châteaux. Monday evenings were the special province of society at the Metropolitan Opera House, where Nordica, Jean de Reszke (his final season), Nellie Melba, Schumann-Heink, Gadski, and Antonio Scotti sang as stars. (In 1903, they would be joined by a newcomer named Enrico Caruso.)

A widely publicized sporting set found life even more enjoyable. To the red-blooded man who preferred bird-bottle-and-girl midnight suppers to Fifth Avenue cotillions, New York offered endless delights. The husband who dared to leave his wife at home—and in double-standard days what sporting man did not!— was free to dabble in a city offering fantastic varieties of pleasure. Its depths lay in the accomplished depravities of the Tenderloin dance halls like the Haymarket, here to be found the youngest and prettiest of the city's twenty-five thousand girls-for-hire, while outside (clogging the sidewalks along Broadway from Twenty-third to Thirty-fourth Street) a legion of streetwalkers plied their trade. No passing male was safe from the importunate cry, "It costs a dollar and I've got the room."

Beside this was the rare luxury of the Broadway and Madison Square hotels—Hoffman House, Gilsey House, St. James, Holland House, Brunswick, Martinique, and two dozen others. The stimulating possibilities open to the sporting gentry was plainly visible at the new and luxurious Waldorf Astoria. Here a man could drink copiously with other men at the Men's Bar. Only a few steps away was the scandalous Peacock Alley, where dewy-eyed maidens invitingly dropped handkerchiefs when a prosperous-looking man walked by.

Along a two-mile stretch—mainly along Broadway, but also along Sixth and Seventh Avenues and on side streets—ran a world-famous theatre district. Indeed, New York with forty-one legitimate theatres possessed more than any other city in the world, for London had only thirty-nine and Paris twenty-four. Officially, the theatre district began at Twenty-third Street and continued up Broadway and side streets as far north as the Casino, the beautiful Empire Theatre at Broadway and Fortieth Street, and the Broadway Theatre at Forty-first. Between these extremes were to be found such playhouses as Palmer's, Garrick, Wallack's, Daly's, Harrigan's, Imperial, Majestic, Savoy, Park, Weber and Fields Music Hall, Knickerbocker, Standard, Star, and a host of others.

From Twenty-third to Thirty-fourth Street, New York's celebrated theatres (many twenty or thirty years old) ran like a string of pearls through the blackhearted Tenderloin. But

with Thirty-fourth Street, Broadway began a transformation
into the Great White Way. As dusk fell, lights from theatre
marquees snapped on, joining with the Metropolitan Opera
House, Hammerstein's vaudeville Victoria, and the blazing
windows of the great lobster palaces to turn night into mazda
day as far north as Captain Churchill's restaurant on Forty-ninth
Street. Diamond Jim Brady, a man capable of sentiment as well
as able to consume a barrel of oysters at a sitting, one night
stepped out of a restaurant into Broadway's full dazzle and
found himself coining a phrase in tribute. "The Street of the
Midnight Sun," he called it. . . .

Aware of the fact or not, playgoers attending Great White
Way theatres, together with the hundreds of thousands seeing
plays more prosaically on the cross-country Road, were observing a period of transition in the American theatre. An established order was fading, opening the way for the new. Since
the end of the Civil War the great theatregoing public had
seemed eager to watch the same actors in Shakespearean repertory or appearing over and over again in the same (or similar)
modern plays. Actors like Edwin Booth, Joseph Jefferson (in
Rip Van Winkle), Lawrence Barrett ("An actor sculptures in
snow," this clever fellow once remarked), Helena Modjeska,
Clara Morris, James O'Neill (*The Count of Monte Cristo*),
Fanny Kemble, Dion Boucicault, Charlotte Cushman, John
McCullough—all these were content to establish a role, then
keep it in lifetime repertory. "They preferred to pasture, rather
than pioneer," a thoughtful critic wrote.

In addition, the plays in which the pasturing was done were
usually long, often five or six acts. As a great star grew older, or
thoroughly familiar with a role, he might begin to act only for
what the profession called *points*—that is, coast along until the
best scenes, or what he considered his best scenes. Then he tore
loose, wrenching passion to tatters. Having made this point, he

would lapse back until the next big moment arrived. Audiences as well as actors became aware of the point system and patiently waited for the big scenes.

"The player, not the play, is the thing," one critic paraphrased. But now the titans had begun to vanish into death or retirement. Nor were great actors the only ones departing the theatre scene. In New York, the two top managers, Lester Wallack and A. M. Palmer, were gone. Augustin Daly, who believed in company playing as opposed to the star system, was losing his hold on the actors he refused to publicize above one another. John Drew, his most polished male actor, had left him to become a star under the banner of another producer. Without her leading man Ada Rehan, Daly's famous lady actress, seemed at a loss. From now on, acting to her, in the words of a caustic commentator, would seem more of a duty than a pleasure.

With old-line producers and old-line stars losing their hold, it seemed the play might now become the thing. Indeed, several American plays had already been tremendously successful. Steele Mackaye's *Hazel Kirke*, a play so sweet it had no villain, played 486 performances in New York City, after which ten different companies simultaneously performed it on the Road. Bronson Howard wrote *Shenandoah*, which rose to a climax as General Phil Sheridan (played by Henry Miller) dashed across the stage astride a horse. Lottie Parker Benjamin's *Way Down East*, a play about New England types, featured a cow on the stage and played year after successful year.

The most talked-about new producer of the time was Charles Frohman, who consistently favored plays from England, by English playwrights. Frohman's nearest rival in producing was steadfastly American in his outlook, but he was a curious native son, nonetheless. His name was David Belasco, and over the past twenty-five years he had risen from boy-around-theatres in his native San Francisco, to Davido the Circus-Boy Wonder, to a precocious Uncle Tom in *Uncle Tom's Cabin*, to a top West Coast playwright, to an important theatrical personality in New York. A man with a knack for lurid melodrama, he had first won notice in the East as a playwright-director at the important Madison Square Theatre. Belasco was co-author of *The Girl I Left Behind Me*, the first presentation at Frohman's beautiful Empire Theatre, and author of *Men and Women*, *Pawn Ticket 210* (the ticket redeemed a baby), *Lord Chumley*, and *The Wife*. However, Belasco would never remain content with merely writing plays; every aspect of the theatre burned in his blood. Of him, William Winter would eventually write: "In all my study of theatre history, I have not encountered a person more downright daft, saturated in every fibre of his being, with passion for the stage and things dramatic." Belasco himself followed through on this by always referring to the theatre as "My adored calling."

Yet anyone observing Belasco on a Broadway sidewalk during one of his infrequent excursions outside the walls of a playhouse would hardly think him such a man. Rather, he looked like a priest on a meditative stroll. Carrying through on his love of the deeply dramatic, Belasco had early made a momentous decision. The best backdrop for his rich personality, he concluded, was the severe, white-collared garb of the Catholic priest. Not quite daring to wear actual priestly attire, he successfully gave the impression by reversing his stand-up collar and affecting what was then called a Stanley necktie (or ascot) which, when ironed flat, resembled a clerical bib. Belasco was a short man, with eyes brooding and soulful ("the eyes of a woman of genius," it had been said), thick eyebrows, and a sensitive mouth. Above the dramatically white turn-around collar, his square face was milk-pale, topped with a picturesque mane of silvery hair, the forelock of which drooped over a high forehead. His favorite and almost constant gesture was to tug at this lock of hair.

Belasco's manner was that of a man gently tolerant of the world and its foibles. His voice was orotund and theatrical, his gestures benign and fatherly, the liquid eyes brimming with human understanding. But it was all highly misleading. Beneath the mellow mantle of white-maned benevolence Belasco was a better actor than most of those with whom he came into daily contact. The true man was wily, self-centered, and lecherous, a determined despoiler of would-be ingenues. It was widely believed (though never proven) that a requisite for any Belasco leading lady was that she double as the priestly looking man's number-one mistress.

In 1900—and indeed forever after—Belasco's most celebrated protégée was a flame-haired belle named Mrs. Leslie Carter. Over recent seasons the Great White Way had watched fascinated while an unusual relationship developed between these two. Like Belasco, Mrs. Carter could look back upon a full life. Born Caroline Louise Dudley, in Louisville, she had at an early age captured the romantic interest of Leslie Carter, an elderly Chicago millionaire whose fortune stemmed from Carter's Little Liver Pills. They married, but shortly a life of bountiful wealth palled on the Kentucky queen. According to her husband, she took a series of lovers, one of them the dashing matinee-idol actor Kyrle Bellew.

Leslie Carter sued for divorce; his wife countered. *The New York Times* branded the resulting trial "The most indecent and revolting ever heard in a Chicago court." Leslie Carter won, at which Mrs. Carter found herself alone in a hostile world with no one but her mother at her side. Possibly because of dalliance with Kyrle Bellew, she decided that her next step should be the stage. Accordingly, she sought out David Belasco, asking him to teach her to act. The first meeting between the two gave no hint of wonders to come. Belasco was unsure of the prospects

of a woman who was both notorious and theatrically inexperi-
enced, for he firmly believed that only those who dreamed of the
theatre from childhood could succeed at it. "One cannot begin
to dream too soon if one expects to transform the dream into
reality," he was fond of saying. Mrs. Carter did little to allay
such doubts. Asked if she desired to enact comedy or tragedy,
she responded flashingly, "I am a horsewoman and I should like
to make my first entrance on horseback, jumping a high fence."

Belasco politely ushered the lady out, but she returned. Now
she fell to her knees to vow, "If being hurt by people can make
me act, I can act." Belasco weakened and agreed to become her
mentor. If Mrs. Carter anticipated a pleasant period of guidance,
she was much mistaken. Belasco proved to be the harshest of
taskmasters. "Mrs. Carter was an amateur and very crude," he
recalled later. "She was full of mannerisms, a society woman
without any knowledge whatsoever of the stage. I first taught
her how to walk . . . showing her for hours how to enter a room."

He next discovered that, like many beginners, she was afraid
of the sound of her own voice. He drilled her endlessly in the
rendition of dramatic poems, together with one-act plays like
The Conjugal Lesson. Four times daily he paused portentously
to hear her recite the Second Player's Speech from *Hamlet,* the
six lines of which he considered a particular test of diction.
Gradually Belasco became more specific, training her in scenes
from well-known plays. Here he used absolute realism. Years
later he reputedly jabbed a hatpin into the derrière of an actress,
making her emit a proper scream for the climax of one of his
plays. Now, rehearsing Mrs. Carter in a scene from *Oliver
Twist,* he "dragged her around by the hair, just as Bill Sykes
dragged Nancy. I would hit her head on the floor and haul her
around until she reached the proper pitch and could express just
what she felt."

Finally Mrs. Carter appeared ready. The first production in which Belasco starred her was *The Ugly Duckling*. "As outstanding as a lighthouse, but less subtle," one critic said of her performance. Others, however, thought her promising and all admired the glowing fire-red hair which when set free (this happened at least once in all her plays) tumbled down to her knees. One scribe found her hair a shade hotter than Titian.

Mrs. Carter was never a beauty. Her mouth and nose were too prominent. But she had striking gray-green eyes and a restless, lissome grace. Further, she seemed able to dominate a stage. Belasco decided to proceed and for her wrote *The Heart of Maryland*. In this, Mrs. Carter was cast as heroine Maryland Calvert. The handsome hero was played by Maurice Barrymore, who offstage was the father of three growing youngsters named Lionel, Ethel, and John. At the climax of *The Heart of Maryland*, Mrs. Carter mounted to the top of a forty-foot bell tower and, grasping the clapper of the bell, swung back and forth against a Civil War landscape. With the bell thus silenced, Maurice Barrymore, as a Northern soldier unjustly accused of spying, was able to escape. This stunning theatrical tour de force was rooted in Belasco's boyhood worship of the poem "Curfew Shall Not Ring Tonight." *The Heart of Maryland* was Belasco's first hit as a producer. It was also a personal triumph for Mrs. Carter. As the two took repeated curtain calls, soaking up the applause which meant fame and fortune, Belasco bent to whisper in her ear. "Do you know what this means?" he asked. "It means that never-never-never again shall we have to eat in a Third Avenue restaurant!"

In 1900 David Belasco was forty-two—or was his age forty or forty-four? (The picturesque man swore he could not remember such trivial facts.) *The Heart of Maryland* had been presented in England, where critic George Bernard Shaw disliked the play but approved Mrs. Carter's skills. Now Belasco was offer-

ing her in *Zaza*, wherein a Paris courtesan finds redemption in
contact with her lover's clear-eyed child. *Zaza* was a sinful play
for the times, adding spice to the gossip about Belasco and Mrs.
Carter. With such a ravishing creature at his side, Belasco seemed
more capable than ever of making mistresses of all his stars. He
and Mrs. Leslie Carter, Broadway firmly believed, offstage led a
tempestuous, sin-drenched existence. But could Broadway be
wrong? Certainly any relationship between two fiery personalities must be tempestuous. But was it sin-drenched? Mrs.
Carter lived with her mother in the Fifth Avenue Hotel on
Madison Square, and most nights after *Zaza*, Belasco could be
seen escorting her home. After an interval—far too short to be
sin-drenched—he reappeared, waving from the sidewalk to Mrs.
Carter as she stood in the window of her suite. Then he prosaically mounted a Broadway trolley car and rode to his quarters in
the theatre district.

Such was the Broadway of 1900. Its great successes were Julia
Marlowe in *Barbara Frietchie*, by Clyde Fitch; William Gillette
in his own adaptation of *Sherlock Holmes*; *Ben Hur*, with Wil-
liam Farnum and William S. Hart; Richard Mansfield in *Dr.
Jekyll and Mr. Hyde;* John Drew in *Richard Carvel*, with Ida
Conquest; James A. Herne in *Sag Harbor*, with a beginning
Lionel Barrymore; and the musicals *Fiddle-Dee-Dee* with De
Wolf Hopper and Fay Templeton, and Alice Nielsen in *The
Singing Girl*.

Now in November came *Florodora*, with its first-night audi-
ences free after the gay opening to continue on to the Café
Martin, Shanley's (on the site of the present Paramount
Theatre), Reisenweber's, Café Metropole, Café Boulevard,
Bustanoby's, Churchill's, the Astor, Murray's A La Carte, and
other Great White Way playgrounds. Though many of those

who arrived in these fashionable cafés and lobster palaces had already enjoyed a full pre-theatre dinner at Delmonico's or Sherry's, they did not hesitate to partake of a midnight supper which might consist of cocktails, lobster (or perhaps planked steak), wine, salad, more wine, ices, champagne, demitasse, and a settling cordial.

Tonight the better-known members of the *Florodora* audience—together with a backstage contingent of at least Edna Wallace Hopper, Willie Edouin, and the newly famous girls of the Sextette—would follow the example of rotund Diamond Jim Brady by traveling four blocks uptown to the lobster palace known as Rector's. This was the Sardi's—and infinitely more—of its time. Housed in a yellow-fronted building between Forty-third and Forty-fourth Streets on Longacre Square (it would not be Times Square until the Times Building opened four years hence), Rector's was so famous that no name was needed on its façade. Only the illuminated figure of a griffin—that peculiar agglomerate animal with the body of a seated lion, forked tail of a devil, eagle's head, and perked-up collie ears—hung suspended over its mid-block entrance. Rector's had opened only a year before, offering not only excellent food (emphasis on lobsters), but the first revolving door the city had ever seen. On opening day a knot of timid folk gathered to study this strange new object. No one dared push through to enter until Gentleman Jim Corbett, heavyweight champion of the world turned successful actor, rounded the corner and boldly revolved his way inside.

"I found Broadway a quiet little lane of ham and eggs in 1899 and left it a full-blown avenue of lobsters, champagne, and morning-afters," George Rector once declared proudly. Again he quipped, "When Broadway sought to sleep, I turned night into daze." Both statements were true. It was hard to imagine the Great White Way without Rector's, which was called

Broadway's Supreme Court of Triviality, Cathedral of Froth,
Bourse of Gossip, and Clearing House of Rumors. No theatrical
triumph was complete unless followed by an after-theatre appearance at Rector's. Actors, society playboys, Wall Street
plungers, prizefighters, opera singers, gamblers, playwrights,
songwriters, jockeys, explorers, journalists, statesmen, theatrical
impresarios, polo players, visiting Englishmen—all these nightly
crowded inside.

Ceiling-high mirrors covered the walls of Rector's. The décor
was Louis XIV, colors green and gold. There were one hundred
tables downstairs and seventy-five upstairs (Siberia, a wit called
this unfashionable region), together with four private dining
rooms. Table linen was imported from Belfast, with the famed
griffin interwoven in the fabric. In such surroundings (on New
Year's Eve the place was festooned with American flags) could
be seen the genius, beauty, and talent of America. Seated unobtrusively at one Rector table on any midnight might be the
gnomelike writer who called himself O. Henry. At another table
would be the far more conspicuous figure of the best-selling
novelist David Graham Phillips. In Rector's one night Phillips
observed a swan-necked Broadway butterfly sprinkling perfume
on lumps of sugar, then contentedly munching the lumps. After
that, what could Phillips do but make the girl the heroine of a
novel—which he did!

Society at Rector's might be represented by Reginald Vanderbilt, Alfred Gwynne Vanderbilt, the dandified E. Berry Wall,
polo-playing Larry Waterbury, and Freddie Gebhard. Novelists
and playwrights might include Booth Tarkington, Rex Beach,
Eugene Field, George Ade. The two best-looking young men
in the establishment would certainly be the journalist-novelist-
playwright Richard Harding Davis and Charles Dana Gibson,
the popular artist of the day. Gibson had not only created the
Gibson Girl, that paragon of female poise and loveliness, but

had used his friend Davis as the model for the strong-jawed
Gibson man who was the Gibson Girl's beau ideal.

Yet any after-midnight gathering at Rector's would be pre-
dominantly theatrical. "While others paid to see stars of the
theatre," George Rector said, "the stars paid to see Rector's."
Actors, working late, were prepared to dine after work, while
other Rector patrons supped—to the rest of the world the lobster
palace was a place to see and be seen, but actors truly needed
Rector's. As a consequence there were always numerous theatre
personalities visible. On this night in November 1900, Sarah
Bernhardt might be there, for the great French tragedienne, who
at the age of seventy could play girls of twenty, was appearing
in New York in *La Dame Aux Camellias*, *L'Aiglon*, *La Tosca*,
and other repertory. Dining with her might be the French male
star Benoit Coquelin, who was appearing with Bernhardt and
also starring in his famous French version of *Cyrano de Bergerac*.
From England might come Ellen Terry and Sir Henry Irving.
So might beauteous Lily Langtry, since the celebrated Jersey
Lily was tentatively testing America's two-a-day vaudeville.
Also Herbert Beerbohm Tree, smarting under a devastating
three-line demolition of his recent interpretation of Shylock.
"Shylock as Mr. Tree," critic John Palmer wrote.

Still, domestic actors far outnumbered distinguished visitors
from overseas. Reflected in Rector's mirrors might be the fami-
liar-to-playgoers faces of John Drew, Richard Mansfield, Kyrle
Bellew, Eddie Foy, Henry Miller, Raymond Hitchcock, Maurice
Barrymore, William Collier, Henry E. Dixey, William Gillette,
Francis Wilson, James O'Neill, James A. Herne, Wilton Lackaye, Nat Goodwin, David Warfield, Chauncey Olcott, James K.
Hackett, and many others. At one table might be Victor Herbert, Broadway composer on the way up. At another, Paul
Dresser ("On the Banks of the Wabash," "My Gal Sal"), Broad-
way composer on the way down. With Dresser might be his

young brother Theodore, who had never bothered to change his name from Dreiser. At another table might be Reginald De Koven, composer of *Robin Hood* with its haunting "O, Promise Me." With him might be collaborators Rennold Wolf and Harry B. Smith.

Seated with the men at Rector's would be the beautiful girls (and women) of the Great White Way. Since Rector's catered to a compact sporting and theatre set, there was much interchange of feminine friends among regulars. Arriving wih a new wife or sweetheart, a Rector male might well find himself seated beside an old wife or sweetheart. Back home after an arduous trip to the Klondike, Wilson Mizner took a long look around Rector's mirrored dining room. "Same old faces," he muttered finally, "only they're paired off differently."

Mixed with the nightly familiar faces would be an exciting vermouth of new, pretty ones. For many males inevitably were accompanied by Broadway butterflies, young girls from the stage doors, hotel lobbies, or even the pavements, who for a bottle-and-bird supper at Rector's would cheerfully leap into bed with the man who paid for it all. A popular joke of the day had one Broadway butterfly saying to another, "I got a pearl out of an oyster at Rector's." To which the other girl replies, "That's nothing, I got a whole diamond necklace out of a lobster." To such girls Rector's had a unique distinction—it was the peak of the primrose path. To reach it was to reach the summit of the Great White Way. No girl could possibly rise higher.

To the Broadway butterfly, Rector's was an overpowering place. But to the famous beauties of the day—and Broadway had so many!—it was just another stage on which to make an entrance. To see Frankie Bailey, possessor of the most perfect legs in America, make her nightly appearance at Rector's was to see feminine success and vanity at its apex. In 1900 gorgeous Frankie turned up after a night's labor in the musical comedy *Whirl-i-gig*, where she appeared in geranium-colored tights and stockings. Frankie Bailey's utterly symmetrical limbs were so famous that at the turn of the century women's legs were not called legs but Frankie Baileys. Said a wit of the day, "Frankie Bailey gets two rounds of applause every time she appears on a stage—one for each leg." At Rector's, Miss Bailey (as well as other beauties) posed dramatically on the threshold, waiting for the violinist from the gypsy orchestra to establish himself at the foot of her train. Only then was the maître d' permitted to lead her to a table, with the violinist following after, serenading her softly.

Similar ceremony was accorded the entrance of the saucy French singer Anna Held. Her legs, too, were dazzling—so much so that a critic had accused them of causing sexual unrest. Together with dazzling legs, petite Anna Held boasted an eighteen-inch waist. Still, it was her eyes which really provoked the unrest. To males who saw her on the stage Anna Held's eyes, wide open or winking, seemed to extend an open invitation to French frivolity, especially during the song, "I Just Can't Make My Eyes Behave." Her other famous numbers, delivered in fetching Gallic accent, were "Won't You Come and Play Wiz Me?" and "It's Delightful To Be Married." Anna Held was currently appearing at the Herald Square Theatre in the trifle *Papa's Wife*, which abounded in bare legs and naughty humor. The producer of *Papa's Wife* was Miss Held's new husband Florenz Ziegfeld, and in offering his wife in such a daring epic, Ziegfeld was going contrary to the advice of George Lederer, dean of Broadway's girl-show producers. Said Lederer, "A girl's limbs are pretty largely in the degree that they are *not* seen. Or, when seen, in the degree that they are seen only momentarily. I make my girls wear fluffy skirts and pass them off as modest and lively creatures."

With the appearance of each new beauty, talk at Rector's stopped. Women present assimilated the gown of the evening, while men thought male thoughts. This also was the moment for gossip. What had one heard lately about dear Frankie or about Anna Held and Flo Ziegfeld? Or what did anyone know of the six new toasts of the town, those Florodora Girls? Sometimes cleverness popped from the gossip, for a few beauties of the day had surprisingly sharp wits. One clever girl was Edna May, tiny and ash blonde, who scored a tremendous success as a Salvation Army lassie in the musical *Belle of New York* ("Men never proceed to follow the light, but they always follow me," she caroled). Eventually *Belle of New York* traveled to London, where dukes and belted earls in profusion began to woo the American star. Edna May was the daughter of a Syracuse mail carrier, and the warmhearted girl wanted her father at her side in this hour of triumph. In New York, the Rector's set wondered how Edna would explain her parent's lowly status to titled friends. The young lady jumped the hurdle neatly when the moment came to introduce her postman father to English nobility. "An American man of letters," she called him.

2: PLAYS AND PLAYERS

The revolving door which propelled diners into Rector's was eternally fascinating. Who next would step on the high-piled plush carpet of Broadway's Cathedral of Froth?

Nearly every night a *swoosh* of the door produced a short, sharp-faced, friendly looking man. Immediately after came a lean, taller man with sensitive features. It can hardly be said that the appearance of these two caused a wave of laughter to sweep through the lobster palace. But certainly the pleasurable relaxation of *remembered* laughter touched all present. For here were Weber and Fields—Joe and Lew offstage, Mike and Myer on! No matter what one called them, they were the two funniest men of the time.

Weber and Fields were even more. They were an institution —proud owners of their own Music Hall, employers of a group of scintillating talents known affectionately as the Weberfields Company, and from coast to coast famous as a top act in vaudeville. What the Weberfields offered New York was comedy and high burlesque—true burlesque. Nothing more daring than Frankie Bailey in her tights (*Whirl-i-gig* was at the Weber and Fields Music Hall) ever adorned a Mike and Myer stage. Nor were the suggestive lines of a later kind of burlesque ever heard there. Joe Weber (Mike) played a comic fat man in a squat derby, rotund stomach filled to bursting with pillows. Lew Fields (Myer) was the fast-thinking bully who abused poor Mike. With these identities, and a multitude of stunts and ideas, Weber and Fields had no need for off-color comedy. Indeed, students in the Columbia classes of Professor Brander Matthews were surprised to hear him compare the art of Weber and Fields to that of Aristophanes. "Theirs is comedy for the ages," the professor intoned. "Rush downtown to see it." Whether the two low comedians ever heard of this comparison to the Greek is not known, but it is possible to gauge how they might have reacted if they did. "When in doubt, kick Weber," was the motto of the act. A startled Lew might have kicked dumpy Joe in the pants over Aristophanes.

Weber and Fields were born into cellar-style poverty on New York's East Side. While in short pants, they teamed up for the amateur nights, then a popular weekly feature in theatres around the lively Bowery. The time was the 1870's, an era dominated by Tony Pastor, whose theatre at Broadway and Prince Street was the cradle of American vaudeville. The two talented boys failed to make the grade at Pastor's and set about beating their way around fleabag vaudeville circuits the country over. Their developing lives became a series of battles with the Gerry Society, which sought to keep children off the stage, and tussles with railroad conductors who thought kids who earned a living should pay full fare on trains.

In the early phase of this career, the two boys stepped onstage singing, *"Here we are, a jolly pair."* They would then swing into an Irish, blackface, or German act, depending on the audience. Slowly, however, they evolved a new type of comedy. It was loud and low, a rough slapstick that came to be called Dutch-knockabout. With it went German dialect. "There had been German-dialect comedians before but no such interchange of twisted, strangled speech as this," writes Felix

Isman in his biography of Weber and Fields. Weber would begin, "I am delightfulness to meet you." "Der disgust is all mine,"
Fields politely replied. Sometimes the pair commenced by
emerging from the wings backward. Or two men made up in
the familiar Weberfields costumes appeared, acknowledged applause, then walked offstage—at which the real Weber and Fields
appeared exactly like the other two.

But ordinarily the act started with the agonized cry from the
wings, "Don't poosh me, Myer!" Weber, pillow-huge, stumpy,
and much set-upon, appeared first. On his heels was Myer,
irately waving a cane. "Didn't I telling you, vatch your
etiquette?" Myer shouted. Mike feigned outrage. "Who says I
et a cat?" he demanded. This was the cue for Myer to achieve
fury. Bending over little Mike, he punched the pillow-chest
with a harsh finger as he bellowed, "Ven I'm avay from you I
cannot keep mein mind from off of you. Ven I'm mit you, I
cannot keep mein hands from off of you. Oh, I luff you, Mike!"

So began the famous knockabout portion of the act, for Myer's
"luff" was expressed in rude ways. He grabbed Mike and proceeded to choke him violently, or gouge out an eye. He might
kick Mike murderously in the padded stomach, or hit him over
the iron derby with a pool cue or any handy object. A peak
moment came as Myer reached out with a crook of his cane, en-
circling Mike's neck. Jerking the cane, he threw Mike sprawling
on the floor. But no Weberfields roughhouse was totally one-
sided. Much-abused Mike carried his own cane. On his feet
again, he hooked this around Myer's neck and proudly hauled
him around the stage.

With all this went a barrage of jokes and catchwords. During
a war scene, Weber shouted, "A soldier has been shot!"
"Where?" Fields wanted to know. "In the excitement," Weber
yelled back. Weber and Fields were responsible for perhaps the
most famous of all American jokes. "Who vass dat lady I seen

you with last night?" Weber inquired. "She vass no lady, she vass my wife," Fields answered. At times the more presentable Myer attempted to overawe Mike. "Vy, I come from a very rich family," he boasted. "Ve hadt a shoffer, a botler . . ." Mike's derisive snort shut him up. "Don't try to kidding me, Myer," he snapped. "I know how it vass you lived. Your family got t'rown out on the street so many times that your mother had to buy curtains vot matched the sidevalk."

By the mid-nineties, Joe and Lew commanded a touring unit called Weber and Fields Own Company. Each made $500 a week, a highly respectable theatre salary for the period. Still, they were dissatisfied and hatched the idea which would carry them into the $5000-a-week class. The two began to think of a theatre in which they would surround themselves with stars of top magnitude. *Stock variety with an all-star company* is the professional terminology. Oscar Hammerstein and other impresarios of the time could find no virtue in such a wild idea, so in 1898 the team decided to go ahead alone. Renting a tiny theatre at Broadway and Twenty-ninth Street, they renamed it the Weber and Fields Music Hall. Around them, as the Weberfields Company, they gathered Sam Bernard, Pete Dailey, Louis Mann, and other talented comics. The first top star hired was Fay Templeton, who for $400 a week sang (among many other numbers) "Rosie, You Are My Posie," the most famous song to emerge from the Weber and Fields Music Hall. Each program had an over-all title like *Hoity-Toity*, *Whirl-i-gig*, *Pousse Café*, or *Fiddle-Dee-Dee*. The first half of a bill was musical nonsense and comedy by Myer and Mike and others. During this part of one Weber and Fields show a custard pie was thrown by one comedian into the face of another for the first time.

The second half of a Music Hall bill was given over to burlesque of the Broadway hit of the past week. The first play to receive this attention was the Belasco-Mrs. Leslie Carter *The*

Heart of Maryland, parodied as "The Art of Maryland." Second came "The Geezer," for *The Geisha*. At first the two parts of a Music Hall show balanced, but as time went on the rare comedy of the first half was surpassed by the irreverent skill of the burlesques. A few voices of protest were heard over these. Miss Annie Russell, a Broadway star, claimed that after seeing Weber and Fields poke fun at her vehicle she could never again give a serious performance. The burlesques usually changed weekly, and the critic Alan Dale complained that he could not properly enjoy new shows because he kept wondering what Weber and Fields might do with them next week.

But such opposition was rare. Stars, producers, and authors were anxious to have their efforts parodied, for to be kidded by a Weber and Fields burlesque became a top accolade. The haughty Richard Mansfield was currently rehearsing his English version of *Cyrano de Bergerac*, which became one of the most popular plays in American theatre history. He urged the Weberfields to attend a dress rehearsal, thus preventing any delay in a parody called "Cyrano de Bric-a-Brac." Music Hall matinees were given on Tuesdays for two reasons. It allowed the Weberfields Company to attend a Wednesday matinee of the play to be burlesqued next. It also permitted the cast of the play to see the burlesque. The Weberfields technique was to sit through a new play, then rush back to the Music Hall stage, where mad inspiration was allowed to run loose. Not the least funny parts of Weberfields burlesque were the titles. *Quo Vadis* became "Quo Vass Iss?" *Barbara Frietchie* was "Barbara Fidgety." A play called *The Highwayman* was insanely transposed into "The Way High Man."

In addition to a regular company, the Weber and Fields Music Hall offered such top stars as Willie Collier, Marie Dressler, Frankie Bailey, and De Wolf Hopper. At one point, an offer of $3000 a week was made to the opera singer Lillian Nordica, but Weber and Fields fled in confusion when it became apparent that she thought this sum was for one performance. Controlling so many towering talents and temperaments in a small theatre was a Weber and Fields feat saluted by Hopper, who said, "Half a dozen stars managed by two other stars! There is no parallel for it in my knowledge of the theatre." Asked how he and Weber contrived to keep the peace among so many star-studded associates, Fields explained, "We're always wrong and they're always right."

In the galaxy of stars revolving around Mike and Myer, the most inspired help came from a pleasant, wide-smiling young man with an underslung jaw. His name was David Warfield. Born David Wohlfelt, he had been a singing newsboy in San Francisco, where a somewhat older David Belasco often bought from him. A born mimic, Warfield hung around theatres until allowed to perform an imaginative impression of William Shakespeare and a more practical one of Sarah Bernhardt as the expiring Camille. After suitable vicissitudes, he arrived at the Music Hall, where Weber and Fields recognized the full range of his talent. Like other comedians among the Weberfields— Bernard, Dailey, Mann—Warfield was tremendously funny in dialect and horseplay. But he had the added quality of pathos. It has been said that most comedians can make an audience laugh and shed tears simultaneously, but Warfield was exceptional in that he could pull forth a second set of tears. He was also full of tricks like putting the wrong shoes on the right feet and achieving a pre-Chaplin shuffle.

Another who recognized Warfield's unusual talents was David Belasco, who had failed to see anything remarkable in the sing-ing newsie of San Francisco. Warfield had been a Weberfields stalwart for four years when Belasco was noticed in the audience night after night. He sent Warfield a note, but backstage at the Music Hall was as disorderly as center-stage and the comedian

thought it a practical joke. Then Belasco made his intentions
known. He wanted Warfield for serious drama. After much
hesitation, Warfield left the Music Hall. His first play for Belasco was *The Auctioneer*, a moderate triumph. His next was *The
Music Master*, one of the towering hits of the era. Over the years
Warfield also excelled in *The Grand Army Man* and *The Return
of Peter Grimm*. From these (with the help of wise investments)
he was able to amass $12,000,000 from that ability to squeeze
forth the second set of tears.

Weber and Fields lost others besides Warfield, for the Music
Hall with its ceaseless hurly-burly was a rare showcase for varied
talent. When Fay Templeton stepped into her own show, the
two producers were truly baffled, for a successor to such a
formidable personality would be hard to find. Then Joe Weber
had an idea. "Do you suppose we could get Lillian Russell?" he
wondered.

Here was a bold notion indeed. Burnished-blonde Lillian,
with her magnified-hourglass figure, was America's Golden
Beauty. Born Helen Louise Leonard in Iowa, she radiated a
serene beauty and a calm confidence in her own loveliness that
dwarfed anyone threatening her great eminence. In 1900
beauteous Lillian had reached the interesting age of forty, but
it made no difference. "The years never rested more lightly on
a woman's head," says Felix Isman. Further, Miss Russell had a
roaring passion for food, especially rich-buttered corn, and as a
result was unabashedly hefty. Even so, her name shimmered
across the land as the synonym for contemporary loveliness. On
the stage Miss Russell delivered lines with dignity or humor,
and sang in a voice which high-domed James Huneker com-
pared to a teakettle. She was able to hit High C without apparent effort, and one night the singer Nellie Melba visited
backstage to advise her to cut down the number of times she did

this. Miss Russell accepted this wisdom graciously, as she did everything. But she continued to hit High C whenever she felt like it.

Weber and Fields were at first afraid to approach such a goddess with an offer from the rowdy Music Hall. But at the race track one day they spied Lillian picking winners by the unique system of jabbing a hatpin through the program, betting on the horse the hatpin pierced. Stepping forward, Lew Fields suggested, "Why not use a fork and pick them one-two-three?" This sally so delighted the Golden Beauty that she listened to the offer of an engagement at the Music Hall. The two comedians were amazed to hear her accept. "But on my own terms," she added ominously. Lillian wanted $1250 a week, with a guarantee of thirty-five weeks, and all costumes paid for by the management—a large item in the case of a Golden Beauty. Weber and Fields gulped and agreed.

The announcement of Lillian Russell's appearances at the Music Hall made front-page news. Reporters hastened to interview her and one ventured to ask her whether she would appear in tights in the manner of Frankie Bailey. Miss Russell looked modestly down at her lap. "Nature has been too kind," she murmured. At her Music Hall debut she was surrounded by Weber and Fields, Sam Bernard, Warfield, and Pete Dailey. Before the audience saw her, she sat for five minutes hidden in the depths of a stage tree while Mike and Myer cavorted below. Suddenly Mike paused to cock an ear at the base of the tree. "I seem to hear a rustle up there," he stated. With that, lovely Lillian descended. To her Pete Dailey sang the song, "Say You Love Me, Sue." For the first time she rendered a lively coon-song—its name, "When Chloe Sings Her Song." In the second half she appeared with Warfield (as millionaire Sigismund Cohenski) in a burlesque of *The Girl from Maxim's*. After polishing off a meal in this elegant restaurant, Lillian said to the

waiter, "You might bring me a demitasse." Says Cohenski:
"Bring me the same, and a cup of coffee."

As 1900 moved toward 1901—and that year raced toward
1902—Lillian Russell was likely to precede Joe Weber and Lew
Fields through the revolving door at Rector's. She had been
joined by De Wolf Hopper at the Music Hall, and both offstage
and on seemed more beautiful and serene than ever. Delightful
Lillian was far too sensible and straightforward to pause while
the Rector's violinist arranged himself at the foot of her train.
Instead, after taking quick leave of Joe and Lew, she moved
alone toward the center table where Diamond Jim Brady sat
with pretty young Edna McCauley. Also seated at this table
was the millionaire Jesse Lewisohn. He waited for Lillian.
Nightly this group made up the Great White Way's most celebrated foursome, and all Broadway expected that any day Jim
would wed his Edna, while Lillian married her Jesse and his
multi-millions. But this was not to be. In a few years Edna and
Jesse astoundingly toppled into love and married, leaving Diamond Jim and Lillian Russell to console one another.

This, however, was yet to come. . . . Tonight the Brady table
seemed as happily close-knit as that of Weber and Fields, who
sat a few feet away with their wives. Joe and Lew had shared
the same dressing room from childhood and at their moment of
top fame still did so. But recently Broadway had been swept
by rumors of friction between these partners of thirty years.
Joe and Lew finally heard the story—the principals are always
the last to know—and quickly scotched it by sitting all one afternoon atop the bootblack stand outside the Music Hall, eating
peanuts from the same bag. This show of amicable solidarity
appeared to render the rumor forever dead. . . .

Jim and Edna—Lillian and Jesse—Mike and Myer . . . all
seemed well in their wonderful world. And why not? They
were wealthy and famous, with Fortune busy dealing high cards

into their eager hands. Weber and Fields, especially, seemed lucky. One of their all-time-best burlesque possibilities had just been presented to them in a play received on Broadway with mingled shock, excitement, and indignation. At that moment it seemed the most scandalous opening night in all theatre history.

Such churning emotion was aroused by *Sapho* (the Music Hall parody called it "Sapolio," after a contemporary soap powder), an adaptation of the Alphonse Daudet novel by the playwright Clyde Fitch. *Sapho* opened at Wallack's Theatre with an English-born actress named Olga Nethersole as its star. The next morning a reviewer said: "This is an exhibition of such unblushing, unvarnished immorality as the town has never witnessed before."

Sapho was the story of sultry Fanny LeGrand, a Camille-like lady of departed morals who was accomplished in the art of using her gleaming flesh to trap men. But Fanny finds herself ensnared by the lusty vigor of a male named Jean. The first shock of *Sapho* came when Fanny abased herself before this hunk of glorious manhood. Abjectly she begged, "I'll blacken your shoes, if only you'll let me stay!" (In the Music Hall version Joe Weber at this point hands Sapho a shoeshine kit.) Up to now girls who abased themselves before men on the American stage had done so to beg honest favors or to protect their own noble purity. But here was a girl in the throes of fleshly passion!

The second jolt of the evening came with a masked ball which to the audience looked suspiciously like an orgy. (Today it would be tame.) This was followed by the real shocker. After a wrestling-match love scene at stage level, Miss Nethersole's leading man (Hamilton Revelle) lifted her in his arms, carried her to the foot of a flight of stairs. At the top of these stairs, the audience knew, lay a bedroom. Slowly, for Olga Nethersole was no light burden, Jean mounted the stairs. At the top he paused to utter a fervent, "At last!" She replied with a cryptic, "So soon!" With these romantic sentiments, the couple entered milady's boudoir.

Stage lights dimmed and the Wallack's curtain dropped to denote passage of time. Members of the audience, greatly horrified, might well have departed the theatre at this pregnant moment, but there is no record that any did. The audience remained rooted until the curtain rose again. This time the stage was suffused by the pale light of dawn, while the twittering of mechanical birds sounded from the wings. Tentatively the bedroom door opened. Then it opened wider, allowing Jean to slip through the door and steal guiltily down the flight of stairs.

From theatre seats came a collective gasp. Most of the audience sat in the grip of outrage but a few rose, muttering angrily, to stride from the theatre. Next morning reviews united in calling *Sapho* an affront to fair womanhood, a sentiment crystallized in the *New York Journal* by William Randolph Hearst, who took pen in hand to write in a stinging editorial: "We think there exists in this country a respect for decent women and for young girls. We expect the police to forbid on the stage what they would forbid in streets and low resorts." Before word of the fury she had aroused reached her, Miss Nethersole was awakened from slumber by representatives of the New York police. In purple gown, matching hat, and fur muff she was led to the nearest precinct and booked as a corrupter of public morals.

Hard as all this was, it may have aided the career of Olga Nethersole. Brooding, flashing-eyed, with a full-blown figure impossible to disguise under the cumbersome female attire of the day, she had already been seen in New York in *Camille*, *Carmen*, and *The Second Mrs. Tanqueray*. As Carmen she had generated comment by kissing her leading man full on the lips. Across the country this had become famous as the Carmen Kiss, and proper folk loudly disapproved. Such notoriety should have made Olga Nethersole a potent theatrical drawing card, but for some strange reason did not. One producer summed up this unfathomable mystery as he sighed, "There is only one thing wrong with dear Olga as an actress—people just won't go to see her."

With her arrest for appearing as scarlet Sapho, the actress seemed at last in a position to remedy this flaw. On advice of her lawyer, tricky Abe Hummel, she demanded a jury trial. So the case received glorious publicity day after day. Despite continuing cries from outside the courtroom, the jury saw fit to acquit her. That night *Sapho* triumphantly reopened, and Olga Nethersole found herself a popular favorite at last. But if that lady's woes were over, those of a male member of the cast were not. He was ordered to remove his eleven-year-old daughter from a fashionable school for young ladies. "Several mothers of several students have seen the play in which you appear," the letter of dismissal read, "and they cannot consider Margaret a fit companion for their daughters in consequence."

Flirtatious Florodora, the Weberfields rambunctious knockabouts, sinful Sapho—these are a sampling of the Broadway theatre at the turn of the century. Shakespeare was always represented in New York playhouses and now, in addition to Sothern's *Hamlet*, playgoers might view Nat Goodwin and Maxine Elliott (man and wife number three) in *The Merchant of Venice* and Modjeska in *Twelfth Night*. From the wings of a world theatre came vibrations from a new Irish-English playwright named George Bernard Shaw and the European Henrik Ibsen, whom critics had labeled "the nasty Norwegian." Ibsen and Shaw wrote plays of realism, but Broadway's realism was *Sapho* and *Zaza*, together with William Faversham, Guy Standing, and Margaret Anglin in *Brother Officers*, Eleanor Robson and Vincente Serrano in *Arizona*, and Nat Goodwin and Maxine Elliott (with the closing of *The Merchant*) in *When We Were Twenty-one*. "Just as the new realism was edging in, the old

romance was bowing out in a blaze of glory," Walter Prichard
Eaton has written of this moment. "It was a superb theatre to be
young in—it was a great world to be alive in."

Yes—the old romance was dying out, but its vanishing blaze
of glory continued to make the fact hard to believe. It was a
moment of huge best-sellers among books, and what swifter
road to predictable success than dramatization of a novel everyone was talking about? The step from best-seller to hit-play was
almost automatic, so that nearly all the truly box-office plays
seemed to be adaptations of novels. William H. Crane was appearing in *David Harum;* Mrs. Fiske in *Becky Sharp;* John Drew
in *Richard Carvel;* Viola Allen in *The Christian;* William Gillette in *Sherlock Holmes;* Richard Mansfield in *Dr. Jekyll and
Mr. Hyde;* Blanche Bates in *Under Two Flags;* James O'Neill in
Monte Cristo; William Farnum in *Ben Hur;* Robert T. Haines in
In the Palace of the King; and Mary Mannering in *Janice Mere-
dith.* In prospect were Cissie Loftus and E. H. Sothern in *If I
Were King;* Richard Mansfield in Booth Tarkington's *Monsieur
Beaucaire;* Virginia Harned and William Courtleigh in *Alice of
Old Vincennes;* and Maude Adams in *Quality Street.*

Of the rush to turn novels into plays, producer Charles Frohman said, "The trend is antagonistic to good dramatic art, but
it keeps theatres filled." This was no exaggeration. In and out of
Broadway's nearly fifty theatres (adding six vaudeville and several Hebrew theatres to the forty-odd legitimate) moved a bewildering number of plays and musicals. Rare indeed was the
in-season night when only one show opened on Broadway.
Usually three or four were simultaneously unveiled, bringing
headaches to city editors of newspapers employing a single
drama critic. On some high-season nights ten plays opened, giving the city editors true breakdowns.

With so much activity, it would seem to follow that the
Broadway theatre district would be both busy and prosperous.

Never had there been so many plays, so many theatres, so many new areas into which the drama could develop. Turn-of-the-century Broadway was indeed, as Ward Morehouse would later say, a small world, tumultuous, congested, self-obsessed.

On closer scrutiny, however, this happy Broadway displays a seamy side. Certainly there never had been—or ever will be again—so many functioning theatres or varying plays shoving in and out of them. But it has always been a truism that the theatre has more actors than parts, and it was so then. In this early era an actor's existence may have been uncluttered by the need for an agent, allowing him to do his own job hunting. This became a process somewhat reminiscent of the auction block of slavery. First arrivals in a producer's office grabbed the few chairs. The rest jammed the office or stretched in lines out of the room, into the corridor, and sometimes to the street.

In a day when a Broadway play could be presented (often by the canny use of secondhand scenery) for only $3000 to $5000, the producer was the indisputable cock of the Broadway walk. From his initial investment it was often possible to reap from $500,000 to $1,000,000 in profit. Producers facilitated the process by investing in each other's productions, interchanging top stars, and altogether behaving like members of a group as exclusive as the United States Supreme Court. This, in some cases, resulted in an arrogance which made the producer the natural enemy of actors and playwrights. Often the personage whom actors waited so patiently to see was highhanded, crude, or sadistic. Some were downright ignorant. When Clyde Fitch's *Major Andre* failed, its producer was asked how he expected a play about a spy to succeed. "How the hell did I know Clyde was going to make him spy?" he whined.

Even without the stupidities of producers—or managers, as the breed was more frequently called—job hunting along Broadway could be a wearying business. A breathlessly lovely girl named

Ethel Barrymore sat for six long months in the anterooms of various managers, though she was the offspring of not one but two famed theatre families. Finally her patience was rewarded—young Ethel got the job of understudying Elsie de Wolfe in *The Bauble Shop*. Columns of *The Dramatic Mirror*, a *Variety* of the day, bulged with job-wanted advertisements in which actors listed their unique skills and past triumphs. At the end of each came the gallant admission *At Liberty*.

Once an actor was hired, he encountered other headaches. For one, he was expected to rehearse without pay as long as the producer or director deemed necessary. Contemporary rehearsal periods usually lasted three or four weeks, but were known sometimes to stretch to nine or ten. After this a show might be so bad that it closed after a night or two, leaving the actor with just that much pay for several weeks' arduous work.

Rehearsals, in turn, brought other pitfalls. An actor could be summarily dismissed at any point during this period. It was even possible to fire him just before the curtain rose on an opening night. He could also be dismissed anywhere on tour and left to get back to New York on his own. Thus producers and stars had absolute control over those who worked for them. One young playwright, sitting unobtrusively (as a young playwright should) through a rehearsal of his first play, was astounded to hear the star call a sudden halt to the proceedings. Then the actor scathingly fired all members of the cast. The young man never forgot the looks of disappointment—or was it heartbreak?—on the faces of the actors.

Hardly less than actors, playwrights stood at the mercy of producers, stars, and nearly everyone else except the lowly thespian. The English playwright Henry Arthur Jones may have dispatched his handwritten manuscripts to the printer to be set in impeccable book-type the moment he wrote "Finis" on a play. But Jones was a towering figure in the theatre, a master of the

well-made play, so secure in his eminence that no one dared
change a syllable of anything he wrote. Few other playwrights
could afford to be so sure of themselves. Even managers of out-
of-town theatres outranked the playwright. One author of a
play being tested out of town was struck by the inspiration of
inserting a tableau of The Last Supper into his brain child. Next
he found himself buttonholed by the theatre manager, who told
him the stage looked empty during that scene. "But," the playwright protested, "there were only Twelve Apostles." "I know,"
the manager replied, "but gimme twenty-four anyway." Even
so, theatre managers stood higher on the human scale than some
who were privileged to judge plays. One author, informed by a
producer that his play had been accepted, was astounded to find
it returned to him. Rushing to the producer, he demanded,
"What happened?" "My chauffeur didn't like it," the producer
replied.

In still another abuse, producers often employed staff playwrights, or house authors. Usually these were hack writers paid
a small weekly sum to improve plays bought by the manager.
Often a new playwright had the pleasure of watching another
hand rewrite his play according to old formulas. Sometimes the
house playwright wrote a play of his own, in which case the
producer considered it office property. The immensely lucra-
tive *Hazel Kirke* was written by Steele Mackaye while that
wildly talented eccentric was under contract to the management
of the Madison Square Theatre. *Hazel Kirke* grossed millions,
but Mackaye never received more than a small weekly wage.
In 1887 the actor-manager Richard Mansfield paid young Clyde
Fitch thirty-dollars a week to write a play based on the life of
Beau Brummell. In addition to this amount Fitch was promised
seven and a half dollars a performance until the total of $1500
was reached. By 1900 Fitch had become America's most celebrated playwright, and presumably had no great need of money.

But he never got more than $1500 for *Beau Brummell,* though it remained a bulwark of Richard Mansfield's repertory.

It is odd to report that few of Broadway's many plays remained on New York stages for spectacular runs. There was a good reason for this. In those halcyon days the Great White Way functioned chiefly as a showcase for the remainder of the United States, a robust and growing country where over a thousand theatres—large, small, impromptu—sprawled across the land. These numerous outlets for drama were referred to generally as the Road, and in 1900 no less than 400 touring and stock companies catered to the greatest theatre thirst the country would ever know. The Road was a highly remunerative and seemingly limitless territory, and with it this way managers could be satisfied with a run of two or three weeks on Broadway. It was even astute to carry these Broadway performances at a loss, for then a play could be billed cross-country as *Direct from Successful Broadway Run.*

Serene in the knowledge that almost any deficit could be retrieved by a tour on the play-hungry Road, producers dispatched company after company, sometimes of the same play, and kept them out for years. Looking back on his apprentice days, De Wolf Hopper recalls, "For four years we played as far south as New Orleans and Texas, then up to Kansas City and San Francisco, and back by way of Canada, one-week stands in larger cities, one-night stands between. It was the routine in the theatre at the time." Eventually Hopper turned this agony of touring into laughter at the Weber and Fields Music Hall. Reminiscing of long tours and sleeper jumps he concluded, "And when I got back to New York and a stationary bed, I couldn't sleep. I had to hire two men to shake the bed all night and another to pour cinders down my neck."

With the wide-flung Road so healthy, many actors of note

never bothered to appear in New York. Or, if they did, it was
for only a week or two. Yet playgoers in the hinterlands, as well
as other large cities, were not altogether lacking in discrimina-
tion. Some plays folded on the Road, while others did badly.
For actors in bad plays, Road tours were one-night stands which
could be a severe trial to body and spirit—not to mention talent.
Even worse perhaps than physical hardship was the ever-present
fear of being stranded. This happened so often with companies
on tour that the company manager who absconded, leaving his
actors in the lurch, became a cliché figure of the time.

For top stars, the Road was a different story. A performer of
magnitude had his (or her) private railroad car. "I wouldn't
think of going to Philadelphia, even, except in my private car,"
statuesque Maxine Elliott informed a round-eyed Billie Burke,
newly arrived from London. In Seattle, Lily Langtry peremp-
torily demanded that a carpet be put down between her dressing
room and the stage, to keep the hems of her dresses from becoming soiled. The obliging management came up with a red carpet—
which is how *that* began. Anna Held's private car was equipped
with fancy lace curtains and a grand piano on which the saucy
star practiced "I Can't Make My Eyes Behave" and "Won't
You Come and Play Wiz Me?" Lillian Russell, of course, had a
private car, as did Sarah Bernhardt. The Pullman of Richard
Mansfield, who toured steadily in *Beau Brummell*, *Cyrano de
Bergerac*, and *Monsieur Beaucaire*, was an elaborate rolling suite.
Those fortunate enough to receive letters from Mansfield as he
ranged the country found them written on stationery elegantly
embossed *Mr. Richard Mansfield's Tour*.

No less than a Broadway which seemed prosperous and contented on the surface, the seemingly thriving Road offered a
deceptive appearance. Actually it was in the throes of a giant
subsurface struggle.

Up to the year 1896 proud stars, managers, and actor-managers booked their own tours over the sprawling Road. This had been done in an informal, haphazard, personal manner which has been recalled as charming chaos. When booking a Road show, the ideal was to arrange consecutive one-night stands between longer weekly or monthly stands in cities. This kept down travel expenses, allowing the company to achieve the ultimate in profit. Yet this ideal was seldom achieved. Few managers or stars had the patience to become adept in the complicated art of booking a show around the country. The resulting chaos was expensive rather than charming, with companies shuttling wastefully over long jumps.

Meanwhile, the United States had entered the era of mighty trusts, with small industries gobbled up and turned into huge, collective corporations like Standard Oil and United States Steel. Lincoln Steffens, Ida Tarbell, Will Irwin, and other muckrakers fulminated against the evils of mighty monopoly, but a naïve nation found it hard to see evil in such colossal enterprise.

On a day in 1896—with the heady atmosphere of trusts, corporations, and octopus combines permeating the New York air—a group of theatre owners met (by chance, they always claimed) at lunch in New York's Holland House. Present were Charles Frohman, who, though New York's most cosmopolitan manager, also owned a chain of theatres in the West; Marc Klaw and Abraham Lincoln Erlanger, who controlled theatres in the South; Samuel F. Nixon and J. Frederick Zimmerman, theatre owners in Pennsylvania and Ohio; and Al Hayman, co-owner with Frohman of the lovely Empire Theatre in New York.

Over a six-course meal these hardheaded gents deplored the eccentric manner in which Road plays were booked. Viewing with alarm, they agreed that because of such clumsy procedures the American theatre might be destined for ruin. Over Coronas and coffee, they arrived at a conclusion. Salvation lay in a merger of the theatres under their control and other theatres into one tight, monopolistic cross-country chain. The strongest link of this would be a central booking office, set up in New York, which would book plays over the country. In this way a traveling attraction could prepare an economical tour in New York, then travel the bumpy Road with a minimum of trouble, effort, and expense.

In theory (and on paper) this efficient system—which Broadway immediately christened the Syndicate or the Trust—had merit. But its virtues immediately evaporated when operation of the booking-office hub was turned over to Klaw and Erlanger. The trouble was not so much Marc Klaw, who functioned largely as the legal brains of the Trust. Kentucky-born, suave, and self-effacing, Klaw is best remembered around theatres for a memorable *mot*. He was once asked to characterize the people attending Great White Way opening nights. "Theatre habitués and sons of habitués," he answered promptly.

Abraham Lincoln Erlanger was different. Buffalo-born, he had entered show business as the boy-manager of balloon ascensions in the Middle West. Outspoken, overbearing, and dynamic —so squat and broad of beam that he appeared somehow to have been stepped on—Erlanger discovered in the Syndicate the opportunity of a greedy lifetime. So rude and dictatorial was he that behind his broad back he was already called Little Napoleon. When he heard this, Erlanger obtained perverse revenge by beginning a collection of Napoleonana which in time became valuable. Yet in his inner soul Abe Erlanger appeared to see himself as other than Napoleonic. One merry summer day he and a group of managers journeyed to Coney Island on a picnic. There Erlanger noticed a lion's cage being cleaned. He jumped inside, pulling the bars shut behind him. For the next fifteen minutes he gave an exhibition of four-legged roaring, snarling, and rampaging that thoroughly awed his friends. Later, attired in a striped bathing suit, the broad little man waded into the surf up to his knees. Urged to go farther, he answered with cold logic, "*Me*—with all my money?"

The list of Erlanger's iniquities is long. Reminded of something he might forget, he would glare back and state, "Once I've heard a thing it is marked on my mind *indeliably*." On occasions when he took time off to play golf, Erlanger could be seen crassly kicking his ball to more advantageous positions. Yet his choler was so greatly feared that no one dared take him to task for such lack of sportsmanship. A remorselessly early riser in a late-sleeping theatrical world, Erlanger tormented actors by setting eight a.m. appointments. Having showed his power by doing this, he snarlingly added, "You are dealing with a *busy* man, so be on time."

Placed in charge of a nationwide theatre chain, Erlanger began displaying a truculence which one mild historian has called a non-asset. Quickly this developed into a manic drive for control of all American theatres, together with as many as possible in Canada and Australia. Using his power ruthlessly, Erlanger drew increasing numbers of theatres under Syndicate control. Any owners who refused to co-operate with him were denied the shows booked by the Syndicate, and almost immediately the Syndicate had won the right to route the best Broadway plays. At the same time any Broadway manager who tried to by-pass Erlanger found himself unable to find a theatre in major cities.

The Syndicate strangled competition by lavish use of money and gigantic pressures. One tactic for snapping managers into line was exactly what the Syndicate was set up to prevent— productions jumped over such great distances that profits were eaten up. Erlanger's favorites were awarded rich Christmas- week engagements in big cities. His enemies found themselves unable to book a stage for any sum. From Weber and Fields Erlanger demanded such a high commission for a summer vaudeville tour that Mike and Myer booked themselves into the relatively minor Stair and Havlin West Coast circuit. Erlanger waited until Weberfields arrived on the Coast, then forced Stair and Havlin to cancel.

The Klaw and Erlanger Syndicate was a trust without the customary attributes. For one thing, it had no capital. Only if the demon industry of Abe Erlanger could be counted as a visible asset did it begin to resemble other great combines. Its office was to be found in a most unprepossessing spot—a grubby theatrical building on West Forty-second Street. Its mounting profits were quickly siphoned into individual pockets, so that its main money-in-the-bank was the fear inspired by the lionlike Erlanger. "No theatre man was so feared, because no one ever had so much to give," the playwright George Middleton says.

Yet Erlanger's increasing megalomania seemed to bring scant peace of mind. Aware that his ruthlessness made him the most hated man in the business, he himself began to live in fear. He ordered an office door a foot thick, strongly reinforced at the hinges. Suspicious of everyone, he glared especially at the barber who came daily to shave the heavy Erlanger jowls in an office barber chair. His fevered mind told him that someone might have approached the barber overnight, bribing him to slice the Erlanger throat from ear to ear.

In view of Abe Erlanger's awesome personality, together with the number of weapons at his disposal, it is heartening to report that (unlike some other trusts of the time) he met obstacles. At first these stemmed from top actors. Joseph Jefferson, James O'Neill, Nat Goodwin, Francis Wilson, Richard Mansfield, and Minnie Maddern Fiske—each accustomed to booking tours in pleasantly individual fashion—array᾿d themselves in firm defiance of Klaw and Erlanger.

At the urging of the *New York World*, *Collier's* magazine, and other crusading publications, the actors banded together as The Association for the Promotion and Protection of the Independent Stage in the United States. Its members unanimously signed an agreement promising to appear only in theatres where managers dealt with them directly. In the unlikely event that a manager of a Trust theatre dared act independently, Association members were free to deal with him.

In the mind of the public, the prime mover in this determined group appeared to be the great actor-manager Richard Mansfield. At the moment the agreement was signed, Mansfield was honoring a prior commitment by playing *Cyrano* in a Philadelphia theatre controlled by the Trust. Each night he insisted on making a curtain speech denouncing Abraham Lincoln Erlanger and his tactics. On orders from Erlanger, the theatre orchestra nightly attempted to drown the actor out as he spoke. Once he was nearly knocked down by a sudden drop of the curtain. Audiences became so enraged at these actions that the management was forced to allow the actor to finish his speech.

Next, a meeting of the Association was scheduled at Mansfield's New York office on Madison Square. Lawyers with papers waited to assist the group in incorporating and soon everyone was present except Mansfield. Then a messenger arrived with a letter from him. The member who read it first emitted a deep groan. "He has gone over to the Trust body and soul," he said. "He was the biggest prize in our camp and they offered him a fortune for joining them. In the letter, he questions our sincerity and advises us not to fight any longer."

It was a thunderbolt, most dastardly of betrayals! Only Minnie Maddern Fiske, who had begun her acting career at the age of two, could find a reason for it. The English-born Mansfield had come to this country with the first touring company of *Pinafore*. He had also sung Koko in *The Mikado*. A broken ankle ended his pleasant career as a frolicking Savoyard, and for the following two years the proud man lived a life of desperate poverty. Finally, the then Minnie Maddern offered him a part as a dramatic actor in the play *In Spite of All*. The rest was history, and the compassionate Mrs. Fiske thought Mansfield was still haunted by this period of struggle in his past. "I think I understand why he has done this," she stated now. "He's afraid that if he fights the Trust he may be driven to starvation again. He will destroy himself piling up money and honors he doesn't need—trying to bury the suffering and humiliation, trying to deny what has already happened."

With the apostasy of Mansfield, opposition to the Trust faded. Even the *New York World* momentarily turned mute. Over the next four years the stars of the ill-fated Association gradually yielded to the Syndicate—all, that is, except Mrs. Fiske. That dogged lady, aided and abetted by her producer-husband Harrison Grey Fiske, refused to truckle. As a consequence, the increasingly powerful Erlanger refused to allow her to play good theatres. Mrs. Fiske was reduced to giving *Tess of the D'Urbervilles*, *Becky Sharp*, *Leah Kleschna*, and other of her popular performances in lodge halls, hastily converted churches, and auditoriums like skating rinks.

More opposition to Abraham Lincoln Erlanger came from David Belasco, under whose creamy surface lay unexpected steel. Like Mrs. Fiske he vowed that never would he bend before the Syndicate. But after assuming this noble posture he, no less than other producers, found himself in a hopeless spot. He had launched David Warfield successfully in *The Auctioneer* and needed to follow with a first-class Road tour of the play and its new star. Now he discovered that only second- and third-class playhouses were available to those defying the Syndicate. For Warfield's sake (the producer said) more than his own, he bent to Erlanger, who, living up to his reputation, demanded fifty per cent of the profits of the tour. Belasco reluctantly

agreed, but as *The Auctioneer* profitably roamed the hinterlands he came to regret it. He sued the Syndicate, claiming that
he had been forced to sign with a dummy partner, thus rendering the contract invalid. Erlanger countersued, accusing Belasco
of hiding his status as co-author of the play. Into the hopper, he
tossed charges of plagiarism as well.

The trial of this complex case was almost as exciting as a play,
and from it the American public obtained its first graphic picture
of Syndicate operations. Wearing his clerical garb on the wit-
ness stand, Belasco tugged dramatically at the tumbling forelock and scored a telling point when in tremolo tones he orated,
"I think Mr. Erlanger is the most abhorred man in the country."
When his turn came, Erlanger strove hard to curb a native
truculence. He failed. His most damaging admission came as he
boasted (under shrewd cross-examination by Samuel Unter-
myer) that it was impossible to secure a good theatrical booking
anywhere in the country without the Syndicate. Having been
led into this damaging statement, he began to sulk, answering
all other questions, "My best recollection is that I don't remember."

At trial's end, the judge reserved decision. So it was twelve
long months before David Belasco heard the staggering news
that, in part because of legal technicalities, he had lost his case to
Erlanger. By this time, he was again fighting the Syndicate, and
in the battle he, Mrs. Fiske, and the few others of the opposition
had received unexpected reinforcement from the city of Syracuse. From that upstate region, where they began by peddling
programs at the Grand Opera House, Sam S., Lee, and J. J.
Shubert had arrived in New York. The boys from Syracuse
were so young in appearance that it was easy to mistake them
for their own office boys—a slip made by the embryo playwright
Channing Pollock among others. Yet they visualized themselves
a trio of Davids fully equipped to battle the Syndicate Goliath.

Today it is hard to visualize the Messrs. Shubert as heroes, for after outlasting Erlanger (and to a large extent vanquishing him), they became over thirty years something of a Syndicate themselves. But at this point, the bold young men were arrayed strongly on the side of virtue. Sam Shubert, the oldest brother, had arrived on Broadway first. He promptly used Syracuse money to lease the drafty old Herald Square Theatre, which Erlanger considered beneath notice. Sam Shubert needed an impressive star for the under-new-management opening of this theatre. The most impressive imaginable would be Richard Mansfield in *Monsieur Beaucaire*. Taking the wildest of chances, the young Shubert set out after Mansfield, finally tracking him to his yacht. The famous actor-manager roared with laughter at the idea of opening his new season at the Herald Square. "I couldn't possibly do it," he declared. "I must have a first-class theatre." Sam Shubert rose to this. "If you play there, it will *be* a first-class theatre," he answered. This so delighted Mansfield's outsized ego that, despite his strong connection with the Syndicate, the baffling man agreed to appear at the Herald Square.

Hearing this, Abraham Lincoln Erlanger emitted a mocking laugh. Beyond this, he did nothing. Years later he was asked why he did not stamp the Shuberts out of existence when this could so easily have been done. To this he gave an uncharacteristically charitable reply.

"The boys were Jews," he explained, "and I didn't want to do any more harm to Jews."

3: MR. THEATRE

Into the category of theatre-conscious Americans at this moment fell nearly every solvent citizen of the country, together with a large proportion of their growing offspring. The results might have been surprising had these theatre-minded folk been asked to name the first person who jumped to mind after mention of the word *theatre*.

They might not dip into a grab bag of star-studded actors to pull out a name like Richard Mansfield, John Drew, Maxine Elliott, William Gillette, Robert Mantell, Mrs. Fiske, Henry Miller, Arnold Daly, Joseph Jefferson, James O'Neill—or even a dashing swell like John Drew or Maurice Barrymore, or a scenery-nibbling matinee idol like James K. Hackett or Kyrle Bellew, or even an ethereal actress like Maude Adams or a red-headed, fetching one like Billie Burke.

Rather the name might be that of a short, round man who waddled as he walked. His soulful eyes were set large in a sallow moonface, above a neck so thick that in the high starch collars of the period he looked like a porpoise and seemed to have no neck at all. His full, wide lips were usually curved into a half-smile that reflected inner humor and a mocking confidence in his ability to win a way in the world. "A queer little strutting man, always sure of himself," is the way a contemporary recalls him. He was plump, and fast growing plumper, for he had an inordinate love of sugar pastries.

Nor did he believe in making a motion when someone could be paid to make it for him. He detested all kinds of physical exercise and made his home in a hotel as close as possible to his own theatre. He was full of paradoxes. Looking insensitive and callous, he had impeccable theatre taste, a simmering sense of humor, and was able to sketch deft caricatures while immersed in talk of business. He never carried a watch ("Why should I, when everybody else has one?"), yet was fabulously punctual. He never carried money on his person (associates shelled out for meals and hansom fares, later collecting from the office till), yet he took millions out of the theatre. He had, most of all, an almost hypnotic ability to inspire loyalty among others. Such a man, who had none of the physical accouterments of drama, was Mr. Theatre to the United States.

His name was Charles Frohman, and he was the number-one producer of his time—perhaps of all time. Frohman was, of course, a founder of the Syndicate, one of those present at the original Holland House luncheon. Indeed, the actual idea of the Syndicate may have sprung from his mind. In middle years Charles Frohman stood before the world as the most international of managers, yet as a young man he had booked plays around the tortuous Road with an efficiency amounting to genius. But if Frohman conceived the Syndicate, he did not wish the world to be conscious of it. The Syndicate ended his close association with David Belasco, and for this and other reasons he professed to be irritated by the existence of the theatrical monster he could have created. "All I ever get out of the Syndicate is trouble," he often complained. Yet realistic souls to whom he said this made a mental note that he also got money.

But while condoning the Syndicate, and banking money from its operations, Frohman was far prouder of the fact that he presented plays by Oscar Wilde, Victorien Sardou, James M. Barrie, Arthur Wing Pinero, Alfred Sutro, Henry Arthur Jones, and the native-born Clyde Fitch, Augustus Thomas, and William Gillette. Simultaneously he guided the tangled destinies of actors. By keeping his right hand fully aware of what his left hand did, Frohman had become the most successful theatrical figure alive. He also produced plays in London, 124 in all. This, at a time when England considered every American an intellectual boor, was a staggering feat. In New York, London, and (several times) Paris, the words CHARLES FROHMAN PRESENTS meant top theatre quality. It brought the round little man a great sense of the dignity of his position, and in time he grew vain of his eminence and invited flattering tribute. To a few close associates he might be C.F., but to the wide world he remained Mr. Frohman. Throughout his career, nothing infuriated him more than to see his name abbreviated to Chas. Frohman.

Like his onetime friend Belasco, Frohman was downright daft about the theatre. But where Belasco wrote plays and personally waded in to direct them, Frohman preferred the aloof role of the producer who provided the money and whose shrewd stage directions and script suggestions were invariably honored. All of which appeared to make him a completely happy man. "My work is to produce plays that succeed, so that I can produce plays that will not succeed," he liked to believe. James M. Barrie saw him this way: "Having once seen a theatre, he never saw anything else." For Charles Frohman was another of those fortunate boys—there seemed to be many at the time!—who on first viewing a theatre performance found the world of make-believe forever superior. On learning that it was possible to make money in this bright new wonderland, Frohman (no less than Belasco and others) never considered devoting his energies to anything else. He remained stage-struck all his life. To him the playhouse was the real universe; outside, all was wearying and bothersome.

Born in 1860, Frohman was just eight years old when he saw his first play. Fittingly enough, this was *The Black Crook*, at Niblo's Garden on lower Broadway. Young Charles, alert, lively, and cheerful, saw this musical milestone because his two older brothers were as stage-smitten as himself. The three boys were sons of Henry Frohman, a German immigrant who came to this country in 1845. In New York, Henry married Barbara Strauss, a girl he had admired from a distance in Germany. The young couple set up housekeeping in Sandusky, Ohio, where the personable Henry became a successful peddler of pots and pans. After fifteen years the family returned to New York, to provide a more sophisticated spot of upbringing for the clever boys, Daniel, Gustave, and Charles. Papa Frohman, who once dreamed of being an actor, opened a cigar-making shop near Union Square, currently the hub of New York's theatre district. While the older brothers earned money selling programs in nearby theatres, Charles hung around the shop, ogling the picturesque actors who entered to buy cigars. On *The Black Crook* night he was drafted by Gustave to assist in selling programs in the Niblo's Garden lobby. Once the performance began, a benevolent doorman let the big-eyed youngster scamper up to the second balcony.

It is safe to say that from then until his death in 1915 Charles Frohman thought only of the theatre. His family wanted him to be a lawyer, but he refused. He had a slight gift for mimicry, but apparently never thought of acting. From his brothers he learned that money could be made in the theatre by other means than treading the boards, and the fact never ceased to hypnotize him. By holding to the convenient coattails of brother Gustave, he was able to work in the theatre early. At fourteen he stood behind the box-office window of Hooley's Theatre in Brooklyn. Here he showed proper ambition by buying a pack of cards. With them he practiced finger manipulation which made him lightning-fast at dispensing tickets.

When brother Gustave quit Haverly's Mastodon Minstrels (40—Count 'Em—40), Charles took over the all-important post of advance man who traveled the country ahead of the troupe, posting bills, placing publicity in papers, and in every way luring people to the theatre. At this he was an unobtrusive dynamo. He persuaded the noisy Minstrels to make more noise, and in other ways subtly increased business. At sixteen Charles was a small boy—as he would be a small man. But in the depths of his personality lay an optimism which the world ever found attractive. He was energetic—"the energy of a Niagara," Barrie would write. He also had the rare quality of making people anxious to stay in his good graces—"I was obsessed by the desire to please him," Barrie goes on. With these notable qualities, Frohman remained quiet and retiring, saving his Niagara energies for constructive work.

Charles celebrated his twentieth birthday in England, where the then Prince of Wales so enjoyed the Mastodon Minstrels that they became the rage of London town. Back home, he spent two more years criss-crossing the country, learning the Road so well that never would he need to consult a map when routing a show. Meantime, Daniel Frohman—the *tall* Frohman—had leased the Madison Square Theatre in New York. Charles, now a rosy-cheeked twenty-three, was placed in charge of routing over the Road such Madison Square Theatre successes as *Hazel Kirke, The Professor, Esmeralda, Young Mrs. Winthrop,* and *May Blossom.* Here his Road tours were such marvels of travel-economy and financial gain that the shaky finances of the Madison Square were quickly stabilized. But Charles was not content. "I must have a New York production," his biographer Isaac F. Marcosson quotes him as endlessly saying.

Frohman always nursed a fondness for deep-dyed melodrama, and in 1893 he and David Belasco got together on an East Coast production of a lurid Belasco play, *Stranglers of Paris*. This was an elaborate effort, with scenes on a ship carrying caged convicts to Devil's Island. Finally, the craft sinks. All this was expensive and, though well received, the production lost money. Still, it brought the optimistic Frohman new confidence in himself, and he next produced *Caprice*, with the young Minnie Maddern; *A Daughter of Ireland*, with Georgia Cayvan; and *Held by the Enemy*, by William Gillette. Much was expected in 1886 of his production of the *The Jilt*, starring the popular Dion Boucicault. But as the play opened, Boucicault's wife chose to ape the title by involving her husband in a messy divorce suit. Frohman was inclined to be prim-minded and this scandal clinched it. He blamed sin and sex alone for the failure of the play and coined a maxim which covered this area of behavior. "Never engage a star smirched by scandal," he repeated for the rest of his life.

Frohman's first big opportunity came in 1889 with *Shenandoah*. This Bronson Howard play lifted him, he liked to say, into the Delmonico's-for-dinner class and also allowed him to jump from ten-cent cigars to twenty-five-cent Perfectos. With *Shenandoah*, he stepped forth as the consummate theatre man, adept at improving scripts and performances, devising slick stunts to promote them further. He first made suggestions about the script which inspired Bronson Howard. *Shenandoah* was a play of trick climaxes. At out-of-town performances the shot fired at Fort Sumter arched across the sky, bursting before the audience. Gasps of wonder filled the air, but the perceptive Frohman noted that with this moment people grew restive. "The shot that blows up the Fort also blows up the play," he informed

the surprised author. "People get so involved in wondering how
it's done they forget it's a shot that separates the lovers." He
decreed that only a *boom* of the cannon be heard, allowing audiences to keep in mind the unhappy plight of the lovers.

As the *Shenandoah* company arrived in New York for final
rehearsals, Frohman evolved a publicity stunt still recalled with
awe along Broadway. He told newspapers that the only manuscript of the revised last act of the play had been lost. The entire
city hunted for it, with *Shenandoah* on everyone's tongue. Just
a few hours before the opening Frohman announced that the
manuscript had been found—where, he never specified.

Shenandoah opened in the midst of a driving rainstorm, but
there had been so much advance talk that the theatre was
jammed despite the bad weather. The third-act climax (most
plays of the era had four or five acts) came when Henry Miller,
as General Phil Sheridan, galloped across the stage atop a live
horse. The play was an instant hit and at no time during its New
York run did weekly receipts sink to less than a thousand dollars. Road companies were profitably routed and Frohman
quickly produced three more plays that season. In 1891 he began
the kind of mass producing that continued during the rest of his
career. That year he produced nine plays; in 1900, the number
was fourteen. In 1905, it was nineteen.

"The theatre is an art conducted as a business by bad busi-
nessmen," grumbled the novelist Israel Zangwill after the failure
of his dramatized *Children of the Ghetto.* He may have had
Charles Frohman in mind, for with his emergence as a manager
the son of the peddler of pots and pans seemed to view the
theatre in wholesale terms. However, if Frohman might be
accused of looking on the theatre as a business, he could never be
called a bad businessman. He visualized play production in
quantity and often had five or six plays in simultaneous rehearsal.

This emphasis on quantity exacerbated some keenly artistic souls. At the same time, quality was always apparent in his efforts. Frohman never applied himself to the footwork necessary for the discovery of new playwrights and actors. Rather, he preferred to employ his genius for picking those who, already doing well, might do better under his guidance. He paid playwrights (and actors) large sums of money and catered tenderly to their errant whims. Altogether, he managed the careers of others with a firm, autocratic gentleness. Under such a regime both Frohman and the artist prospered.

Slowly a tight web of Frohman influence began spreading over the English-speaking theatre. The euphoric producer's main interest seemed to be playwrights, and now he brought to these shores plays by Oscar Wilde, Sardou, Henry Arthur Jones, Arthur Wing Pinero, and Somerset Maugham. Yet he was no mere importer of established productions. Frohman's enemies claimed that he never read a book unless it had been recommended to him as a possibility for dramatization. Still, it was he who saw dramatic possibilities in James M. Barrie's tremendously popular novel, *The Little Minister*. Frohman decided on the spot that this must be made into a play. He was capable of a refreshing modesty, and always gave a short reply when asked how he argued a reluctant Barrie into becoming a playwright. "Sent him cables," he said. Barrie was happy as a novelist and could see no reason for trying drama. But by the time he arrived in this country on his first trip, the cables had at least made an impression. He paid an unexpected visit to Frohman, who was busy. Frohman suggested that the novelist kill time by watching rehearsals of a play called *Rosemary* on the Empire stage. There Barrie first saw the lucent Maude Adams. Rushing back to Frohman's office, the Scot enthused, "I've just seen the girl to play Babbie."

So—in Barrie, Frohman, and Miss Adams—began a unit unsurpassed in the theatre. *The Little Minister* played 3000 performances in the United States, earning $600,000 for Frohman, $500,000 for Barrie, and giving Miss Adams a star status which shortly enabled her to make $500,000 a year. Barrie never wrote another novel. "I had only one quarrel with him," he said of his long friendship with Frohman, "but it lasted all the years I knew him. He wanted me to be a playwright and I wanted to be a novelist. All those years I fought him on that. He always won."

With his triumphs, Frohman also made blunders. He turned thumbs down on *Arizona* by Augustus Thomas, *Paid in Full* by Eugene Walter, *The Fortune Hunter* by Winchell Smith, and other highly successful plays of the first fifteen years of the century. In part, this can be attributed to an ingrained reluctance to gamble on untried American playwrights. Yet it is also a tribute to the eternal riskiness of play production, a riskiness that Frohman appeared to relish. At times he showed an extreme awareness of the number of play producers who died broke. "We make money for everyone but ourselves," he lamented of his chosen profession. Still, he was capable of graciousness toward those for whom he made money. "Why shouldn't I like actors?" he asked once. "Actors and authors have made me." His failures were dismissed with a true gambler's shrug, as if the hazards of his trade richly appealed to a buccaneer in his nature. George Bernard Shaw sensed this when he paid tribute to Frohman as "The most wildly romantic and adventurous man of my acquaintance. . . . He has become the most famous manager through his passion for putting himself in the way of being ruined."

Several times Frohman was pressed for cash, yet he continued to extol the tightrope aspects of play producing. "If I knew every play I was going to produce would be a success, I'd quit the business," he said once. Again, he confessed, "If I can produce two successes out of four, I think it's fine." More than any other producer's, Frohman's life was a glamorous succession of opening nights. It is doubtful if he enjoyed a single one. He could never face the important ones in person, usually cowering in a nearby restaurant or in his hotel room, where runners brought reports of audience response. He could not bring himself to travel to the world premiere of *Peter Pan* in London, where Nina Boucicault played Peter. Instead, he passed the night at his country home in White Plains, relieving the dreadful tension by acting out the play himself.

Frohman even displayed a fondness for his failures. "Shut up or I'll keep it running," he snapped at a subordinate who expressed sadness because a play was closing. Then he continued, reflectively, "You know, if I didn't keep a grip on myself, my sentiment would be the ruin of me." Always, however, the sentiment was anchored in the theatre. Asked (as he often was) why he never married, Frohman answered, "If I had a wife and children, I could never take the risks I'm called on to take every day."

Frohman functioned like the commander-in-chief of an army constantly engaged. In time he controlled the Empire, Garrick, Knickerbocker, Lyceum, and Savoy theatres in New York, and the Duke of York's, Globe, Comedy, Vaudeville, and Empire in London. To keep these filled with Frohman productions was no small problem. In chain-of-command fashion, he delegated authority to subordinates. One man had charge of weeding out playscripts, one screened actors, one supervised scenery, another hired stagehands.

Frohman's first assistant was an Oscar Wilde-ish fellow named Paul Potter, who came to this country accompanied by a beautiful Italian girl and a St. Bernard dog. (Frohman was dead when this lurid story finally came out.) Girl and dog gave sexual exhibitions before the decadent rich, and for these Potter made the arrangements and collected the fee. At the same time, he was a theatre genius who appeared to remember the plot of every play written. He also believed that any plot could be summarized on the back of a calling card. The office play reader, Theodore Burt Sayre, was equally versed in the theatre. Frohman also depended heavily on Elizabeth Marbury, the first woman to test the career of play agent. Established playwrights were allowed to read new plays to Frohman himself. If he liked a script, Frohman was often so carried away that he raved ecstatically. Once he told an author, "You've done the whole business. You've got pepper and salt, soup, entree, roast, salad, and dessert, coffee. It's a real play and I know it will be a success." After listening to a play by Augustus Thomas, Frohman sat mute, then reverently whispered, "That was almost too beautiful to bear." But he rejected it after showing it to his brother Daniel, who failed to respond.

Every Frohman play-in-rehearsal boasted a nominal director, but when Frohman was in New York he was apt to slip unobtrusively into a seat and take control. Often this became an odd business, for the most eminent man on Broadway was curiously inarticulate. Otis Skinner thought he knew the reason why. "His ideas were so great that their very presence seemed to overwhelm his utterance; the mental pictures he saw he lacked the power to describe," he writes.

True or not, Frohman usually conversed in strangulated phrases, delivering his teeming thoughts in a jumbled kind of cablese. As Billie Burke saw it, "He spoke in unpunctuated telegrams . . . made his wishes known by tight little jabs of his forefinger and by his eyes." Still, he seemed able to make himself completely understood, perhaps because eloquent eyes and forefinger made listeners catch meanings before he spoke. Frohman's ability to communicate at rehearsal was truly remarkable. From the depths of the auditorium he once called to James K.

Hackett, "Jim, that's fine, but just in there somewhere, you know what I mean." Oddly enough, Hackett knew. Again, he said to Otis Skinner, "Er—a—Otis—you know—er!" Skinner also knew. With James M. Barrie, Frohman's problem was simple. The two men spent contented hours in each other's company without uttering a word. "Because we were the two shyest men in the world, we understood each other perfectly," Barrie has said.

At rehearsal the image of Frohman's urbanity sometimes vanished. He lost his temper and, in the words of Billie Burke, "inflated himself like a pigeon, turning red and purple in the face, seeming to grow and tower, Neanderthal-like." With crisis in rehearsal one fact became bountifully clear—C.F. was the boss. When stars became temperamental he forgot the choppy telegraphic lingo to achieve masterful sarcasm. Once he ventured to correct the great Mrs. Patrick Campbell. The formidable Stella whirled in wrath. "You forget, Mr. Frohman," she stated, "that I am a great artist." "Mrs. Campbell," he answered softly, "I will try to keep your secret." At rehearsals of The *"Mind-the-Paint" Girl*, he found it necessary to chide Billie Burke, of whom he was deeply fond. "I know my lines, Mr. Frohman," she protested. "I don't doubt that, Bill," he replied, "but you don't seem to know Pinero's."

In all, Frohman produced more than 500 plays in New York, London, and Paris. The cherubic little man seemed to step on and off ocean liners as often as the average man bought cigars. He established a London office on Henrietta Street, taking abroad with him a young man named Charles Dillingham, who had been drama editor of the *New York Sun*. Dillingham, who would become an important producer in his own right, differed from most of Frohman's business associates in that he was tall, handsome and erudite. He also had a sense of humor. The first visitor at the new London office was an Englishman who ordered Dillingham to take his card into Frohman. "I have no time," Dillingham replied. "Why not?" the Englishman haughtily demanded. "I have to wash the office windows first," Dillingham said.

Though his own appearance hardly suggested a fountain of wit, Frohman too was quick with words. "He mixed jest with life," says Isaac Marcosson, "and it enabled him to meet crisis and disaster with unflagging spirit and smiling equanimity." Frohman enjoyed laughter, calling each day wasted that did not contain at least one hearty guffaw. Buoyed by this inner optimism, he maintained a cheerfulness which allowed him to see a bright world. "Never saw waves so high or receipts so low," he wired his office after an unhappy tryout in Atlantic City. Queried as to which seats in a theatre were best, he replied, "The paid ones." Again he was asked the difference between New York and out-of-town audiences. "Fifty cents," he answered. Frohman could also poke fun at himself. One of his speedy caricatures showed him looking up at the moon and saying, "I'll make a star of you yet."

Other Frohman quips reflected his staccato style of talk. "Do you spell highball with a hypen?" asked an actor. "No, with a siphon," Frohman snapped back. When the English author of a play cabled, "How's it going?" the producer cabled back, "Gone." Georgianna Drew Barrymore (mother of Lionel, Ethel, and John) telegraphed from San Francisco asking fresh costumes for the remainder of her tour. "No!" Frohman wired. "Oh!" Mrs. Barrymore answered back. This brought Frohman his laugh of the day, and in gratitude he dispatched an expensive wardrobe. He was equally delighted when a famous English actress wrote him her terms were a thousand dollars a week. "Accept with pleasure," he gallantly replied. "Thousand for acting, pleasure extra," she cabled back. Frohman laughed again.

To contemporaries Charles Frohman seemed an ever-spinning top (he resembled one physically) whirling cheerfully from one major production to another. Yet beneath the confident, adjusted surface, he nursed problems. He had a gnawing frustration, for he wished to write a play and begged playwrights to give him a quick, magic formula. A more immediate problem was his inordinate love of pastry. At Rector's he favored crabmeat Mornay, followed by sweets and more sweets. "He was so fond of sweets," says Barrie, "that he could never get them sweet enough and sometimes he mixed two in the hope that this would make them sweeter." Next to pastry he liked apple pie, lemon meringue pie, and pumpkin pie, in that order. His favorite drinks were lemonade and sarsaparilla. In his devotion to pastry, he was matched by the elegant Clyde Fitch. The two hesitated to indulge this awful fondness in public and retired to Fitch's home or Frohman's suite in the Hotel Knickerbocker to eat their monumental fill. To Frohman it all brought annoying intestinal disorders and (perhaps) painful neuralgia. Despite the apparent optimism and the determination to laugh once a day, Frohman was also capable of melancholy. To Fitch he once wrote, "I am down with a bad head, *and have been blue for two months.*"

But to the world he remained energetic, forceful, happy. No one who saw him could doubt his oft-repeated: "All I want is a good meal, a good cigar, good clothes, a good bed to sleep in, and the freedom to produce whatever play I like." He was Mr. Theatre, the greatest of international managers, whose vast success was based on a consuming passion for the theatre. It was said that Frohman could watch a play in any foreign tongue, then intuitively describe the plot, quoting dialogue. With English plays he could sometimes tell exactly what would happen from the placement of the furniture as the curtain went up. Together with this instinct he had an unerring good taste which involved not only scripts (he was horrified at any suggestion of vulgarity) but also costumes, scenery, diction, and the million details involved in play production.

Not the least of Frohman's assets was the faith he aroused in others. Those near him seemed to feel a compulsion to bask in his favor. "You wanted to please him," says Billie Burke, echoing Barrie's similar obsession. When Frohman made enemies, he seemed equally able to influence them in his favor. "Men who came to him in anger went away in satisfied peace," says a tribute to Frohman's almost hypnotic influence over his fellow man. Yet Frohman had detractors. They did not object so much to his personality as to his relentless dependence on foreign plays. Says Otis Skinner: "His general importation of material, instead of encouragement of the works of American writers, aroused bitterness."

George Middleton, a young playwright then, puts it this way: "Except for the already established Clyde Fitch and Augustus Thomas, Frohman encouraged no new American playwrights as he became successful. None of us youngsters ever thought of submitting a script to him. His play reader admitted to me that Frohman had never produced an American play by an unknown dramatist, even though he [the play reader] recommended it." Yet—as Middleton is broad-minded enough to admit—Frohman's partiality for foreign offerings allowed America to see excellent productions of plays by Pinero, Jones, Maugham, Sutro, and others, including the classic comedy *Charley's Aunt*. His imports often featured such fine overseas talents as Marie Tempest, Sir Charles Hawtrey, Sir Charles Wyndham, and Irene Vanbrugh.

Others called Frohman a limited human being, whose view of life was bounded by the four walls of a theatre. To him (it was said) all landscapes were stage sets, all people actors, all the world a stage. When accused of this, Frohman cheerfully admitted its truth. But as time went on, he lost a bit of his redeeming humor. His manner became imperative, his self-importance grew. "Shall

I read you the theatre news?" Paul Potter asked him on a train ride. "No, I *make* theatre news," he answered solemnly. With this came a refusal to admit he could be wrong. He liked to believe that all ideas about his plays stemmed from his own fertile mind. His subordinates worked hard to plant seeds of suggestion, hoping they would flower into orders from C.F. Yet his industry, plans, and international triumphs continued undiminished. Frohman remained the consummate theatre man, the world's Mr. Theatre.

Though his productions were the most famous, his theatres the most elegant, his stars the most glittering, his audiences the most sophisticated, he never lost sight of one bedrock axiom.

"Great successes," he often said, "are those that take hold of the masses, not the classes."

4: THE STAR FACTORY

Frohman became Mr. Charles Frohman—the name he really asked of life—with the opening of the beautiful Empire Theatre in 1893. Not only was the Empire a gem of a theatre and for a long period New York's farthest uptown (Broadway at Fortieth), but it was built completely to Frohman's taste. Auditorium and stage were the result of his distilled wisdom, and it is a tribute to him that the Empire remained New York's most dignified and atmospheric playhouse until it was demolished in 1953. The Empire's unusually large foyer-lobby measured fifty feet from doors to ticket-taker, with cushioned benches lining the walls under oil paintings of Frohman stars. On floors above were offices-for-rent, and Frohman's personal offices. The producer's large office on the third floor was the hub of his world: a rafter-ceilinged room with low bookshelves which gradually filled with bound copies of Frohman plays. Dominating the Gothic, cloisterlike room was a large stone fireplace, the mantel of which would eventually have a bronze head of Maude Adams as Peter Pan for its decoration. Against one wall was a heavy leather couch on which Frohman sat while reading scripts, conversing with others, or listening to playwrights read aloud. While sitting on this comfortable couch for any of these purposes, Frohman slipped off his Congress gaiters (he hated confining shoelaces or button shoes) to cross legs and sit like a jolly Buddha.

It is hard to conceive of the elegant Empire Theatre having a nickname. But it did. It was informally called the Star Factory—though it is difficult indeed to associate so utilitarian a word with so lovely a theatre. Yet new stars seemed to rise like comets from the Empire, to become the most envied actors on the American stage. Possibly some of them were not deserving of the unique honor of stardom, but by grace of Frohman they became stars anyway. For just as he changed the outlines of the American drama by lavishly importing foreign plays, so Frohman also changed the accepted contours of stardom.

Until Frohman, the favored beings who won star status battled their way upward by a combination of genius, industry, sweat, and presumably tears. No less than the self-made titans of industry, theatrical stars made themselves, doing it by the power of personality and performance—with a lacing of luck. Edwin Booth, Edwin Forrest, Joseph Jefferson, and others had fought for their own recognition. After it, they had won full right to manage their own careers.

In the personality of Charles Frohman lay qualities which allowed him to view stardom in a different perspective. He saw that the long process of achieving it made most stars middle-aged by the time they became dramatic heroes. Both stage-struck and intuitive himself, Frohman instinctively felt that the public was ready to worship younger stars. "Romance instead of respect," is the way he phrased it. He also believed he could mold stars. With his help, actors lacking the drive necessary for stardom could become stars anyway. The public would not care, so long as it had the stars to worship. "A star has a unique value in a play," Frohman was fond of saying. "He or she concentrates interest, for in some ways a play is like a successful dinner. No matter how splendidly served, the menu should always have one unique and striking dish which, despite its elaborate gastronomic surroundings, will long be remembered. This is one reason why you need a star in a play."

With his mind dwelling on a new kind of star system, Frohman was fortunate in the first top-rank performer he lured under his wing. This was John Drew. Born in 1853, Drew was the son of Louisa Lane Drew, the matriarchal actress who dominated the Arch Street Theatre in Philadelphia. Drew's father, who died at the age of thirty-four, had been an actor of exceptional promise. "Your father," Drew's mother told him, "was one of the fine actors of his day. Had he lived to be forty-five, instead of thirty-four, he would have been great. But too early success was his ruin. It left him nothing to do." Years later John Drew himself would be accused of doing too little on the stage and perhaps failing to find himself. The much-married actor Nat Goodwin settled this forever by saying: "Drew is a gentleman, on or off stage, and while many of the play folk do not consider him a great actor, they must admit that his mother and father were geniuses, which is something of which to be proud."

In our world of cold-war tensions it is hard to visualize the importance of John Drew to a country gracefully rounding the corner of a century. He was the public's idea of a gentleman, the man of eternal good manners, faultless breeding, unvarying grace. The words *nonchalant, savoir-faire,* and *imperturbable* seemed to have been coined only to describe him. "Uncle Jack Drew," wrote Lionel Barrymore years later, "deserves the highest honors of all the male members of our family, for it is so much harder to be a great gentleman than to be a great actor."

Thus bountifully equipped, John Drew became the first actor to bridge the gap between the theatre world and so-called society. He played polo, a game hitherto reserved for the rich. He owned a stable of horses, and easily attained membership in both the Brook and Racquet & Tennis clubs, while also belong-

ing to the actors' Players and Lambs. He spent summers in East
Hampton, Long Island, and in time became citizen number one
of that attractive town where he was devotedly addressed as
Squire. Not only were Drew's manners superb, but his clothes
were the same. He wore shirts and ties from Charvet and made
regular trips to London to be outfitted on Savile Row. Arriving
at Liverpool, he saluted the proximity of his London tailor by
lifting his walking stick to declaim, "Poole and Peal, I'm with
you again." He also remains one of the few men in history who
dressed for bed as well as for the boulevard. He wore custom-
made nightshirts with maroon-stitched seams and French-
embroidered monograms over the breast pocket. Each night before retiring he neatly folded into this pocket a hand-loomed
Irish-linen handkerchief.

Perhaps the world's short memory of the fine figure of John
Drew stems from the fact that photographs usually show his face
dominated by a large, well-kept mustache. This deflects the
eye from the dashing good looks apparent in his younger, pre-
mustache years. Drew was of average stature, with a large head,
impressive nose, and broad shoulders. A prominent (though not-
too-prominent) jaw added deep masculinity to his face. In
photographs all this is blurred by the mustache. Still, it was always the polished manner, the drawling nonchalance, the good-
humored *savoir-faire* that made John Drew a personality. He
had a rare knack of creating an aura about himself. Also, he had
the most priceless gift that can be bestowed on a light comedian.
In his easy way, he seemed to enjoy himself more than anyone
else in the theatre.

From the beginning Drew's offstage personality dominated
his roles. He possessed his glorious nonchalance as a young man,
making his iron-handed mother consider him too easygoing to
appear on the stage. Finally she relented, offering a small part
in a play aptly named *Cool as a Cucumber*. The young man per-

formed with an ease impressive in a minor role. It so distressed his mother that as he exited to the wings she ad-libbed, "What a dreadful young man! I wonder if he will ever amount to anything? He has far too much confidence."

The elder Mrs. Drew was additionally annoyed when John brought home a young English actor named Maurice Barrymore, who instantly became enamored of Drew's younger sister, Georgianna. The elder Mrs. Drew thought Barrymore a theatrical upstart and did not hesitate to state this. Nonetheless, the two married. Their children were Lionel, Ethel, and John—and of course John Drew was Uncle Jack.

In 1875 Drew left Philadelphia for New York, where he became leading man in the famous Augustin Daly Stock Company. Daly was author of the celebrated *Under the Gaslight*, wherein for the first time a character was strapped to railroad tracks in front of an approaching locomotive. Despite this flair for the spectacular he believed in ensemble playing, and over the next fifteen years coupled Drew, Ada Rehan, Mrs. G. H. Gilbert, and James Lewis into an accomplished quartet known throughout the country as the Big Four. During this period Drew played Petruchio to Ada Rehan's Kate, and in this role—if in no other during his career—he subordinated the Drew charm to a part. It is said that his finest acting came with this *Taming of the Shrew*.

In 1891 the thirty-eight-year-old Drew was still playing opposite Ada Rehan. He had established himself as the country's most polished delineator of light comedy. Daly, on the other hand, was wearing down. With elderly irascibility, he offended the Big Four by rescinding an arrangement (based on that of the Comédie Française) which gave actors a share of the weekly profits. Charles Frohman may have learned of this, or merely sensed that John Drew was growing restless. At any rate, he dispatched emissaries to the actor. "Frohman is the coming man," they told him. Next, Frohman invited Drew to take part in a poker game. At this Drew was a splendid winner. Not for years did it occur to him that the canny Frohman had further softened him up by seeing that he won.

What Frohman dangled before John Drew was stardom—the chance to dominate his own company. He also offered an increase in salary, and finally the men signed a three-year contract (at the end of which time it was renewed by a handshake). Drew first appeared under the Frohman banner in a French success, *The Masked Ball,* by Alexandre Brisson and Albert Carre. Any doubts that John Drew in person was as fine a gentleman as those he played onstage vanished as the curtain fell. Drew then stepped forward to pay courtly tribute to his recent mentor, Augustin Daly:

> It is trite and hackneyed, perhaps, to allude to a particular time as the proudest and happiest moment in one's life, but if ever phrase were apt for an occasion, I feel that particular one is befitting this moment. This splendid welcome accorded to me by you—kind friends rather than spectators or auditors, who have with your plaudits and consideration encouraged me for so many years in the past—makes this, indeed, a proud and happy moment for me.
>
> But I feel that all these plaudits and this great greeting might not have been for me, had it not been for one who taught me how to merit and deserve them, who from the beginning of my career has watched and guided my steps, smoothing the way to success for me, and encouraging me in moments of trial and discouragement, and, in fine, striving to make me worthy of this honor tonight.
>
> I feel, too, that this poor and halting tribute of the heart is little to offer after the years of care and trouble he has bestowed on me, but it is from the heart that I wish to offer it. I am glad, too, to offer it before you—his friends as well as mine. I see that I need not name him, my friend and preceptor, Mr. Augustin Daly.

The Masked Ball was a milestone for others besides Drew. A young Clyde Fitch adapted the play into English. After much private cogitation and public speculation, Drew's leading lady had been revealed as Maude Adams, a frail but dedicated girl of twenty. Miss Adams had lately scored a New York hit as Nell, a consumptive factory girl, in *Lost Paradise*. In *The Masked Ball* she played Suzanne, a flighty mademoiselle who simulates drunkenness in order to reform a dissipated husband. Young girls who imbibed were a rarity on contemporary stages and Maude Adams' moment as a tipsy child-wife was a true test of her ability. Attired in an Empire gown of silk brocade, waving a long-stemmed rose vaguely to emphasize aimless remarks, she did so well that audiences called her bewitching. Both Fitch and Miss Adams covered themselves with glory, making Charles Frohman winner all-round. For Drew fully proved his right to stardom, demonstrating a hold on the carriage trade which he never lost.

From now on John Drew's September opening at the Empire Theatre became a theatrical event as stable as Labor Day. Only after this did the new fall season really begin. Then, after a month or two in New York, the Drew company began to tour. One year Drew traditionally made one-week and one-night stands to the West Coast. The alternate year he toured the South.

When reading plays, which he often did while munching chocolates, Charles Frohman kept his stars in mind. He was perpetually on the alert for a John Drew part, a Maude Adams part, an Ethel Barrymore part. The roles he provided for John Drew over the years were drawing-room comedies of lightest tinge. There was—even Drew admitted it—a dreadful sameness to them all. In 1909, seventeen years after this initial Frohman opening, the John Drew play was *Inconstant George*, another adaptation from the French. "An Anglo-Saxon fig leaf over a

Gallic plot," one critic called it. In this Drew, now close to fifty, played a young man named George, described as "gay, irresponsible, delightful." If nothing else, George loved the fair sex—"the more the merrier," he said of females. He was carrying on simultaneous love affairs with both the wife and mistress of a close friend. Also in his heart was Micheline, "a wild, sensitive, primitive child," the ward of the friend and madly in love with George. (Micheline was Mary Boland.) In one scene Drew, lolling in bed in blue silk pajamas, is faced by the indignant friend who brands him a libertine and a louse. Before the final curtain George is redeemed by none other than the wild, sensitive Micheline. Concluded one reviewer: "As he has done so often before in adaptations from the French, Mr. Drew carries the performance on his own shoulders."

Drew was a fellow of wit and wisdom. His young Barrymore relatives hopefully combed encyclopedias and dictionaries, but never found an esoteric question Uncle Jack failed to answer quickly. "Everything he did, in life or on the stage, seemed effortless, and his profound knowledge seemed effortless too," Ethel Barrymore has written. Many theatregoers wished Drew would throw off the yoke of drawing-room comedy to attempt more taxing roles. Drew knew of this, but seemed satisfied to do nothing about it. Indeed, he was so totally relaxed and free of nerves that even opening nights held no terrors for him. He took premieres as lightly as billiard games at The Players. In *The Second in Command*, he was supposed to lie down, simulating sleep. To the horror of the cast, he stretched out on the opening night and actually fell into snoring slumber. At the same time, he always enjoyed his hours on the stage and never let down a performance. "An actor is exactly like a soldier," he once said. "He has to be there, or be dead."

Still, there can be little doubt that Drew wearied of his roles. In an effort to fend off boredom, he played tricks on other actors, whispering amusing or ribald asides into onstage ears. For this, he early found a peerless victim in Ada Rehan, a beautiful lady who could be reduced to helpless giggles by the introduction of any unexpected business. Maude Adams, Drew's next leading lady, was the opposite. She never cracked a wintry smile over Drew's inspired sallies. His niece Ethel, who says Drew possessed a little humorous demon, was often broken up by his antics.

Eventually Drew found the perfect foil in bright, redheaded Billie Burke, who became his leading lady in 1907. Frohman had plucked charming Billie from the English musical stage, at which her producer, Sir Charles Hawtrey, warned her: "You will miss your dancing and singing. You may not think so now, but straight comedy is dry, hard work." Hawtrey went on to explain that in musical comedy an actress directs everything toward the audience. In comedy or drama she plays to her fellow actors—as if in a room with them.

Hawtrey had been a severe taskmaster—so much so that at her first Empire rehearsal Miss Burke asked Drew, "Is this the way you want me to make my entrance?" He looked at her in astonishment and drawled, "My dear child, do it any way you like." Miss Burke was also amazed on opening night—the play was *My Wife*—to find Drew continuing the kind of break-up tomfoolery (gracious japery, she calls it) he had inserted into rehearsals. Miss Burke had dimples on her elbows and during first-night love scenes Drew's fingers searched for them. "Where are they?" he whispered tenderly. "Higher," she whispered, biting cheeks to hold back giggles. The audience noticed none of this and at the end Drew was accorded twenty curtain calls.

John Drew was called "The First Gentleman of the Theatre." Also the "Master of the Monosyllable." Reputedly he could say "Gad!" with a hundred different inflections. During the run of *My Wife* Billie Burke set out to test this. In one scene the pair sat at a table while she drew a note from her handbag. She began pulling out all kinds of preposterous gadgets she had bought during the afternoon. "Gad! What's this?" Uncle Jack asked with magnificent aplomb at each one. "Gad! What's coming next?" Not once did he lose his incomparable poise and he always pulled the play back on course by saying at last, "Well, and it's really the note we're looking for, aren't we?"

Bored or not, Drew never complained. He cheerfully went on earning an excellent living, at the same time establishing standards of manners and dress for the nation. He had married Josephine Baker of Philadelphia in 1880. Turn-of-the-century rumor said he occasionally cast an interested eye on other females, but on the whole he seems to have been pleasantly married. Drew enjoyed drinking, but almost never got drunk. The strict gentleman did not use profanity and never stooped to vulgarity. He expected others to abide by the same code. To a man who undertook to tell him a smutty tale, he said coldly, "I do not think you know me well enough to tell me that kind of story." Offstage his favorite exclamation was "Death!" which he delivered with nearly as many inflections as "Gad!" In moments of strenuous emotion he would utter, "Death and the young sculptor!"—a quotation none of the diligent young Barrymores could ever trace to a classical source.

As much as anyone else John Drew enjoyed several popular stories that swirled about his polished person. One declared he had a glass eye, and from time to time Drew saw fit graciously to deny this. Another was a favored Sunday-Supplement feature which said, in effect: "John Drew is not an actor, he only plays himself"; or "John Drew does not act, he merely behaves." This was a calumny widely believed, but never by members of the profession. Actors knew John Drew was very much an actor. In the words of Ethel Barrymore, "His acting was so perfectly effortless that it didn't seem to be acting." Says Mary Boland: "He was the first of the completely natural school." Nat Goodwin, evaluating Drew's skill, ended: "The most difficult roles to play are those that fall to the light comedian. He must be perfectly human and true, for he is portraying the character one meets every day."

Drew's only complaint against a congenial existence seemed to be the presence on the market of a five-cent John Drew cigar. The nonchalant actor was upset by this and claimed that the cigar had been named in his honor without his knowledge or consent. However, friends believed that during an unusually bibulous evening Drew listened to the blandishments of a cigar manufacturer and gave verbal permission for use of his name. The fact that Drew never sued or otherwise took action bears this out.

Dedicated playgoers of the time thought that, despite the prosperity of the union, Charles Frohman was bad for Drew. The actor's absolute faith in Frohman's judgment, the producer's determination to have Drew play nothing but smooth drawing-room comedy or polite melodrama—these may have kept a fine actor from truly finding himself. But Drew continued to enjoy every moment of his professional life. He liked the Road as much as the Empire Theatre in New York. On the Road, as Billie Burke recalls: "He amused the entire company, entertained us lavishly with dinner parties, ordered cavalcades of carriages for us to go sight-seeing in, and introduced us to his friends in every large and small city en route."

One day Drew encountered the elderly Joseph H. Choate, who had been Ambassador to Great Britain in the days Drew played there with the Augustin Daly company. Ever the gentleman, Drew politely inquired, "Do you remember me, Mr. Choate?"

Choate looked at him and said, "Good God, it's Drew! Mercy, why don't you grow old?"

"I don't know, Mr. Choate," Drew answered, "unless I can

explain it in the words of old Mr. Adam in *As You Like It*, who says, 'Never in my youth did I apply hot and rebellious liquors in my blood.' "

Choate studied him. "Drew," he inquired sharply, "is that entirely true?"

Drew laughed. "No, sir, it isn't. But that's what quotations are for."

It was a pleasant life, and John Drew seemed determined to keep it that way!

Charles Frohman liked to develop his own stars. "He is *made*; I like to *make* stars," he said when the popular Chauncey Olcott expressed a desire to join a Frohman company. But Frohman was also astute enough to know that the producer of twenty plays a season must call on established outside stars for help. As a result nearly every important actor of the day appeared at one time or other under the Frohman banner. Under the impressive CHARLES FROHMAN PRESENTS were to be found such famous names-in-lights as Henry Miller, Viola Allen, William H. Crane, Otis Skinner, Francis Wilson, Edna May, James K. Hackett, Julia Marlowe, Nat Goodwin, Kyrle Bellew, Alla Nazimova, Mrs. Fiske—and, from England, Ellen Terry, Marie Tempest, Charles Hawtrey, Mrs. Patrick Campbell, Charles Wyndham, Constance Collier, and A. E. Matthews. In 1909 Frohman offered a program of Isadora Duncan in classical dances.

Yet the new—or fairly new—actors he helped to stardom were his pride and joy. In addition to John Drew, Maude Adams, Ethel Barrymore, and Billie Burke, these included Annie Russell, William Faversham, Virginia Harned, Clara Bloodgood, Edith Wynne Matthison, Charles Rann Kennedy, William Collier, Margaret Anglin, Fay Davis, Margaret Illington, Marie Doro, Doris Keane, Julia Sanderson, Pauline Frederick, Richard Bennett, William Courtenay, Bruce McRae, Donald Brian, Elsie

Ferguson, Pauline Chase, Richard Carle, John Emerson, Blanche Bates, and Grace George.

Next to John Drew, Frohman's most formidable male star was the actor-playwright-director William Gillette, who had known Frohman from the days of the Madison Square Theatre. Gillette's frosty charm has been etched by Gene Fowler: "Slim, straight, he had the face of a tomahawk, the manners of a curator, the mind of a professor of Romance Languages. He had been educated to the hilt: forged at Hartford, tempered at Yale, sharpened at Harvard, and finally damascened at the Massachusetts Fine Arts Institute. He painted in oils and enjoyed a membership in the American Academy of Arts and Letters."

Frohman had booked over the Road Gillette's first great success *Held by the Enemy*, then personally produced its successor, a comedy called *Too Much Johnson*. In a sense Gillette—austere, Lincolnesque, unapproachable—rivaled John Drew as the first gentleman of the American theatre. Billie Burke, who yields to none in her admiration of Uncle Jack, considers Gillette the great aristocrat of the theatre. In Drew a bedazzled public found the quintessence of the urbane, cosmopolitan gentleman. Gillette was more American: crotchety, individualistic, caustic. Even when young he showed a demon integrity bordering on the eccentric. As a fledgling author he attended the opening night of an established playwright who might have aided his career. In the lobby, after the show, he encountered the man. "Great house, splendid performance, bad play," Gillette barked, and vanished into the night.

This abundantly talented man—he had reached his forties by the turn of the century—enjoyed wearing his stage costumes offstage. (At one point pedestrians saw Sherlock Holmes stalking the avenues.) He loved cats, tinkered with the works of clocks, collected old bird cages, and corresponded in varicolored inks. Like Frohman and Belasco he was stage-struck from boyhood, and with his multiple talents seized on playwriting as the shortest way to theatre eminence. Still, he saw no reason why he should not act in his own plays and direct them as well. With his match-thin body, incisive face, staccato diction, and spareness of gesture, he carved out an acting realm as exclusive as Drew's. It was said that with his studied underplaying he could steal a scene with a glance or a nod. Others thought he tailored his own plays so that he could stand still while the other characters dashed furiously about, leaving him always center-stage, the focus of all eyes. "This," said one pundit, "is a splendid trick but only permissible to actors who pay their own royalties."

It was Frohman who conceived the idea of having Gillette adapt and play Sherlock Holmes, a part he would revive repeatedly, for the final time at the age of seventy-four. Frohman sought out Sir Arthur Conan Doyle, who agreed to an adaptation provided no love interest was inserted. Nonetheless, the theatre-wise Gillette added a dash of *l'amour*. Frohman sat fidgeting while Doyle perused the script. At the end the author merely said, "It's good to meet the old chap again."

A string of hits allowed Gillette to build a large estate near his home town of Hartford, Connecticut. There he indulged his expensive whims and a desire for patrician solitude. Among other novelties, he built a miniature railroad to run over the acres of the estate. The few allowed to know Gillette well admired his mordant wit. He never married, but one of his most quoted quips was beamed at the noble institution. Speaking of a middle-aged actor wed to a young wife, he said, "She adores him passionately and annoys him in other ways." For all his surface arrogance, Gillette could make fun of himself. When the playwright George Broadhurst visited the Hartford estate, Gillette took him on a tour of the grounds. Two goats poked noses through palings to lick Gillette's hand. "Up here even the goats love me," the actor said proudly. Broadhurst snorted. "Love you!" he answered. "They only want to be fed." Gillette fixed him with his famous glare. "George," he said, "there comes a time in every man's life when he calls that love."

Gillette's performances were individual and striking, all eyes riveted on his stark person. His every movement was accomplished with dignity and skill. The same could not be said for other popular actors of the day. Some of Gillette's contemporaries were disparagingly called Cuff-Shooters. This stemmed from the fact that before the telling lines of a play they importantly shot their cuffs. At the truly meaningful line of a script—usually the one containing the play title—Cuff-Shooters shot cuffs twice.

It is said that (of the Frohman stable) William Faversham was a Cuff-Shooter. Another who sometimes acted for Frohman was the lean-faced and brooding James K. Hackett, who in some circles was deemed untalented. Indeed, a cruel theatrical witticism said the K in Hackett's name stood for Kant-Act. Hackett was a matinee idol with a striking profile and the bravura mannerisms of the breed. Young women flocked to theatres when he appeared, swooning over his exploits and weeping copiously into lace handkerchiefs at his unhappy stage predicaments. With such a devoted following Hackett perhaps had no need to become an expert actor. He was also a man on whom Lady Luck once turned a most beaming smile. At a low point in his fortunes —possibly because of Kant-Act—Hackett found himself the unexpected beneficiary of several million dollars, willed by a relative he barely knew. He promptly threw a sumptuous dinner party for all his creditors, putting under each plate a check for the exact amount he owed. This hardly scratched the surface of the lucky man's fortune. Next he bought two elegant town houses, knocked down the intervening wall, and lived in splendor for the rest of his life.

If James K. Hackett was never taken seriously, Richard Mans-

field was treated with the utmost respect. Here, despite bewildering facets of personality, was the country's most dedicated actor. Like Gillette, he was a man of multiple talents. He
was a sculptor, painter, linguist, and brilliant conversationalist.
His roles ran an unusual gamut, from Koko and Brummell to
Brutus and Shylock. Mansfield was the far-seeing actor who
introduced George Bernard Shaw to this country. He presented
Arms and the Man in 1894 and *The Devil's Disciple* in 1897.
Later, he placed *Candida* in rehearsal, but decided he was not
physically equipped to play the poet Marchbanks. Mansfield
made *Cyrano de Bergerac* his own. When he died (in 1907) he
had just concluded an impressive pioneering run in Ibsen's *Peer
Gynt.*

Offstage as well as on, Mansfield played the flamboyant actor,
often seeming as gaudy as his famous Beau Brummell. He wore
yellow silk dressing gowns, collared and lined with mink. His
talk was grandiloquent, with suitable facial emphasis. Despite the
vast sums he earned, Mansfield was often impoverished—which
may have abetted his fear of the Syndicate. Yet on the surface
this never appeared to faze him. While hard pressed financially,
he toured elegantly in a private railroad car, spent summers on
his yacht or at a mansion in New London. Elizabeth Marbury
sat in Mansfield's Madison Square apartment one afternoon while
the landlord pounded on the door demanding rent. Mansfield
finally routed him by roaring, "Cannot you realize that it is I,
Richard Mansfield, whose mere presence in this despicable
house has filled it to overflowing, and thus raised the price of
these apartments? You consider that I owe you rent? Bah! A
preposterous idea! I have brought you fortune and fame, and
should be paid by you rather than I should ever pay *you*." After
observing the great actor in this and other embarrassing situations, Miss Marbury concluded with admiration, "No one I have
ever met could owe money as gracefully as Mansfield."

"A nerve-wracked devil, given to explosions of temper and wild rages—moods governed his every action," one contemporary wrote of Mansfield. In restaurants he was capable of erupting into temperament-tantrums so violent that he threw lamb chops at offending waiters. His outsized ego never betrayed him. As he rose to acknowledge plaudits at a testimonial dinner given him in an auditorium once known as Metzerdot's Music Hall, his eye glimpsed a faded M still visibly entwined on a pillar. "What a charming tribute," he murmured. Yet he could view himself with amusement, and liked to tell of a visit by Sarah Bernhardt to his private car. Seating herself, the aging French actress tightly wrapped a leopard skin around her legs. "To protect her virtue, I assume," Mansfield purred.

Mansfield's vibrant personality and the stimulating scope of his theatrical vision kept critical attention focused on him through the years. William Winter produced two long books devoted to his art. But though his performances were much admired, Mansfield never received wholehearted acclaim. Like Henry Irving in England, he seemed a personality first, actor second. Ever arresting, he appealed to the mind rather than the emotions. One ingredient lacking was the magic one of sentiment. He was much admired for effects, yet these were flamboyant tricks of overplaying or technical tricks. Possibly preoccupation with them kept him from his moment of truth as an actor. "He touched his art, but never assaulted it," one critic opined. Another, pondering why Mansfield had become an actor when so liberally endowed with other talents, wrote devastatingly: "He does everything wrong, well." Once in his career Mansfield undertook to appear in London. At intermission an Englishman was told that he was watching the performance of America's greatest actor. The man's eyebrows rose. "Really," he said, "what an extraordinary country!"

But if his performances seemed more indebted to energy than

to inspiration, Mansfield at least viewed himself and the theatre in heroic size. He unhesitatingly tackled the hardest roles he could find: from Shakespeare to Shaw, Cyrano to Mr. Hyde, Brummell to Peer Gynt. Offstage he was an infuriating man—"His channels were the deep dark waters of the uncanny." But he satisfied audiences. Departing the theatre after a Mansfield performance, most of those who had seen him thought, "Tonight I have truly seen a performance."

Frohman walked among the actors of his Star Factory with ease and assurance. He understood them, and they him. Even the most rampant ego found him tolerant. But with playwrights, Mr. Theatre seemed oddly ill at ease. He appeared to feel that writers were an uncongenial group. Several of his utterances show a lack of sympathy for the author and his problems. "I get two kinds of plays," he once grunted, "those I like to produce and those I don't like to produce." Again, testifying in a lawsuit, he was asked, "Mr. Frohman, these authors, when they bring plays to you, they think the plays are good, don't they?" "No," Frohman answered icily. The lawyer was taken aback. "They don't think they're good?" he demanded incredulously. "They *know* they're good," Frohman snapped.

The writers Frohman preferred were the ones with careers already fashioned. Barrie, Pinero, Jones, Galsworthy, Maugham—these were gentlemen, as behavior-perfect as their plays were well made, in company as restful as the excellent cigars they proffered. They were, of course, Englishmen, behind them centuries of practice in controlling unruly emotions. . . . Yet Frohman might also point with pride to his native land, for in one case at least America had produced his own kind of playwright. Clyde Fitch—now there was a fine fellow! If Americans had to write plays, their plays should always be like Fitch's. More, the playwrights themselves should be personally like Fitch. . . .

No—there were no rough edges to Clyde Fitch, nothing un-couth or blatantly American. He was what Frohman most ad-mired—a consummate theatre craftsman. Frohman did not pro-duce all Fitch's plays—at the peak of his career the prolific author wrote enough to keep several managers busy. But with *Barbara Frietchie*, the first original Fitch play on which the two com-bined, Frohman learned the full measure of his man. Like other busy producers Frohman owned several storehouses full of scenery, furniture, and décor from past plays. Fitch spent several happy days poking around among this, which in Frohman's ex-perience no playwright had ever done. From then on Fitch kept in mind what props and scenery resided in the warehouse. For his Frohman plays he drew on this inexpensive backlog when-ever possible.

In Frohman's book, Fitch was almost in a class with Barrie, Pinero, and Sardou. He too seemed a bridge between the theatre of the Old World and that of the New. A neophyte drama critic named George Jean Nathan saw this somewhat differently. "A graceful, pretty kleptomaniac," he said of Fitch, "who pilfers the counter of European comedy." The fact that Fitch's comedies bore a European gloss never bothered Frohman; it did not seem remarkable in a playwright who adored Italy, loved France, and seemed to step aboard ocean liners as often as Froh-man himself.

In other ways, Fitch was an unlikely American. In a day where men dressed conservatively, he was fastidious and color-ful in his attire, wearing high starched collars, English hats, and fawn-colored spats. He liked rich colors in clothes and was a pioneer in wearing unmatched coats and trousers. All this caused an alleged friend to whisper that Fitch's clothes seemed to lead him into a room. Yet Fitch seemed willing to be thought a dude. Better than anyone in the theatre (with the exception of John Drew) he knew how high society behaved. When he bewailed the fact that no American actor knew how to handle a silver dining service properly—as Fitch once did—the edict had the ring of full authority. Yet Fitch's interest in the production of his many plays progressed beyond the realm of table manners. He was an indefatigable scrawler of notes to everyone involved in a production, and from abroad bombarded managers with messages that said, "The lace must be coffee-colored—NEVER WHITE. The pink must be deep rose—NEVER PALE." Yet ultra-fastidiousness never completely blinded him to reality. Criticized for putting a certain actress in a play, he answered, "She has that warm quality of cheap emotionalism which is just what I need." He could also be wickedly acid, and remarked of another actress, "She is so damned dramatic that she couldn't take a boiled potato off the dish without stabbing it."

With all this, Clyde Fitch was one of the dazzling figures on contemporary Broadway. He was a solid-looking five-eight in height, with olive skin, receding dark hair, a silky turned-up mustache, and heavy lids over shy eyes. He was also likable, witty, unfailingly polite. "The essence of Continental courtesy and culture," an observer called him. After becoming interested in the drama as a chi-chi undergraduate at Amherst, Fitch wrote in over twenty years thirty-six original plays, a-dapted twenty-six from the French and German, and made five dramatizations of popular novels (among these, of course, was the salacious *Sapho*). As a result he came to average $250,000 a year in a pre-tax era. At one dazzling moment of his career, Fitch had five plays running simultaneously in New York—a record no other playwright has ever achieved. On another enchanted evening, two Fitch plays opened along the Great White Way. One was *The Truth*, his favorite play and the one which has best worn the test of time. *The Truth* opened at the Criterion on the night of January 7, 1907. As its curtain fell the audience clamored for a curtain speech. Fitch obliged, and while he did a friend called, "Hurry! They're shouting for you across the street." Fitch cut short his words at *The Truth* and dashed across to the Astor, where the curtain had fallen on *The Straight Road*. There he made a second felicitous speech.

New York critics did not approve *The Truth*, though in England it was a smash success. "The only man sure of favorable criticism in America," the playwright said once, "is the dramatist on his way up or on his way down." Fitch, so industrious and likable, had somehow incurred the hostility of the New York press. Perhaps this was because he was widely believed to be a homosexual—or was it envy for the ease with which he apparently created? Whatever it was, New York critics seldom gave him a break and seemed actually to enjoy downgrading him. Other pundits, in less biased judgments, also found things to disparage in his plays. He was (they said) a supremely skillful craftsman who gave the impression of never fully believing in his work. His work seemed to be the product of a facile mind rather than a beating heart. "He embroiders his plays," one writer charged. Fitch's own actions sometimes bore this out. For *Her Own Way*, he created a hairdresser who spoke East Side slang. The character made a hit, which both pleased and annoyed him. Shrugging impeccable shoulders, he said, "If they like that sort of thing, I'll give them twenty such." He did, writing a play called *Glad of It* entirely in East Side vernacular. Where one character had been right, twenty proved too many. *Glad of It* was a rapid failure.

Fitch's approach was often called feminine—a later age might say bitchy. "The sensitive predominates in his work—delicacy, tact, and a feminine manner in apprehending the meanings of life," the towering James Huneker wrote. Together with this he displayed a gift for sharp observation and quick psychological insight. "With a kind of smiling irony," a critic said, "he can plunge down beneath the crust of life." Fitch never seemed

anxious to pioneer or expand the outlines of American drama.
Rather he was content merely to utilize a remarkable instinct
for what audiences wanted. "His preoccupation with the idea
of successful Entertainment was a blemish on his work,"
Huneker adds. Four years after graduating from Amherst he
had made a mark as a coming playwright. Historical and costume
romances were the rage and his *Nathan Hale, Major Andre*, and
Barbara Frietchie (a young girl who says, "Shoot! You've taken
a life already dearer to me than my own. Shoot, and I'll thank
you! But spare your flag!") fitted perfectly with the times.
When drawing-room comedy emerged, Fitch was even more at
home, for most of his life was passed in drawing rooms. Women
always dominated his plays (his closest American rival, Augustus
Thomas, created men with blood in their veins). Fitch wrote devastatingly of women, but nonetheless appeared able to please
them. On the surface his society women seemed elegant and
fastidious. The playwright's four-act scalpel usually ended by
exposing them as shallow, venal snobs. One of his most successful efforts was *The Climbers*, in which a social climber and her
two daughters, in funeral mourning, bargain over the sale of a
now-useless fall wardrobe.

Because of his fondness for high-toned backgrounds, it is easy
to imagine all Fitch's plays resounding to the tinkle of teacups
and the pitter-patter of sophisticated dialogue. Yet he was a
knowing theatre craftsman who nursed a Belasco-like affection
for realism and stunts. Much of *The Stubbornness of Geraldine*
took place on a pitching ocean liner. *Captain Jinks of the Horse
Marines* (Ethel Barrymore's first success) boasted a stunning
replica of the Hotel Brevoort in 1870. In a play titled simply
Girls, Fitch outdid himself. The story of three bachelor girls in
New York City, this included the clamorous banging of steam-
pipes, a singer practicing across the air shaft, fights with an
unfriendly janitor, and the washing of handkerchiefs in a

washbowl, with subsequent drying of same on windowpanes. Fitch was thirty-five years old at the magic moment when five of his plays ran simultaneously on Broadway. Usually, he directed his own works, casting the parts from a select group of actors with whom he preferred to work. With his soaring prosperity went a compulsive eagerness to work, and personally to transact all possible business. When in New York, he was easily visible around the theatre district, the cut and color of his modish attire spoiled by playscripts jammed into his pockets. To new playwrights, he was encouraging, understanding, and ever friendly. "If you will come in Saturday at six I will be delighted to see you for a word, a puff, a sip," he wrote aspiring George Middleton.

Those who did visit Fitch found other rewards than advice and encouragement. For the sybaritic style in which the playwright lived was an inspiration (or would it be the opposite?) to those who hoped to wrest a living from the theatre. Few men have lived so splendidly on Manhattan Island, for Fitch's five-story town house at 118 East Fortieth Street (Telephone: 6302-38th) was a private museum of art, as elegant and colorful as a European palace. The entrance hall at street level was white and dimly lit, on one wall a Della Robbia "Mother and Child." A marble mantel displayed five Wedgwood urns, while a marble fountain shot a shaft of water which tumbled into a basin rimmed with growing flowers. In a niche of the winding stairway leading to the first floor stood a statue of an adolescent Adonis. In the drawing room were Gobelin tapestries, Louis XIV furniture, Watteau shepherds, crimson draperies, a piano of blond mahogany, and the pungent aroma of Oriental incense. The dining room was California redwood, with red brocades, gilt candelabra, and china of Delft, Spode, or Lowestoft, depending on the master's mood.

Fitch's workroom—if it can be called that—was over the drawing room, lined with bookshelves, brightened by a Gainsborough, a Corot, a Diaz, a Meissonier. His bedroom was oak, lined with crimson brocade, with a silver crucifix once owned by the Empress Josephine on the wall beside a huge fourposter. Attending Fitch in these supernal surroundings was a small army of man-servants discreetly attired in blue-and-white livery. In the kitchen was a French chef. To one visiting Englishman, Fitch's home was the finest gathering spot in America. "He collects together the most intellectual men and, to his credit be it said, the most beautiful of women," he reported.

Fitch, who spent so much time abroad, also owned a large house called the Quiet Corner, in Greenwich, Connecticut. This too was jammed with art treasures, so many that eventually the playwright acquired another home in nearby Katonah which he called the Other House. In all these establishments he entertained lavishly, yet managed to keep up his prodigious work output. Daily he peppered friends with lively, heavily italicized notes. After the lukewarm reviews of *The Truth* in New York, he wrote to a friend, "In spite of its rather *feeble press*, I am in *hopes* it will even develop into a success. No *hope* ever springs *so* eternal as that in a dramatist's breast."

Fitch should know. He was *the* dramatist of the day.

5: *PETER PAN*

Who was the brightest of the stars produced by the Star Factory?

Of all the scintillating Frohman personalities, the most glittering always remained a luminous slip of a woman who resembled a lively girl, often played a boy, once portrayed a barnyard rooster, and lived a private life so remote that she might indeed have been a heavenly star twinkling far above this earth.

Her name was Maude Adams and beside her ardent following (it included hundreds of thousands of children) the crowds that thronged to see John Drew, Richard Mansfield, and Sarah Bernhardt dwindled into unhappy insignificance. While other actresses of the time were popular, Miss Adams improved on this by having passionate admirers. "Her popularity is such that it amounts almost to unreasoning worship," said her contemporary Forrest Izard. "One can safely say that, at least among the women of America, there is a Maude Adams cult. The mere announcement of her name, without respect to the play she is acting, is enough to fill any theatre in the land."

Miss Adams' earning power equaled her drawing power. Over twenty years (she retired in 1917) this brightest of stars was in a position to earn $20,000 for nearly every week she worked. Often she acted fifty-two weeks a year. It is likely that—in days before taxes—she profited more from her talents than any other performer in the world. Money, though, was the least of her concerns. She lived quietly, splurging only on rare trips to Europe. Merely in a small, spontaneous way might she be called extravagant. From her own pocketbook she often increased the salaries of underpaid bit actors, or of stagehands who pleased her by laboring overtime. Occasionally, as she arrived at the theatre the star would spy a schoolgirl shedding tears outside for lack of enough money for a ticket. Miss Adams would then stop her carriage to buy her one, or would issue orders from backstage that all balcony seats be lowered in price to let such girls in.

But such human aspects of Miss Adams were little known, for this was a time before personal press-agentry and rapacious newspaper columnists. To the playgoing public she merely represented the perfect Charles Frohman star: the docile girl who permitted the master-producer to pick her roles, dictate her life, and in every way act as a Pygmalion. This was entirely true, and Miss Adams was always unstinting in her praise of Frohman for his guidance.

In return for tender care, Frohman extracted his own price from her and the other stars he employed. The first requirement was a high standard of moral behavior, for C.F. never forgot his experience with Dion Boucicault or changed his mind about never-engage-a-star-smirched-by-scandal. He not only insisted on spotless offstage conduct by his stars. He did not even like them to have active social lives. "Nothing so kills the healthy growth of an actor," he pontificated, "and brings usefulness to an end as soon as the idea that social enjoyment is a means to public success and that industrious labor to improve himself is no longer necessary."

Frohman went beyond this and strongly opposed his stars appearing in public places. Eternally stage-struck himself, he believed that if glamorous theatre folk were seen too often in public the glamour wore off, with the result that the public became less interested in paying money to see them. He even objected when John Drew strolled Broadway. "If he must walk, let him walk on Fifth Avenue," he muttered one day, when from a window of his Empire Theatre office he saw passers-by stopping to gape at Uncle Jack holding court across the street. Naturally, his greatest power was exerted over his female stars, of whom he once said, "In all my experience I have seldom known of a very rich girl who made a finished actress on the stage. The reason is that daughters of the rich are taught to repress emotion. In other words, they don't seem able to let-go their feelings. Give me the common clay, the kind that has suffered and even hungered. She makes the best star material."

Few of Frohman's girl stars were from the common clay. Yet all were deeply indebted to him and felt obliged to obey his orders without protest. He fought valiantly to keep Ethel Barrymore, Maude Adams, and others mysteriously shrouded from the public eye. When Billie Burke arrived from London, where she made a sensation singing "Put Me in My Little Canoe" in *The School Girl*, he treated her in Frohman fashion. Miss Burke recalls: "He introduced me to New York quietly, avoiding publicity stunts, strictly forbidding me to appear in public or even to see other plays. It was his Napoleonic principle that the illusions of the theatre would be shattered if the public saw too much or knew too much about stars."

Those working for Frohman were expected to surrender their destinies completely to his guidance. His handshake became his eternal bond, and he prided himself (after John Drew) on never entering into written contracts with a star. Some who worked for him never knew how much money to expect at the end of a week—this too was left completely to the great man's judgment. Says beautiful Marie Doro: "In all my association with him we never spoke of money. I never knew what my salary was to be until I got my pay envelope." Actors who demanded outrageous salaries sometimes found Frohman willingly paying them. The English actress Julie Opp named a high sum because she did not wish to journey to America. "Of course, you are joking," Frohman answered after she set her price. "But if you are not I'll pay it." Miss Opp was shamed into lowering her demands. She came to America and presumably found happiness as the wife of William Faversham.

In return for compliance with his edicts, Frohman was capable of the grandest of gestures. Both Ethel Barrymore and Billie Burke enjoyed the supreme thrill of arriving before the theatre one night to find their names blazing forth in the bright lights of marquee stardom. Neither had been told to expect it.

With his girl stars, Frohman freely permitted himself to mix sentiment with business. He thought of himself as an indulgent Pygmalion surrounded by grateful Galateas, each of whom wanted a special place in his affections. Each got it, too. Once he said, "I have often helped these young women to take a brighter view of things and it makes me feel that I am not just their manager but their friend." Most of all, he hated his girl stars to marry, and in this field (as well as others) Maude Adams remained his all-time favorite. She not only made the most money for him and remained the most malleable to his will, but never did she contemplate matrimony. Some thought she and Frohman were married, but both were wed tightly to the theatre.

Frohman's tense struggles with actresses who were determined to marry have become legendary. When Edna May married Oscar Lewisohn she sent Frohman a handsomely engraved announcement across which she wrote, "At Home Thursdays, Four to Six." He angrily scrawled on it, "So am I," and mailed it back. After Julia Marlowe dared marry the actor Robert Taber, she arrived in his office, announcing herself as Mrs. Taber. "I

don't know any Mrs. Taber," Frohman barked, "but Julia Marlowe can come in."

His most heroic tussle came when (eventually) Billie Burke
became enamored of Florenz Ziegfeld, who had astounded the
male population of the country by losing interest in flirtatious
Anna Held. As a producer of bare-legged girl shows, Ziegfeld
was precisely the kind of producer Frohman loathed. Mr.
Theatre's efforts to keep the lovebirds apart grew so fierce that
Billie and Flo were driven to Romeo and Juliet meetings at
Grant's Tomb. On Miss Burke, Frohman imposed flat, staccato
orders: "Stop it. Ruin your career. Mustn't marry. Drop you if
you do. Bad man. Also, can't produce shows." Ziegfeld's answer
on hearing this last was monumental in its gentlemanly restraint.
"Have you ever seen Charles Frohman eat oysters?" he inquired
loftily. Poised on the verge of elopement, Miss Burke felt she
was running away from Charles Frohman more than from her
dear mother. Shortly before the pair eloped Frohman appeared
in her dressing room to announce, "Going to London. Going to
leave my hat here. To remind you not to get married. Don't be
foolish while I'm gone." Miss Burke married and cabled Frohman. "Send me my hat," he replied.

She never saw him again.

Maude Adams—born Maude Adams Kiskadden in 1872—not
only fitted perfectly the exalted Frohman standards of obedi-
ence, but seemed perfectly to match the era's conception of an
actress. The United States was gradually emerging from the
stifling pressures of Victorianism. To the world, rugged Richard
Harding Davis, with his high principles and vaunted virtue, was
even more of a male symbol than sophisticated John Drew. It
was a country ready at last to fall (in the later Hollywood era,
it tumbled overboard) under the spell of the mystique of theatre
stardom. Maude Adams, never visible in public or available to

the press, apparently bereft of an offstage life, seemed the quintessence of it all. She seemed to enjoy the nunlike seclusion Frohman imposed on her. If nothing else, this allowed her to subli-
mate all emotional life into the acting craft, making her dedica-
tion to the theatre complete.

Still, this is hardly enough to account for her gigantic appeal.
What, then, was her magic? "Maude Adams is a moonbeam," a
critic wrote, and this remains perhaps the best description of
them all. Of her voice another said, "There is a pipe organ in
Germany, one note of which will shatter glass—her tones do
exactly that to one's heart." Beyond the age of thirty Maude
Adams could play a piquant girl-child or an elfin boy, each with
a leavening of Irish mischief. Her will-o'-the-wisp charm was
called ethereal, pixie, lambent, and lucent. As Maggie Wylie in
Barrie's *What Every Woman Knows*, Miss Adams herself spoke
the line, "Charm is the bloom upon a woman." Onstage Maude
Adams certainly bloomed. Yet it must be added that this fragile
moonbeam quality does not always shine through in photographs. Every adjective applied to Maude Adams rang a varia-
tion on the word *virginal*, yet in photos she looks remarkably
earthy. This may be because she was so often pictured as a boy.
At the same time, her large round eyes have a level, worldly
look. Slightly prominent teeth bring to her a look of intriguing,
slightly perverse invitation. In all, Maude Adams, moonbeam,
much resembles a precocious and not unknowing teen-ager of
our day.

The contradictions in Maude Adams' pictures match others
in her character. Under the elfin surface reposed a trained
woman of the theatre who viewed herself and the world with
great solemnity. "Genius is the talent for seeing things straight,"
she said once, and straight is the way she looked at most matters
connected with both career and existence. Reasons for this were
no doubt rooted in a hard-working childhood, with only a

mother to lavish any amount of affection on her. Through this mother Miss Adams could proudly trace her ancestry directly back to the Mayflower. Asenath Ann "Annie" Adams was also the offspring of a first-generation family of Mormons. In her teens, Annie was chosen by a wife of Brigham Young to become one of the Salt Lake City Church acting group. She showed exceptional talent.

Several years later one of her performances was watched by a roving Scotch-Irishman named James Kiskadden, of whom it was said, "He seldom let work stand in the way of his enjoyment of life." Kiskadden vowed to wed alluring Annie Adams and in time he did. Marriage may have sobered James Kiskadden slightly, but it never made him a good provider. The honeymooners traveled from Utah to San Francisco in 1869 on the first through train ever run to the Coast. They decided to stay there. A short time later Annie Adams found it necessary to go to work as a professional actress. Maude was nine months old when Annie appeared in a play called *The Lost Child*, in which a baby is carried onstage aboard a platter. Inevitably baby Maude was drafted for this taxing role and so (on an almost-silver platter) her theatre career began.

Annie Adams continued her acting career (Kiskadden fades from the scene like vapor), touring with theatrical companies over the rugged frontier territories of California and Nevada. Maude was with her, playing Little Eva in *Uncle Tom's Cabin*, among other roles. Through her later musings runs a thread of thanks to the theatre as a place for escaping reality. As quoted by Phyllis Robbins in *Maude Adams, an Intimate Portrait*, she believed, "To make our own acquaintance is difficult enough under ordinary circumstances, but if life is begun pretending to be Eva, the youthful heroine of *Uncle Tom's Cabin*, or little Paul in *The Octoroon*, or this or that other little boy or girl, it becomes increasingly difficult to separate whom from which."

And again: "It is one of the many blessings of life in the theatre that we are always so delightfully busy being someone else, that we can scarcely spare a moment to know ourselves. That doubtful pleasure can always be deferred. And what a mercy! If we really knew ourselves, how could we endure it?"

Maude Adams eventually saluted this inability to know herself by referring to her childhood self as "The One I Knew Least of All." Even so, she functioned well as a child performer. As Little Maudie, she not only played speaking parts in the lurid melodramas of the day, but piped between-the-acts songs like "Pretty as a Picture" and "That Yaller Girl That Winked at Me." While still a tot she became keenly aware of the rights and privileges of the person of talent: "At six I liked to be consulted about the business arrangements with my managers—salary and how long the engagement was to last."

At ten, Little Maudie was dispatched to Salt Lake City, there to attend the Collegiate Institute. Later her teachers would recall her as an intelligent, adjusted child, but Miss Adams complains of the fact that she was a celebrity to other pupils. By the age of twelve she was back on the Road, leaping by stagecoach from one gold-coast town to another. Once, she and her intrepid mother toured as far east as New York, where the star of the attraction followed tradition by absconding with the profits. In California again, Maude seems to have realized that she was not a born genius whose talents divinely prepared her for the stage. One play in which she appeared had numerous laugh lines, but she was unable to make the audience laugh at hers. Other members of the cast became annoyed. The leading man worked with her, trying to teach the preternaturally serious girl how to lighten and liven the tones of her voice. Finally, he gave up in despair.

This seems to have persuaded Maude that her strongest weapon as an actress was hard work. Years later she would be hailed for her "tremendous reading, solitary thinking, and extra-ordinary personal application." Now, oddly enough, the harder she labored on herself, the more wispy and fragile her person-ality seemed to become. In 1889 a second Road tour carried her to New York, and following a round of casting offices, she was dispatched to Boston as a replacement in *Lord Chumley,* starring E. H. Sothern. One Eastern critic privileged to cover an early Maude Adams performance called her "a sweet and tender blossom on the dramatic tree."

Maude first attracted New York notice in *A Midnight Bell,* by Charles Hoyt, whose plays of contemporary life were de-scribed as full of American spunk. Hoyt's lively *A Trip to Chinatown* had just run for two years on Broadway, establish-ing a new performance record. In the new Hoyt play, Maude played an Old Maid, but those who saw her seemed to find her rooted in their minds as a young girl. Considering promising talents to cast in a new production, Charles Frohman and David Belasco spoke her name simultaneously. She was engaged for William Gillette's *All the Comforts of Home,* a Frohman offer-ing, which once again brought a shocking reminder of her defi-ciencies as an actress. In one scene she was required to cry, some-thing a trouper of her experience should be able to do at will. Maude Adams could not, though leading man Henry Miller ad-vised her to stare into the footlights until her eyes became teary. Doggedly, she did this, but in two hours of light-staring failed to shed a single tear.

When John Drew became a Frohman star, Broadway won-dered what lucky actress would be chosen as his leading lady. Maude Adams, age twenty, nursed her own hopes. She went to see Frohman, stating that after twenty years of melodrama and tragedy, she would relish a try at comedy. Frohman was a man who enjoyed his little joke. He shook his head, saying, "Per-haps you had better leave the company." Miss Adams sadly gathered up her belongings and started for the door. As she reached it Frohman called, "I'm going to put you in Mr. Drew's company as his leading lady."

From the lighthearted John Drew, Miss Adams learned a few lessons. "One had to be ready for any intrusion his fertile mind injected into the play," the earnest girl wrote, adding, "It was excellent training for a beginner." For five years she appeared opposite Drew, with mother Annie Adams also a member of the company. Then in 1897 it was announced that she had been picked to become Frohman's second major star, in Barrie's *The Little Minister*. To Miss Adams the jump from John Drew's leading lady in *Rosemary* to stardom on her own was "like going from geometry into higher mathematics, it was the same thing, but more so." The profession, ever prone to gossipy doubts, did not share this calm confidence. One writer wondered: "Can a little actress girl, unheralded but grounded in theatrical twists and turns, green to the ways of stardom, take a place suddenly inside a triangle entirely bounded by James M. Barrie and Charles Frohman?"

Well—she could. On opening night Maude Adams discovered a public which enveloped her in an everlasting hug. People cherished her as the fantasy figure of a woman playing a girl— and, later, a boy—a personality both mischievous and clever, but above all innocent and sweet. One critic summed this up by rhetorically inquiring:

> Is this a woman or a child who comes among us with sure tread, surer head? The play . . . might be performed by either woman or child, so Miss Adams gives us an ad-mixture of both. She comes onstage with an odd little tip-toe gait. Forthwith she exhibits the outer accoutrements of charm—a winsome manner, cameo-like, utterly feminine, girlishly effervescent, plaintive. She proceeds subtly, deftly to exhibit the inner qualities of art; she shapes and gradually glows as an actress—all-sufficient word. Her touch is unfailingly light, her spirits unflaggingly high.

In New York Miss Adams gave 300 performances of *The Little Minister*, and on the last night at the Empire Frohman gave every lady in the audience an American Beauty rose. On the Road, she played Lady Babbie for two more years, or 1000 times in all. As an established star, she purchased a small residence at 22 East Forty-first Street in New York and also engaged a Maine-born secretary-companion named Louise Boynton, who remained loyally at her side over years to come. To predatory males of the Great White Way, the attractive Miss Adams presented a complex problem. She was never to be seen at Rector's, or otherwise scrutinized at close quarters, while the parts she played onstage were so unworldly as to discourage the dreams of virile men. Yet the role of Lady Babbie had a certain saccharine attractiveness and a few brave men briefly attempted to pay court to Maude Adams. One discovered the location of her new home and through several long nights this ardent swain paced back and forth on Forty-first Street, lifting his hat each time he came abreast of Miss Adams' door. The actress was aware of this superb devotion and may have peered out at her admirer through a discreetly drawn curtain. But she did no more.

At the same time she was intelligent, well read, and clever. Socially she occasionally mixed in groups with such outstanding males of the time as Richard Harding Davis, Finley Peter Dunne, Charles Dana Gibson, and John Fox, author of the best-selling *Trail of the Lonesome Pine*. But for all her enormous theatre success, Miss Adams continued unsure of herself. "I had very little confidence in myself as an actress," she later said of herself at this time. This lack of assurance may have been behind her increasing passion for isolation. Even Frohman, so carefully guiding her destiny and so much in favor of the isolation, became concerned about the lack of variety in her existence. He encouraged her to become interested in stage lighting, which was making new strides after the development of electricity. Miss Adams obligingly dug into this esoteric art with all her customary thoroughness. During the later years of her retirement she was rated a lighting expert and was often consulted by other experts.

After *The Little Minister*, Miss Adams appeared in *Romeo and Juliet*, a production rendered curious by the fact that it was rehearsed in two parts. Miss Adams, on a triumphant tour in *The Little Minister*, rehearsed dewy Juliet on the Road. William Faversham (Romeo) and James K. Hackett (Mercutio) perfected their roles in New York. Frohman, who had no real feeling for Shakespeare, supervised both. When either side expressed uneasiness about the odd procedure, Frohman demanded, "Who's Shakespeare? He won't hurt you. I don't see any Shakespeare. Just imagine you are looking at a soldier, home from the war, making love to a giggling schoolgirl on a balcony. That's all I see and that's the way I want it played. Dismiss all ideas of costume. Be modern!" Prepared in the midst of such confusion, *Romeo and Juliet* entirely failed to come off. William Winter, most august of critics, dismissed Miss Adams' Juliet as one that could be matched after a little practice by many schoolgirls.

To salve such rebuffs, Miss Adams journeyed to Europe. There, for a brief moment, she toyed with the tantalizing idea of playing Juliet to Sarah Bernhardt's Romeo. Deciding against this, she crossed the Channel to meet James M. Barrie for the first time. It is curious to note that, after being struck so forcefully by Miss Adams as she rehearsed *Rosemary* in New York, the shy Scotsman made no effort to meet her. Nor had he traveled the ocean to watch her much-saluted performance in *The Little Minister*. Now, as Miss Adams waited nervously in his London study, Barrie suddenly burst through the door, alarmingly hauled by a huge St. Bernard dog. In a tense voice he muttered, "How do you do?" Then, giving full attention to the bounding dog, he asked, "Would you like to see us wrestle?" A stunned Miss Adams nodded. Barrie donned a protective mask and assumed a broad stance which encouraged the dog to leap on him. Man and dog then battled back and forth, straining up and down the room, knocking over chairs and tables. Finally the contest ended and a panting Barrie, his shyness thoroughly overcome, was ready to commence a long friendship with Maude Adams.

One result of this bizarre encounter was Barrie's *Quality Street*, the story of an English girl whose beloved goes to the Napoleonic Wars. He seems to forget the girl he left behind and she fades into drab spinsterhood. When he returns she blooms again and the two rediscover love. Miss Adams did *Quality Street* after her first boy-role in *L'Aiglon*, but speaking lines coated with Barrie whimsy, she was once more all girl—"an innocent and lovely girl, ingenuous, artless, buoyant, piquant, brisk." The major product of the friendship between the star and the Scotsman came in 1905, when Maude Adams appeared in *Peter Pan*. This was by far the greatest triumph of the Adams-Barrie-Frohman combination. *Peter Pan, the Boy Who Would Never Grow Up*, became less a play than an institution. Says the critic Eugene Burr:

> Miss Adams played Peter Pan more than 1500 times. Others have played him well, but he will always be identified here with Miss Adams, whose delicate and sensitive charm first gave him life in this country, and made him one of the great modern myth-figures of the English-speaking world. . . . Symbol of the gay, bright innocence of eternal youth, he became an influence and a high ideal to generations of . . . children.

Charles Frohman first heard of *Peter Pan* in London when Herbert Beerbohm Tree dashed up to him on the street to exclaim, "Barrie has gone out of his mind! He's written a play about children flying through the air and crocodiles swallowing alarm clocks. I'm warning you, C. F.–he's gone mad!" Frohman was uneasy as Barrie began to read the script aloud. He was enchanted by its end and immediately agreed to produce the play. Miss Adams, in a similar state of rapture, went to the Catskills to master the unusual part. On long horseback rides she endlessly asked herself, "What will this character mean to the people who see it?"

Peter Pan opened on the night of November 6, 1905. At its unforgettable climax a thirty-two-year-old woman, dressed as a fetching boy, ran to the front of the stage and inquired of a sophisticated audience, "Do you believe in fairies?" Like every other crowd that heard the question, this one fervently did–for the enchanted moment, at least.

Peter Pan established a long-run record at the Empire, then went on spectacular tour. (Miss Adams now traveled with a $30,000 railroad car which held a stage for between-cities rehearsals.) The entire country went into a frenzy over *Peter Pan*. One who recalls a Midwest performance says, "I have never witnessed such emotional adulation in the theatre. It was hysterical. Her devotees pelted the stage with flowers." In response to such tributes, Miss Adams invariably made a brief, breathless curtain speech: "I thank you–I thank you for us all–Good Night." At the stage door mobs of men and women (at matinees, children) waited humbly to watch her depart–this was long before rampaging autograph hounds. They respectfully pulled back as she was guided from the stage door by Alf Hayman, into whose protective custody Charles Frohman entrusted his most valuable property.

Maude Adams did not consider Peter Pan her all-time favorite role. This rare honor was reserved for *Chantecler*, the Edmond Rostand drama in which (1911) she played a barnyard rooster. But Peter was always her next favorite. Among other things, *Peter*

Pan brought her to the pinnacle of her profession. Shortly before *Peter Pan* opened she considered herself finished as a performer: "I had no freshness, no spontaneity, my mannerisms were becoming more and more marked and objectionable." She was unable to sleep, felt physically depleted, and in general thought her career ended.

Appearances in *Peter Pan* quickly changed this sad state of affairs. "No actor lives by bread alone," she concluded, "and to have been part of that lovely play, to have known that wonderful feeling in an audience, is something to refresh one's spirit and one's life, something to make one always grateful." *Peter Pan* also brought a closer spiritual affinity with James M. Barrie. The two seldom met face to face, but they treasured one another nonetheless. To her Barrie wrote, "I believe you have become Peter Pan in such a magical way that my only fear is your flying clear away out of the theatre some night." Miss Adams responded by saying, "Whenever I act, I always feel there is one unseen spectator, James M. Barrie."

Peter Pan seemingly brought full faith in herself, but one cannot tell for sure. Her private life remained a deep mystery. "She hid behind her activities and they formed a worthy rampart," a commentator has said. Her few intimate friends were people outside the profession. In the theatre both Billie Burke and Ethel Barrymore mention her failure to respond to friendly overtures. "For several years," declares Miss Barrymore, "she was perfectly charming and gay, and then she began to be the original I-Want-To-Be-Alone woman. . . . It was very rarely that anyone saw her offstage. . . . She was a rare spirit and I am glad I touched her even lightly."

More than any other actress, Miss Adams was the actress onstage and the mysterious woman off. To De Wolf Hopper, for one, she was all actress. Visiting his friend Richard Bennett backstage at *What Every Woman Knows*, Hopper found himself whisked past watchdog Alf Hayman to an unexpected meeting with Miss Adams. She acted as eager for praise as any unskilled ingenue. "I know you wouldn't have come back to see us if you hadn't nice things to say," she told Hopper. "Now just say them, please."

"I'm afraid to, Miss Adams," the huge man responded. "I might gush."

"Then go right ahead and gush," she commanded. "I am going to sit back, close my eyes, not say a word, and just listen."

Hopper gushed, and at the end she clapped delighted hands. "Beautiful!" she exclaimed. "I feel as renewed as if I had spent a week in the mountains."

Nat Goodwin, who married even more times than the much-married Hopper, felt a more worldly reaction to a similar meeting with Miss Adams. Like nearly everyone who met her, Goodwin immediately thought of a Barrie line. His came from *What Every Woman Knows*: "You are missing the greatest thing on earth—romance."

He continues: "Maude Adams' name is a household word; she stands for all that represents true and virtuous womanhood; at the zenith of her fame she has woven her own mantle and placed it about the pedestal on which she stands alone. And yet, as I looked into those fawnlike eyes, I wondered." The sharp-eyed fellow noted little furrows in the piquant face and sharp vertical lines between her brows. Her skin seemed dry, her gestures tense, her speech jerky.

He ends: "I felt like taking those tiny little artistic hands in mine and saying, 'Little woman, I fear you are unconsciously missing the greatest thing in life—ROMANCE.' "

6: THE WITS

Maude Adams . . . John Drew . . . James M. Barrie . . . Charles Frohman . . . The Empire . . .

These names represented the ultimate in the period's theatre, the summit of new-century drama. Around the summit swirled the colorful community known as Broadway. Its side streets of the Thirties, Forties, and Fifties were lined with theatrical boardinghouses and on hot summer nights actors sat on stoops to talk of past glories, present problems, and dreams of the future. In one of the boardinghouses on Forty-seventh Street—for example—lived a grinning, rubber-faced young man from a ranch in Oklahoma. He did a rope-twirling act in vaudeville and his name was Will Rogers. On his stoop, he spoke vaguely of interspersing the rope tricks in his act with salty comment.

At night the Great White Way snapped on its million mazdas to become an area of din and dazzle. New theatres had been built north of the Empire (Lyceum, Bijou, Belasco) and like others they offered melodramas, dramas, farces, and comedies in profusion. Some of these plays, as the world proceeded to 1905, were *Alice-Sit-by-the-Fire* (Ethel Barrymore), *The Lion and the Mouse* (Richard Bennett), *The Squaw Man* (William Faversham), *Girl of the Golden West* (Blanche Bates), *Strongheart* (Robert Edeson), *Mrs. Leffingwell's Boots* (Margaret

Illington), *Cousin Billy* (Francis Wilson), *The Prince Chap* (Cyril Scott), *The Chorus Lady* (Rose Stahl), *The Great Divide* (Margaret Anglin, Henry Miller), *Rose of the Rancho* (Frances Starr), *Brewster's Millions* (Edward Abeles, Mary Ryan), *The Price of Money* (William H. Crane), *Salomy Jane* (Eleanor Robson, Holbrook Blinn, H. B. Warner), *The Warrens of Virginia* (Cecil B. DeMille and child Gladys Smith who became Mary Pickford), *The Boys of Company B* (Arnold Daly), *Polly of the Circus* (Mabel Taliaferro), *The Silver Box* (by John Galsworthy, with Ethel Barrymore), *When Knights Were Bold* (Francis Wilson, Pauline Frederick), *The Ranger* (Dustin Farnum, Mary Boland), *The Music Master* (David Warfield), and *The Man from Home* (by Booth Tarkington, with William Hodge and Olive Wyndham).

With all this came more plays by Shaw and Ibsen. Indeed, 1905 might well be called the Shaw Year for during it *You Never Can Tell, John Bull's Other Island, Mrs. Warren's Profession,* and *Man and Superman* were produced. Ibsen, too, was receiving attention. Mrs. Fiske had played *A Doll's House* at a special matinee at the Empire, giving a performance which seemed to siphon the nastiness out of the nasty Norwegian. Blanche Bates played *Hedda Gabler* in 1904, but not until the arrival of the vital Russian actress Alla Nazimova did Ibsen electrify as he should.

The Weber and Fields Music Hall was no more, for the whispers throttled so successfully as Mike and Myer ate peanuts on the shoeshine stand turned out to be true. In an eruption of petty jealousy, misunderstanding, and bad advice from friends, the partnership of thirty years burst violently asunder. "Is low comedy doomed?" wondered John Corbin, drama critic of *The New York Times*. Weber and Fields continued to produce and perform separately, while other comedy teams rose to offer comedy not so low as theirs. Dave Montgomery and Fred Stone achieved stardom in *The Wizard of Oz*. Other seasons brought the musicals *Sultan of Sulu* (by George Ade), *The Prince of Pilsen*, *Mr. Bluebeard* (with Eddie Foy), and *A Chinese Honeymoon*, all bigger, brighter, and fresher than musical comedies had ever been before.

In the years before 1910 nearly one-quarter of the Broadway productions were musicals, an art form in which the Great White Way always excelled. Among them were *The Ham Tree* (McIntyre and Heath, juggler W. C. Fields), *Easy Dawson* (Raymond Hitchcock, John Bunny), *The Earl and the Girl* (Eddie Foy), *The Mayor of Tokio* (Richard Carle), *The Vanderbilt Cup* (Elsie Janis), *The Rich Mr. Hoggenheimer* (Sam Bernard), *A Yankee Tourist* (Raymond Hitchcock, Wallace Beery), *The Dairymaids* (Julia Sanderson), *Miss Innocence* (Anna Held), *The Boys and Betty* (Marie Cahill).

Much of the flavor of musical Broadway was contributed by a genial man born in Ireland and educated in Germany, from which country he seemed to have got his beefy looks. His name was Victor Herbert and from his head came melodies of distilled, light-opera perfection. Victor Herbert had played the cello in the orchestra of the Metropolitan Opera House. His urge to compose first led him to write *The Wizard of the Nile*. Songs from this did not sweep the country, but the show's catchword "Am I a wiz?" did. Later, in *The Fortune Teller*, another Herbert operetta provided another national twister. This was a bit of nonsense verse:

> I had a little bird and its name was Enza
> I opened the cage and in-flu-enza.

In 1900 Victor Herbert wrote the music for *The Singing Girl*; in 1903, *Babes in Toyland*; in 1904, *It Happened in Nordland*. Then in 1905 he crashed through to success. His show that year was *Mlle. Modiste*, and it was a rousing hit. Starring was Fritzi

Scheff, a girl with a grand-opera voice and an operetta spirit. Fritzi wore backless gowns and sang "Kiss Me Again" with such sweet fervor that every stylish woman in America dreamed of changing places with her. On Broadway itself another Victor Herbert song ranked in popularity with "Kiss Me Again." On late nights at Rector's big William Pruette, who sang, "I Know What I Want When I Want It" in the show, rose grandly to his feet and rumbled out the song while the supper throng joined in, accenting every *Want* with the bang of fist or glass on the Belfast-linen tablecloths.

When not composing lightsome music, Victor Herbert was a compulsive spender of easily made money, a titanic consumer of Pilsener beer, and a fanatical bettor on horses (horseplayer is a word too ordinary for this gifted man). His gay operettas brought him fame and money, yet he disparaged his talents, living out life in the belief that his melodies would not last beyond him. "Don't kid me," he said, when complimented on his work. "I'm a good tunesmith. Six months after I'm dead no one will remember my name." He tormented himself in other ways. He was a man cheerful and seemingly carefree, but he always moved like lightning, as if driven by a frenzy to get things done at top speed. "He was feverishly industrious," recalls the lyricist Harry B. Smith, who collaborated on fourteen operettas with Victor Herbert, "and always seemed to work at high pressure when there was no need for it. He would dash across a room merely to get another piece of paper, across a street simply to get on the other side."

Herbert astonished his friends by an ability to play the piano with full orchestra effects. His heart, despite inner tensions, seemed as big as his body. He particularly hated to hurt anyone. Over the years an actor friend had dedicated himself to the composition of a musical masterpiece called "Grand Mass in F." Finally, it was done, and Herbert agreed to render an opinion.

"Grand Mass in F" proved a succession of wild dissonances about which Herbert could find nothing good to say. Still, he bent down to peer hard at the sheet music. Straightening, he clapped the composer heartily on the shoulder. "By Jove, it *is* in F," he roared enthusiastically.

On the night of October 21, 1907, Victor Herbert, by now a thoroughly American composer, was shoved aside by a European invasion in the form of *The Merry Widow*, with its lilting, incomparable score by Franz Lehar. This had been known as *Die Lustige Witwe* in Vienna, where it was a smash hit. The robust American producer Colonel Henry W. Savage bought it and for his production hired Donald Brian as Prince Danilo and Ethel Jackson as Sonia. A white-tie opening was succeeded by riots as average playgoers sought to buy tickets. Rather than no-back gowns, women the country over now wore sweeping two-feet-in-diameter *Merry Widow* hats, in emulation of sparkling Ethel Jackson. Men attempted to be as graceful and irresistible as Donald Brian as he swept Miss Jackson into the immortal *Merry Widow* waltz. But soon Victor Herbert fought back with *The Red Mill*, starring Montgomery and Stone. *The Merry Widow* continued to be the popular rage, but the European conquest was no longer complete.

Victor Herbert's niche in American entertainment remained secure. So did that of Florenz Ziegfeld, who further stemmed the European threat by producing his first *Follies*. The idea of a revue glorifying girls was given Ziegfeld by Anna Held, who during her tenure as Mrs. Ziegfeld proved smart as well as fetching. A second assist came from the ubiquitous Harry B. Smith, who wrote the book for the production. Smith borrowed a title from the newspaper column "Follies of the Day." He planned to call the production "Follies of the Year." But Ziegfeld, for all his smooth sophistication (he affected pink shirts, spats, and malacca cane) was a superstitious man. He insisted on a thir-

teen-letter title for his show. So it became *Follies of 1907*. The
first *Follies* was, by later standards, as innocent as the morning
dew. But at the time it was daring—and sumptuous as well. The
original *Follies* girls cavorted in puff-sleeve bathing suits. One,
apparently nude, popped up in a barrel. Altogether, the first
Follies may have inspired Eugene Field to utter his famous
critique, "The talkin' and the dressin', they are both dekolletay."

In the first *Ziegfeld Follies*—to use the name the world later
embraced—comedian Nat Wills sang "If a Table at Rector's
Could Talk." This was a mild melody, hinting at daring secrets
whispered over a tabletop. At almost the same moment prolific
Paul Potter finished his adaptation of a gently sexy French
farce. He needed an American title for this and, ambling toward
his favorite restaurant, thought of *The Girl from Rector's*. Soon
a poster of this delightful miss, peering captivatingly over a glass
of bubbly champagne, advertised such a show.

At the moment, this double use of Rector's name seemed
harmless—little more than belated tribute to the Great White
Way's most popular lobster palace. Yet over years to come these
early references to Rector's combined with others to put Broadway in the Oscar Wilde-ish position of killing the thing it loved.
For Rector's began to gather a reputation. The energetic Rec-
tors, father and son, were unaware of this. Having made a million dollars from the restaurant, they were planning to build a
Rector's Hotel, on the site of the present Claridge. But by the
time the hotel was completed, no traveling male (and most hotel
patrons of the day were men) dared write home that he was
staying at risqué Rector's.

But all this was to come. . . . Rector's was still Broadway's
Supreme Court of Triviality, catering in peerless fashion to the
theatrical profession. So, in a different way, did the many free-
lunch emporiums along the Great White Way. Here, for the
price of a five-cent beer, an indigent actor might help himself to

chicken salad, lobster salad, lobster Newburg, melted cheese on toast, cold corned beef, Virginia ham, and hot chafing dishes with bubbling contents. This, at least, was the glorious amalgam of free lunch offered by Considine's Metropole. This restaurant of tender memory had three entrances, so a man chased out one for eating without drinking might nonchalantly enter by another. This was a favorite stratagem of down-at-heels actors, and one day the Considine bouncers saw a performer who had once been great but now was small repeatedly helping himself to vast portions of the establishment's best Edam cheese. The thespian saw the bouncers advancing on him and drew himself up threateningly. "I warn you, boys, don't think a man is a mouse just because he eats cheese," he thundered.

Some of the theatre's top actors—John Drew, especially—spent off-hours at The Players, on Gramercy Park. But Broadway had a nearer oasis for the solvent male at the Lambs Club on Forty-fourth Street. In this Stanford White edifice gathered the truly robust performers of the time. In most cases they were colorful figures, men of mingled wit and intellect who could sometimes write plays as well as act in them. A bond between woolly Lambs was a devout belief that in liquor was to be found the best cushion for the rough highway of life—better even than the soft flesh of women, though this of course had its place. "Staggering is a sign of strength, weak men are carried home," a Lambs Club imbiber once pontificated. This splendid sentiment was resoundingly echoed by Henry E. Dixey, a star whose career ups-and-downs were called a "frequent leaping o'er the rails of failure into pastures of success." One night a friend asked Dixey why he consumed so much liquor. "Because when I drink, I think, and when I think, I drink," Dixey answered. In the Lambs Club this was rated cold, clear logic.

Staggering or sober, the drinking actors seemed able to give performances unfailingly delightful to those who watched. For this and other reasons, they peered condescendingly down on members of the less raffish Players, whose founder was the great Edwin Booth. For one thing, the Players invited the membership of painters and literary men. Asked once why he disapproved so strongly of the rival club, the double-dipped Lamb William Collier tartly answered, "You meet so few actors there." The Lambs gave an annual Lambs Gambol and often took this lusty entertainment on the Road. On one such tour the Lambs Gambol Special was pulling out of Syracuse when Collier spied a dingy engine pulling a dingier caboose in the opposite direction. "Look, fellows," he called. "There goes The Players Club back to New York."

For a long time the most spectacular of Lambs was Maurice Barrymore. Barry the Magnificent, he was christened by admiring friends. In tribute to him, one colleague invoked the quotation, "The world delights in sunny people." Another defined, "He was pre-eminently a man's man and beyond question a ladies' man."

Maurice Barrymore's contemporaries thought him the most winning of humans. His personality was stoutly reinforced by a physical strength which he used to advantage against drunks who made remarks about his manly beauty and clipped English accent. Nat Goodwin, a fellow seldom given to superlatives, salutes Barrymore as "The most effulgent man I ever met, with a brain that scintillates sparks of wit which Charles Lamb or Lord Byron might envy, a tongue capable of lashing into obscurity anyone who dared enter into verbal conflict with him, the courage of a lion, the gentleness of a saint. . . ."

Barrymore—Barry to friends—landed in this country in 1875, his striking handsomeness embellished by a top hat and monocle. He had been born in India, the son of an English army officer, and educated at Oxford, where he became amateur light-heavy-weight boxing champion of England. The possessor of a dashing stage presence and the knife-sharp profile perpetuated in his son John, Barry rapidly became the most sought-after leading man of the day. For a time he was the highest-paid actor on the American stage and among many other parts played Armand to Olga Nethersole's Camille and (his final role) Rawdon Crawley to Mrs. Fiske's Becky Sharp. Yet on Road tours the prosperous actor could never stay in good hotels. With him he carried a menagerie, usually consisting of mongoose, racoons, and miscellaneous birds and monkeys. Because of these beloved animals he was reduced to patronizing hostelries that were close to flophouses.

On occasions when he recalled family responsibilities, Barrymore was a splendid husband to his wife Georgianna Drew. To his children, he was a stimulating and imaginative (if will-o'-the-wisp) figure who told exciting stories of his childhood in India and had a clever answer to every question. But he seldom remembered his family—somehow he felt far more at home with an elbow on the Lambs Club bar or between the perfumed sheets of a strange bed. After one overnight absence he staggered home on Sunday morning to find his wife arrayed for church. "She was made up perfectly for the part and had a prompt book with her," he told friends later. The sight caused Barrymore to feel a stab of guilt. "Oh, by the way, Georgie dear," he tried to explain. "I spent the evening with Will Lackaye." "Indeed," answered his wife crisply. "I always thought Will Lackaye was a man."

Possibly no man ever took fatherhood as lightly as Maurice Barrymore. When John was a toddler, his father often took him to the Lambs. There debonair Barry checked the child in the coatroom while he passed hours at the bar. Later, when his ravishing daughter Ethel became the toast of London, she fell in love (or thought so) with Laurence Irving, son of Sir Henry. She cabled the exciting news of her engagement to her father at the Lambs. His return cable read, CONGRATULATIONS LOVE FATHER. Soon a heartbroken Ethel cabled that the engagement was over. CONGRATULATIONS LOVE FATHER, read the answering cable.

After arriving in this country so impeccably attired, irresponsible Barry became a notoriously careless dresser—a sloppy Apollo, one friend called him. Still, he was to the Lambs what his immaculate brother-in-law John Drew was to The Players. On Broadway he rapidly achieved fame for his ability to fend off bores. "Don't you recognize me, Mr. Barrymore?" a stray drinker inquired. "I didn't at first," Barrymore responded, "but when you didn't buy, I knew you right away." When a boastful Englishman shouted, "We could take our fleet and beat the daylights out of America any day," Barrymore asked quietly, "What, again?" In the course of a night's carousing he found it necessary to call a truculent Texan a son of a bitch. The man rose in fury. "If you were in Texas I'd kill you for that," he raged. Barry shrugged. "Of course, if your mother's virtue is a matter of geography," he said airily. "I'm a self-made man, sir, a self-made man," a loudmouth told him. "What interrupted you?" Barrymore wanted to know.

On rare occasions Barrymore could be prevailed upon to eat. Once a friend proudly escorted him to an Italian restaurant where a full meal, together with red wine, cost thirty-five cents. "Excellent meal for the price, wasn't it, Barry?" the man asked at meal's end. "It was that," Barrymore answered. "Let's have another."

On the stage Maurice Barrymore was a forceful actor who was often unsure of his lines. This caused Helena Modjeska, whose leading man he was, to complain of his lazy gaiety. One night he blandly led the Polish-born actress from one play into the heart of another. The bewildered Madame doggedly followed, but with the dropping of the curtain exploded into wildest temperament. "You ingrate!" she shrieked. "I have given you position, I have made you!" Barrymore patiently heard her through, then said, "Made me! I was famous in New York when people didn't know whether you were a woman or a mouthwash." His feeling for fellow actors was one of gentle tolerance. Told by a friend he must see E. H. Sothern's *Hamlet*, he replied, "My boy, I don't encourage vice." Joseph Jefferson, elder-statesman actor, had a passion for painting and occasionally held exhibitions of his work at the Lambs. Pausing briefly before a bright landscape by Jefferson, Barry murmured, "Summer isn't as bad as it's painted." When fellow actors took him to task for appearing at Hammerstein's Victoria in a play deemed off-color, Barry defended himself by saying the barnlike vaudeville house was so large that few in the audience could hear his purple lines. "Hammerstein's is a theatre where one may be obscene and not heard," he finished.

One night Barrymore asked a bartender to hand him a pencil. He then composed his own epitaph:

> He walked beneath the stars
> And slept beneath the sun;
> He lived a life of going-to-do
> And died with nothing done.

For years this downbeat prophecy appeared to be all too true. Barrymore talked constantly of writing a play, but never did. Barry the Magnificent, man of incorrigible drinking habits, also had an irresistible appeal for Broadway maidens. For dalliance, he maintained a number of bedroom hideaways. Papers scattered over the floors of these testified to the actor's efforts to write a play. His wife, who continued to adore him withal, claimed that on these papers and others found at home were only one line—"Act One, Scene One: A Ruined Garden." In time, Barrymore amazed everyone by finishing the play. He invited friends to a reading and, after importantly clearing his throat, began: " 'Act One, Scene One: A Ruined Garden.' " His listeners dissolved into helpless laughter.

The completed play was *Nadjesda*, and Helena Modjeska played it in San Francisco, with Barrymore in the cast. But for all his rapier wit, Barry was excruciatingly modest about his own work. Friends urged him to press Modjeska for a New York production, but he merely shrugged philosophically and ordered another round of drinks. Finally, he sent a script of the play to Sarah Bernhardt. Two years later Bernhardt opened in New York in *La Tosca*, which bore a suspicious resemblance to *Nadjesda*. Whether this was plagiarism or mere coincidence the world will never know. Though heartbroken, Barrymore steadfastly refused to sue.

For a while afterward he talked of dramatizing *Les Miserables*, but the sole result of this was another celebrated Barrymore quip. Informed of the projected adaptation a friend remonstrated, "But, Barry, you'll never get a New York manager to produce it!" "Produce it!" Barrymore exclaimed. "I can't get a Broadway producer to *pronounce* it!"

Another of the sharp wits in the group frequenting the Lambs bar was Wilton Lackaye, who in the course of a long career appeared in such varied plays as Sheridan's *The Rivals* and Channing Pollock's *The Pit*. He was the offspring of well-to-do parents in Washington, D.C., who pronounced the family name "Lacky." So did Wilton during early acting years. Then he scored a notable success as Svengali, the hot-eyed hypnotist of *Trilby*. From then on he pronounced his name "Lack-*eye*." "It's the least I can do," he explained.

Lackaye—friends called him Will—was big, bluff, solid. He

resembled John Drew in that his English was impeccable and his wit seldom (if ever) relied on profanity or vulgarity. It was said of Lackaye that he could shade the English language so delicately that often the victims of his sharp thrusts wondered what the laughter was about. Lackaye had such soaring standards of behavior that an admirer once asked him to define a perfect gentleman. "The perfect gentleman," replied the actor unhesitatingly, "is the one who opens the door of a bathroom, sees a lady in the tub, and backs out closing the door, meanwhile saying, 'Excuse me, sir!' "

Wilton Lackaye could be caustic. Hearing that one star's company had given a charity performance in a prison, he said, "It must have been a great relief to him to have an audience that couldn't get away." Once he was forced to sit through a recital by an Irish tenor. "A tenor voice is a disease of the throat," he whispered loudly at one point. When the dramatic actor Arnold Daly announced plans to appear in a musical comedy someone asked Lackaye, "What's Daly doing in a musical?" "Hadn't you heard?" the bluff man responded. "He's lost his voice." Lackaye was himself the proud author of a song. He wrote "My Intimate Friend," done with some success by Fay Templeton. It told of a stage-struck girl who could always be sure of a part in a certain producer's plays. Why? *An intimate friend of a friend of mine*, the song went, *is an intimate friend of his.*

Wilton Lackaye could be caustic. Hearing that one star's com-made the Sahara desert seem like a lush meadow). Usually there was a kernel of hidden wisdom in what he said. When wonder was expressed at the smart chitchat in theatrical circles, he interjected, "Repartee is largely a matter of repertoire." Another of his specialties was the gentle sigh of humor that demolishes its object. One night E. Berry Wall, the era's most splendiferous dude, strolled into Rector's. Lackaye glanced quickly at his ornate attire and said, "Add spats and stir with a cane." Another item of apparel sparked Lackaye's most famous line. Losing an expensive cuff link, he pinned its mate to the bulletin board at the Lambs. Under it, he wrote: "LOST—The mate of this cuff link. Will buy or sell."

This was an era when actors were considered the finest possible after-dinner speakers, and Lackaye was much in demand at public functions. He avoided them whenever possible, but sometimes found himself trapped. At one dinner the clergyman who was to deliver the invocation fell ill and Lackaye was asked to take his place. Rising, he said, "There being no clergyman present, let us now thank God." He always claimed this was a slip of the tongue, but friends doubted it. Later, he was guest of honor at a dinner given by a suburban drama society. The toastmaster was so impressed at the honor of introducing Wilton Lackaye that he rambled for nearly an hour. Finally he turned to the fuming actor. "Now the guest of honor will give his address," he said. Lackaye got up. "My address is the Lambs Club," he shouted and stalked out.

Lackaye remains one of the few actors who ever turned his wit on an audience. On tour he said something which gave offense to the populace of a Road town. Onstage that night he was greeted by hisses. Lackaye stepped to the footlights. "Snakes and geese hiss," he informed the audience. "Which are you?" The hisses stopped. Yet with his remarkable composure went a few quaint conceits. Lackaye was bald, wearing an obvious toupee. It was his naïve belief that no one knew this. His favorite position at the Lambs bar was opposite a revolving electric fan. As this rotated in the summertime, the toupee rose and fell—a sight which delighted some drinkers but drove others to the wagon. Once Lackaye was summoned by a manager who was casting the part of a bald-headed man. This fact was stated and the eyes of cast members swung to Lackaye in the hope that he would voluntarily offer to abandon his precious hairpiece. He guilelessly returned the looks. "Of course, I'd have to wear a bald wig," he sighed.

With this dash of vanity went another. On tour Lackaye traveled with a dresser, and boldly scrawled on hotel registers, "Wilton Lackaye and valet." In one town an intrepid unknown was the next person to register. Under Lackaye's strong hand he put down, "John Smith and valise."

Lackaye was almost impossible to surpass in tests of wit, and few dared fence verbally with him. Once a bibulous Lamb undertook to bait him, with results so bloody that a visiting member from the West saw fit to intervene. "Mr. Lackaye," he said sternly, "I don't know what game laws are in New York, but in Colorado we consider it unsportsmanlike to shoot mackerel in a barrel."

If anyone could top Lackaye, it was the sprightly William Collier. On at least one occasion Willie did. This happened during one of the few periods when Lackaye was at liberty— that is, without work. Collier, on the other hand, was starring happily in a hit. As Collier bounced into the bar one afternoon Lackaye asked sourly, "How's the matinee idol?" "Fine," Collier retorted. "How's the idle matinee?"

Like his fellow actor-wits, Willie Collier was popular as an after-dinner speaker. He too served time enduring long speeches preceding his. At one military dinner he followed a long-winded general and a tiresome admiral. "Now I know the meaning of the title 'The Army and Navy Forever,'" Collier stated when at last he got to his feet. On another occasion, Collier was consulted by a producer trying to salvage a sinking play. "Don't you think I'm right, Willie?" the producer asked. "All that play needs is an end?" "Well, how about Saturday night?" Collier suggested. Collier was unimpressed at meeting a prominent person. "You should have been more cordial," he was chided. "He's rotten with money." "He's rotten without it," Collier shot back.

Nat C. Goodwin, slight, sad-faced, red-haired, lantern-jawed, ran away from home near Boston to become a boy-actor in a play called *The Bottle*. At moments during later years this title seemed to have been prophetic. But for the most part Goodwin was a distinguished trouper who outstandingly played Shylock, Bob Acres, Nathan Hale, Fagin (in *Oliver Twist*), and a host of other difficult roles. During most of a long career, Goodwin was an actor-manager, which is another way of saying star. As such he surrounded himself with the strongest possible casts. Other stars might fear the competition of skillful supporting talent, but Nat Goodwin never did.

Also he was a wit who could hold his own with his fellow man in and out of the Lambs. He specialized in wry, self-deprecating humor. As a prominent actor he was honored at a banquet given by the Boston city fathers. Goodwin's father had been a gambler in the old home town and the actor began his remarks by saying, "I'm glad to receive this honor from the citizens of a town where I dwelt, and my father dealt, so long." As an actor-manager-star Goodwin took his company on a long tour of Australia, where he played in *A Gilded Fool*, *The Prisoner of Zenda*, and other favorites. The performances were well received, but Goodwin found Australia totally lacking in appeal. "You travel ten thousand miles and you get to Newark," he complained. Nat Goodwin probably performed as many important roles as any other actor of his time. He never failed to suffer attacks of extreme vertigo and jangling nerves on opening nights. "My boy," he once said to Augustus Thomas, "a first night is a hoss race that lasts three hours."

Nat Goodwin was popular and highly esteemed as an actor, but he achieved notoriety as a marrying man. He married seven times—or was it eight? The public became confused, meanwhile relishing the wry remarks the actor made about his matrimonial upsets. "Marriage for me has become an incident, not a conquest," he told an interviewer. After shedding one mate in favor of another, he lamented, "I fled from Cleopatra to find a Borgia." Goodwin and his friend De Wolf Hopper appeared to be engaged in a wedding sweepstakes, and it was traditional for each to escort a new bride to Rector's for a wedding supper. When the newlyweds appeared the orchestra stood to render "The Minstrel Boy to the War Has Gone."

Goodwin discoursed a great deal about his marriages and from his words a curious pattern emerges. By his own testimony he was never a dashing fellow who swept women off their tiny feet. Rather, he was a well-meaning man constantly victimized. His first marriage (when young) was to an actress ten years his senior. This was also his most successful venture and he afterwards looked back on it fondly. This wife, on her part, paid him the ultimate tribute. By the time she died Nat Goodwin was the husband of young bride number four. Nevertheless, his first wife left him all her money in her will.

Goodwin's second shot at a lifetime of happiness was a comedy of errors whereby the gallant chap made a phony proposal to a girl in order to get her away from a cruel husband. This accomplished, the actor found public pressures so great that he was forced to marry her. "What else could a real American do?" he asked when recounting the episode.

Shortly he was rid of wife number two. Then at Rector's one night he glimpsed statuesque Maxine Elliott, a girl from Maine destined to become one of the great beauties of all time. Maxine was the daughter of a Maine sea captain who liked his daughter to stand by his side on the gale-swept bridge of his ship. Her name then was Dermot, and she performed a neat trick in finding and marrying a man named McDermott. Now she had left him to find a career on the New York stage, and her radiant loveliness hit Nat Goodwin like a bomb-burst. His company was poised to embark on its Australian adventure, but he informed his business manager that Maxine Elliott must be hired as leading lady. "You're insane," the manager exploded. "She hasn't got the emotion of an oyster."

Undaunted, Goodwin got the signatures of Maxine and her sister Gertrude on a contract. On the way to Australia they rehearsed, and on arrival Nat and Maxine read that their respective divorces had simultaneously been granted. This was the spark needed to make Australia, together with the rest of the world, believe that the actor and the beauty planned to wed. The notion was also taking possession of Nat Goodwin. His affection for beauteous Maxine—he called her Max—had become so great that not only did he coach her in the mysteries of acting, but he advertised her as well. "I first printed her name in support of me," he explained later, "but as I became more enamored of her charms the type gradually became larger until it equaled mine." Goodwin also had reason to be impressed by Maxine Elliott's unusual judgment. It was she who eventually called his attention to *An American Cousin* and *Nathan Hale,* two of his top successes.

Returning to the United States, the couple found the playgoing public firmly convinced they were man and wife. So inevitably they sought out a preacher and had the knot tied. Goodwin now found himself in the uncomfortable position of a man whose wife looked down on him in more ways than the physical. Maxine began to find fault with his grammar, clothes, manners, friends, and opinions. In New York, she displayed a partiality for the company of Wall Street financiers (some say she was the the mistress of J. P. Morgan) from whom she collected valuable tips on the stock market. She hustled her protesting mate to England, where she moved with grace among nobility and crowned heads. Soon Nat Goodwin allowed his third wife to divorce him. As years passed and Maxine became an international celebrity, proceeding (it was whispered) from J. P. Morgan to England's King Edward VII, a remark of Goodwin's helped keep the magnificent lady in perspective.

"Being married to Maxine," Nat said once, "was like being married to a Roman Senator."

Goodwin met his fourth wife (he says) because of a partiality for fishcakes. While eating them, he could be talked into anything. He was enjoying a five-fishcake breakfast at the Café Metropole when a silver-tongued producer sold him on investing financially in a new play. Its leading lady was luscious Edna Goodrich, who began her career as a Florodora Sextette replacement. Nat was introduced to Edna, who seemed immediately to tumble in love with him. So did her mother, who could hardly be persuaded to leave the pair alone. When Nat wed Edna, he found himself spliced to her mother as well.

Gradually it dawned on him that a shadowy fourth person inhabited the ménage. One afternoon he strolled by a pawnshop, to see one of his valued watches dangling prominently in the window. He hired detectives who found that Edna was bestowing gifts, money, and mid-afternoon favors on a younger man. A sad result of this was that Nat Goodwin never was able to enjoy fishcakes again, but he never lost his appetite for matrimony and became a bridegroom four times more. In his short periods when not married, he always teetered on the happy brink.

If Nat Goodwin seemed a victim of predatory females, his rival-in-marriages De Wolf Hopper more than righted the balance. Six-foot-four, handsome, with heavy features and the deepest of voices, Hopper was a chap women found easy to adore. On the stage, he was usually seen in operettas and liked to call himself a clown—his autobiography is titled *Once a*

Clown, Always a Clown. But he never was a clown to the fair sex—that is, until after the girls married him. He and Nat Goodwin matched each other until bride number five. Then Goodwin forged ahead. Hopper married six times—or was it seven? His next-to-last was a stage-struck girl from Altoona named Elda Furry, who has become the Hollywood gossip columnist Hedda Hopper.

The son of a wealthy New York lawyer, De Wolf grew up in the social whirl. When the boy reached his early twenties, the elder Hopper died, leaving $50,000 to a stage-smitten son. Overnight De Wolf reached a status most actors take years to achieve. He became an actor-manager, using a large part of this inheritance to organize his own company. The New York appearances of the Hopper troupe were a dismal failure and the remainder of the money was spent on a Road tour of a masterpiece called *One Hundred Wives*, a title which may have given the young man his big ideas. This too failed, and after his glorious fling De Wolf Hopper returned to New York to take his place at the bottom of the theatre ladder.

He intended to train his basso voice for grand opera, but was sidetracked into musical comedy where he discovered a knack for comedy. He played in *The Pied Piper, Panjandrum*, and other operettas, while offstage his personality developed in other directions. Like Maurice Barrymore, Hopper was both a man's man and a ladies' man, but his accent was on the latter. Rennold Wolf, a brother Lamb back from Europe, reported that in Rome he had examined newly discovered excavations. Over the door of a temple sacred to vestal virgins, he vowed, was the inscription YOU CAN'T KEEP DE WOLF FROM THE DOOR.

Of Hopper's blooming brides, the most famous—until the emergence of Hedda Hopper—was tiny Edna Wallace, the star of *Florodora*. She once put her amorous husband through the acid test of cuckoldry. It may be said that he passed gloriously—perhaps better than any other male who ever lived.

It came about after Hopper rented an elegant town house for himself and petite Edna. One afternoon he led a group of convivial Lambs uptown for a tour of the fine dwelling. On entering the place he expatiated on the wonders of the first floor, then took his friends upstairs. Flinging open an imposing door, he intoned, "This is the bedroom." The Lambs duly filed in, to stop aghast. In the four-poster bed, deliciously nude, was Edna Wallace. Beside her, equally nude, sprawled the English jockey Tod Sloan. Both were fast asleep, obviously exhausted from the transports of rapturous love. The Lambs swiveled horrified eyes to huge De Wolf. What would he do about this ultimate in manly disgrace? Hopper slowly walked to the side of the bed and peered down like a connoisseur at the two small, naked, perfectly formed bodies. "Aren't they beautiful?" he quietly asked.

For all his insistence on being thought a clown, Hopper was a sensitive, knowing performer with great respect for acting as a craft. About the actor's quicksilver world of make-believe, he once said:

> Acting is an art, not a spasm. The actress who makes her hearers weep is not the one who weeps herself, but the one who *seems* to weep. Had she not been completely self-possessed, making her every move deliberately with shrewd pre-knowledge of its effect, she would have had no effect. Had she lost control of herself for an instant, that instant she would have lost control of her audience. . . . The secret of fine acting is suggestion, the inflaming of the spectator's imagination; and the secret of suggestion is studied repression.

An actor's life was rendered especially congenial for De Wolf Hopper by the fact that he was one of the fastest studies the profession has ever known. Those rehearsing with him were frequently infuriated to find him letter-perfect in a part after carousing all night. Once he departed the Lambs bar to memo-

rize Gilbert and Sullivan's "Nightmare Song," aptly named because not one of its words bears relation to the one before. In an
hour Hopper returned. The pals who had so recently bade him
farewell made bets that he had not mastered the troublesome
song. Hopper waited until the wagers had reached interesting
proportions. Then he proved that he knew every syllable.

Like Nat Goodwin, Hopper's great skills were obscured by
another factor in his existence. This was not so much wives as a
poem. In those days shows often increased attendance by advertising social nights. For a Baseball Night, Hopper was handed
a poem clipped from a newspaper to deliver. It was called "Casey
at the Bat" and from that instant on, at nearly every Hopper
performance until his death (aged seventy-seven) in 1935, audiences clamored for him to repeat it.

He always did—and it is a measure of De Wolf Hopper, actor,
that he never did it quite the same twice.

Lambs Club wits not only enjoyed striking sparks off fellow
wits. They also relished stories about others.

Nat Wills, who sang "If a Table at Rector's Could Talk" in
the first *Follies*, was the hard-luck subject of endless anecdotes.
Once he escorted an adorable young lady home to Brooklyn in
one of the first limousines-for-hire available in the city. In the
middle of Brooklyn Bridge, the chauffeur stopped the car. "Keep
going," Wills ordered. The chauffeur ran down his glass parti-
tion. "The girl said, 'Stop!' " he retorted. The girl glared at him.
"I didn't mean *you*," she said icily. Eventually, Wills married a
beautiful circus bareback rider. Years of balancing on the rump
of a white horse had given her marvelous co-ordination, plus
muscles of tempered steel. In the course of an argument she
hurled Wills through the solid-wood paneling of her dressing-
room door. Carefully Wills picked himself up. "I should have
married the horse," he muttered.

Most actors of the day rested heavily—how times have changed!—on the crutch of alcohol. Henry E. Dixey, star of *Adonis*, was a drinker who scorned soda, water, or ice, to demand his whisky neat. He warned the world: "The continual use of ice in drinks will develop a race of people with black and blue upper lips." Yet liquor never slowed Dixey's lightning wits. At Rector's one night he was introduced to a lawyer named Ira Leo Bamberger.

"I didn't catch all those names," Dixey said.

"Ira Leo Bamberger."

"Oh, yes! Three nice boys!"

Another unusual drinker was Jack Prescott, who nightly felt obliged to partake in every bar between his theatre and the Lambs Club. When he played near Madison Square the number of his stops became formidable. Prescott made an elaborate ceremony of imbibing. First he requested a dash of absinthe in a whisky glass, with bourbon on top. After downing this, he extended a hand to the bartender, who splashed it with absinthe. Prescott then rubbed palms together, sank his nose between them, and inhaled.

On special occasions he requested a second dash of absinthe. This he ran over his eyebrows and dabbed into regions behind his ears. Young John Barrymore, observing this solemn rite for the first time, gave out with a respectful gasp. "Christ, I never thought of *that*," he said admiringly. It was the beginning of a lifelong friendship.

But perhaps the most notable of drinking actors was **Pete Dailey**, who after the dissolution of the Weber and Fields Company succeeded on his own as a musical-comedy comedian. Among other things Dailey, who weighed 250 pounds, was **one** of the better soft-shoe dancers of the day.

"O, rare Pete Dailey," a contemporary has rhapsodized. "He spikes the stale beer of the casual barroom group with the old wine of his personality and yawns flee before him." At the end of a performance Dailey retired to his dressing room where he simultaneously opened a quart of whisky and a quart of champagne. Before leaving the theatre he had emptied both, using the champagne as chaser. Anyone who paused at the dressing room was invited to join him. When this invitation was accepted, Dailey broke open two more bottles.

Like Maurice Barrymore, Dailey turned night into day. "A working man knocks off at six and has his evening for fun," he explained. "When I get done at eleven, I want mine." This somewhat complicated life for a devoted wife, who on one occasion was bold enough to complain of her lot. "Come along with me," Dailey urged heartily. For three nights Mrs. Dailey accompanied her husband on his round of barrooms. Then, forever mollified, she stayed home.

Dailey lived as close to his theatres as possible. When playing with Weber and Fields, he stayed across the street in the Norfolk Apartments, Broadway at Thirtieth Street. While he slept through the daylight hours his wife stood stern guard and no one was allowed to interrupt his slumbers. On matinee days she allowed him to sleep until the last possible second. Then, half-dressed, unshaven, and breakfastless, he tore across the street to the stage. Even without breakfast in his ample stomach, Dailey could hold his own in brushes with other actors. When a bald-headed actor named Bigelow undertook to needle him during a performance, Dailey's first riposte was aimed at Bigelow's head. "Put on your hat, you're half-naked," he bellowed. Turning attention to Bigelow's red tie, he whipped it out from under the vest. "Your nose is bleeding," he roared.

Yet of all stories of drinking actors, one that ranks high concerns a fellow who was no actor. He was a bookkeeper in a producer's office and when a snowstorm kept a small-part player from showing up the young man volunteered to take his place. Quickly he memorized the necessary lines. Then the enormity of what he had undertaken began to dawn on him. He started to drink whisky to stoke ebbing courage. By curtain time he was bleary-eyed but game. Pushed out on the stage, he stood revolving slowly. "Face the audience," the stage manager whispered hoarsely.

"Where is it?" the young man wanted to know.

These robust wits and meaty talents added a sprinkling of high spirits to the era. They were bravura types, inclined to address friend and foe with a courtly "Sir!" But even as they flourished, with the world laughing at their sallies, the harbinger of another kind of Broadway had appeared on the local scene. His would be a White Way brash rather than gay. On it, ego would pay off no less than talent, while friend and foe would not be greeted as "Sir," but rather as "Sweetheart" or "Kid."

This augur of a new Broadway was to be found in the brisk person of George Michael Cohan, aged twenty-eight in the year 1907, and the brashest young man ever to appear in a profession where brashness can be a virtue. If Charles Frohman was Mr. Theatre, young Georgie Cohan seemed destined to become Mr. Broadway. And—this whirling planet being what it is—Broadway seemed certain to eclipse the Theatre.

George M. Cohan was the Theatre's Tot. He was born on July 3rd—close enough to the Fourth to claim it later as his day of birth. His parents were vaudevillian Jerry Cohan and his wife Helen and the bouncing baby's cradle was an open tray in a dressing-room trunk. Georgie went to school for only six weeks in a rich, full life—the theatre being the only seat of learning that could ever contain his talents. In the same life span he read only three books—all by Mark Twain. From the moment he was able to speak, Georgie displayed an ego unprecedented in show biz. He *knew* he was the best the world had yet produced and he saw no reason why civilization should not be aware of this. While in knee pants, he freely offered wisdom to older performers, telling established vaudeville performers just what was wrong with their acts. "Say, are you trying to get a laugh or are you just naturally fresh?" his elders asked in amazement. The answer was simple. Georgie was just naturally fresh, and when subjected to the hard knocks traditional in life, his cockiness seemed to grow rather than diminish. Once the boy-genius was told he would be paid exactly what he was worth for a performance. Ripping open his pay envelope, he found six dollars inside. His cries of anguish rent the air and an older performer blandly asked, "What's the extra dollar for?" Such sharp-edged sarcasm was totally lost on Georgie Cohan.

With his pretty sister Josie, the boy early became a working member of the Four Cohans act, which was greatly favored in New England, upper New York state, and Pennsylvania. The Four Cohans became on occasion The Cohan Mirth Makers and Jerry Cohan's Irish Hibernia. In the course of strenuous trouping Georgie played his mother's father in one skit. Again he donned skirts and a blonde wig to dance beside his sister. This he loathed.

By the age of ten he was a trumpet player, loudly maintaining that his was the finest horn the world had ever heard. He expressed a desire to master the violin and his long-suffering father duly arranged lessons. After three of them Georgie came home with a note. "Impossible to teach this boy any more," it read. "HE KNOWS IT ALL." Following this, the elder Cohan decided to put his problem child in a New Jersey community where a family friend would see that he attended regular school. During this sojourn Georgie was hit across the face by a baseball bat, an injury which forever twisted one side of his mouth into a quizzical droop. It was providential, making him look every bit as sure of himself on the surface as he felt inside. But the effort to fit Georgie Cohan into the conventional mold was a failure. After a few weeks the family friend led the youth to the railroad station, to put him aboard a train. "Tell your father, mother, and sister that we think just as much of them as ever," he said, in parting.

Georgie was put to work selling song books in theatre lobbies, where he rapidly earned the title of "The Freshest Song-Book Boy in America." Reunited as one of the Four Cohans, he delivered lines out of the side of his mouth, sang through his nose, and danced as if his legs were pistons. By sheer drive he made himself into an infectious singer and a highly capable buck-and-winger. "He sang without a voice and danced without steps," a description of him states. An added burden came from the fact that his relentless bragging antagonized members of pit orchestras, who played tricks with the music while he danced and sang. He also annoyed the stagehands, who contrived noisy distractions as he performed. Yet he continued to proclaim his own magnitude. His father seems to have been one of the most lovable men in show business, and for the sake of Jerry Cohan, Georgie's tireless braggadocio was forgiven. "He's just a boy with big ideas about himself," Jerry Cohan would explain, and this gentle answer turned away wrath.

At the age of thirteen, Georgie appeared with his family in a vaudeville sketch based on *Peck's Bad Boy*. He was ideally cast as Henry Peck—"incorrigible lad with a heart of gold." By this early age he had also begun writing songs. His first, soon published, was called "Why Did Nellie Leave Her Home?" Needless to say, he wrote words and music himself—under what conceivable conditions would George M. Cohan need a collaborator? In a long lifetime George M. never walked—he strutted. Now the prodigious youth sashayed up and down the Great White Way buttonholing members of the profession to whom he rendered his song. "I'm a great little guy, I am," he announced at the end. "My mind is working every minute."

It was. Georgie turned out songs, parodies, sketches, and skits in a geyser flow. At the age of eighteen he wrote a song called "Hot Tamale Alley," sung successfully by May Irwin. Simultaneously the Four Cohans—never a top attraction in vaudeville —were hired for a touring farce called *April Fool*. The star of this was Gus Williams, a tried-and-true favorite in Road towns. Young Georgie immediately endeared himself to Williams by stating, "I make more in a day than you do in a week." He next offered to improve *April Fool* by subjecting it to a speedy rewrite. An apoplectic Williams informed him that *April Fool* had been a financial success for the past two seasons. Georgie shrugged this off and quick-talked the personal opinion that it still stank.

At rehearsals he balked at playing his role in the country-bumpkin style of his predecessors. (Here, for the first time, sweet Jerry Cohan took a swing at his son.) Williams threatened to fire all four Cohans, and Georgie was forced to give in. But on opening night he reverted to smart-aleck style. Backstage, Williams again threatened to fire the Cohans and Georgie backed down for the second time. After the final curtain Williams insisted that he apologize before the full company. Georgie did this with such grace that Williams was deeply touched. "I thought you had a swelled head, Georgie," he said. "I'm sorry."

This was all Georgie needed. Out of the side of his mouth, he set the record straight by saying:

There's nothing swelled head about me at all! I'm too smart to get that way. I could have had a swelled head a long time ago if I'd wanted to. Why I've published over two hundred songs. Right now, May Irwin is making the hit of her life with one of them. Look at all the sketches I've written for variety teams! I've a dozen of them playing around the country at this moment.

But I don't go around bragging about it. No, sir, there's nothing swelled head about me. . . .

The conflict between this most conceited of youths and the established star continued unabated over a long tour. At times Williams scored. "There's one thing I'll say about you, Georgie," he jabbed once. "You've convinced me that capital punishment is absolutely necessary." Williams also got in the last word. After the final performance of the tour, he found himself entering the same hotel elevator with Georgie. As always, the young man began a rapid-fire monologue extolling himself. Williams went berserk, shouting, "I've been listening to you all season and if you get into this elevator, so help me God, I'll grab the lever and run it through the roof!"

From the time he became conscious of his own importance, Georgie urged his father to make a frontal assault on Broadway. Gentle Jerry hesitated. Then Georgie wrote a sketch called *The Governor's Son* for the Four Cohans. It was a sensation in vaudeville and Georgie expanded it to a full-length play. A Broadway booking was arranged.

With this came an event that cast a long shadow. On the evening *The Governor's Son* was scheduled to open, a small theatrical union called the White Rats (rats being *star* spelled backward) decided to call a strike in protest against no-pay-for-rehearsals and other abuses. To Georgie Cohan, so famished for Broadway success, this was a terrible blow. The frantic young man ranged the theatre district, begging the White Rats to give him a dispensation to open his play because he was also author and coproducer. At the last moment, the White Rats agreed. Yet the frustrations of the episode did what life itself had always failed to do to George Michael Cohan. He was thrown off balance. On the opening night of *The Governor's Son* at the

Savoy Theatre his own performance was ragged and others in the cast were similarly affected. *The Governor's Son* was a flop and in his seething mind Cohan saw fit to blame it all on the White Rats union.

However, his ballooning ego seemed to push this setback aside. He took *The Governor's Son* on tour, after which he popped brightly into the Syndicate office of Abraham Lincoln Erlanger to announce that he had written a musical comedy called *Little Johnny Jones*. "Best thing I've ever done," he declared from the side of his mouth. Impressed by this sublime assurance, Erlanger offered to provide backing for the show. With his jaunty straw hat and crooked grin, George M. now strutted Broadway hiring cast, scenery, costumes, and even ordering programs and posters. What he alone knew was that only a title existed for the musical comedy *Little Johnny Jones*.

Georgie became so happily involved in details of big-time production that ten days short of the opening he still had only the title "Little Johnny Jones." At this fateful moment George M. was introduced to Sam H. Harris, a young man from New York's East Side who had produced ten-twenty-thirty melodramas and managed the prizefighter Terry McGovern. Harris offered to handle management details for a firm to be called Cohan and Harris. The young producer sought out William A. Brady, who had given up management of Gentleman Jim Corbett to become a theatrical producer. Harris told Brady he too was quitting the fight game. "Quitting it!" Brady roared. "Hell, fellow, you aren't quitting it—you're just getting into it deeper than ever!"

With Harris behind him, Cohan was free to devise an old-fashioned plot which he embellished with new-fashioned songs like "Give My Regards to Broadway." His Fourth-of-July birthday had made him conscious of the fertile soil of patriotism, and for himself in the leading role he wrote, "Yankee Doodle

Dandy." The flag-waving occasioned by this breezy number became a staple of early Cohan shows. Even so, New York critics
did not like *Little Johnny Jones*. One called Cohan, "a swagger-
ing, noisy vaudevillian, entirely out of place in the first-class
theatre." Reeling from this, *Little Johnny Jones* fled to Philadelphia, where a theatre miracle occurred. The show was a hit, so
much so that—in a reversal practically unheard of in theatre an-
nals—it was brought back to New York. This time *Little Johnny
Jones* caught on. Georgie celebrated by beginning a weekly
newspaper called *The Spotlight*, in which he aired his refreshing views on critics, actors, and plays.

At last the world had become aware of George M. Cohan. "I
don't care what they say about me so long as my name gets in
the papers," Georgie proclaimed, the straw skimmer aggressively
over one eye. Everyone he met was "Kid." Success hid (if it
did not mellow) some of his pristine aggressiveness, and successes now came fast. In 1905 he wrote *Forty-five Minutes from
Broadway* ("So Long, Mary"; "Mary Is a Grand Old Name").
In 1905–1906 his show was *George Washington, Jr.* ("It's a Grand
Old Flag"). He and Sam Harris suited each other, and an interviewer has recalled a scene in which Cohan struts blithely into the Forty-second-Street office of Cohan and Harris. To Harris
he calls, "Say, kid, I got an idea for a new show this morning."

"Swell," Harris answers, "but I hope you'll write a second act
before we go into rehearsal. I always like to start with a complete show."

"Listen, kid," Cohan replies. "There isn't gonna be any second
act until we start rehearsing the first. We might have to change
the first and that'd mean changing the second. So there isn't
gonna be any second until we see. It's my system."

Broadway suited George M. Cohan and the Yankee Doodle
Boy suited Broadway. His songs and lyrics rang with tributes to

its Great White Way—"The Man Who Owns Broadway"; "Too Many Miles Away from Old Broadway"; "I Long for the Hustle Bustle of Hurly-Burly Lane, Where Midnight Is as Noisy as Midday." In 1907 the Cohan show was *The Yankee Prince* and in it he was joined by the other Cohans. This enabled him to advertise in bright lights GEORGE M. COHAN AND HIS ROYAL FAMILY.

Observing this, a Broadway wit said, "George M. Cohan and his family royalties!"

A new Broadway had indeed arrived!

7: PLAYWRIGHTS

One afternoon during the winter of 1907 a tall Harvard student walked by a Salvation Army meeting on a street corner in a poor section of Boston. A cluster of bums and derelicts was being exhorted toward the Faith by a young Salvation Army lassie whose face under the red and black bonnet was extremely pretty. Yet over it lay a patina of experience which hinted a provocative past. The young Harvard man—his name was Edward Sheldon —had just left a class in George Pierce Baker's celebrated course in Playwriting Techniques. He made a mental note that in the sweet-hard face of the girl with the tambourine lay the germ of a dramatic situation.

Handsome Ned Sheldon, dark-haired, high-colored, with deep brown eyes, firm chin, and serious face, was the Golden Boy of Harvard. Indeed, from the time of childhood in a wealthy Chicago home, he had shown himself lavishly endowed with the indefinable something called Charm. "Talk flowed from him like a bubbling fountain," a friend said. Yet the owner of this magic ability to win friends was no self-centered egoist. With his rare magnetism, Sheldon was deprecating, friendly, generous. His mental powers fully matched the high-voltage charm and he was in the process of zipping through Harvard in three rapid years.

Almost on the eve of graduation, Sheldon had made up his

mind to become a writer. But what kind? As a child he had played theatre with his toys and Professor Baker's course had rekindled a bit of this early enthusiasm. His interest in the theatre gained further impetus from the felicitous manner in which he got along with stage folk. When Mrs. Fiske visited the Harvard Stylus Club she was so entertained by young Sheldon that the distinguished Professor Edward Townsend Copeland was obliged to write her a note: "Dear Minnie—When you are finished talking with Ned Sheldon, may I see you?"

In accordance with the regulations of Professor Baker's course Sheldon had written his first play. It was called *A Family Affair*, and the Professor had been impressed by it. He suggested that Sheldon send it to Alice Kauser, a play agent who had studied the craft under Elizabeth Marbury, then ventured forth on her own. In Cambridge, Sheldon was accounted the luckiest of lucky young men and now his luck stretched out to New York. Seated in her office in the Empire Theatre building, Alice Kauser picked up the script of *A Family Affair*. Her first impulse was to reject it unread, since it was ineptly bound. But she began to read. The plot paralleled a play already on Broadway, but the scenes were expertly built and the dialogue flavorsome. Miss Kauser dictated a wire to Cambridge.

When Ned Sheldon arrived at her office, he seemed so young that her secretary advised through the intercom, "It's a boy!" Though forewarned, Miss Kauser still thought the actual author must have sent his son to see her. After discovering otherwise, she inquired whether Sheldon had more ideas for plays. He mentioned the Salvation Army lassie on the Boston street corner.

So was born *Salvation Nell*, the most-talked-about play of the year 1908 and a milestone in theatre realism. For up to this moment playwrights hesitated to employ seamy backgrounds. Pleasant pastoral backdrops and elegant drawing rooms were deemed superior. Why should playgoers wish to see bums and beggars

on a stage when they avoided the type on streets? Sheldon, the
well-brought-up young man, first tried to write his play without
coming into contact with bums and prostitutes. It did not work.
The first draft of *Salvation Nell* failed to ring true, and he began
haunting Salvation Army meetings. The result was the script
sent to Alice Kauser in January 1908. Miss Kauser had already
mentioned the play to Margaret Anglin, an actress so effective
as a tear-jerker that it was said her audiences could be recognized
by red-rimmed eyes. To her subsequent regret, Miss Anglin
turned it down. Taking a long chance, Miss Kauser submitted
the script to Minnie Maddern Fiske, then appearing in *Rosmersholm*. Once again the Sheldon luck held. Mrs. Fiske had grown
weary of Ibsen and thought longingly of a contemporary American play. She read *Salvation Nell* and—the story is—immediately
sent out for an assortment of Salvation Army bonnets.

On the stage of 1908, *Salvation Nell* passed for extreme realism.
It told the story of Nell Sanders, barroom slavey, who rises
from the depths of sordid love to find redemption in God. Jim
Platt, Nell's common-law husband, is a denizen of Hell's Kitchen
in New York, a thief and proud of it. The two have a son named
Jimmy, and when big Jim urges Nell to join him in a life of crime
she blurts out, "For God's sake, Jim, let's be straight and give
our kid a chance—we never knowed it until it was too late."
When Jim's heart fails to soften she clasps the child to her and
cries, "Come on, Jimmy! We're goin' to pray—we're goin' to
pray for your dad, Jimmy, an' we're goin' to save him! If we
only believe—if we're only sure in our hearts—God'll do it."

The real shocker in *Salvation Nell* came with the locale. It is
Christmas Eve in Sid McGovern's heavy-oak Empire Bar, Tenth
Avenue and Forty-eighth Street, the heart of Hell's Kitchen.
The Yule season is saluted by MERRY CHRISTMAS written in stale
beer across bar mirrors and by shabby decorations festooning the
joint. The patrons are an assortment of loafers and down-and-

out bums. A little girl comes in for a bucket of beer; a one-legged fiddler plays a tune. In the backroom gather the street-walkers and female drunks. Next door a house of prostitution is raided and one of the madame's girls eludes the cops to duck into McGovern's. Into all this drunkenly stumbles brutal Jim Platt. A bedraggled scrubwoman leaves her bucket and rag to greet him fondly. He retaliates by forcing her to give him money for more drinks. Jim Platt is the excellent actor Holbrook Blinn. Nell, the scrubwoman, is Mrs. Fiske.

One of the McGovern bums attempts to steal a Christmas kiss from Nell, and in a rage over such poaching Jim nearly kills the man. Then he falls in a drunken stupor, head cradled in Nell's loving lap. For assault, he is sent away to Sing Sing for eight years, during which time Nell travels the Glory Road to the Salvation Army. She is Captain Sanders when finally Jim is sprung. Daily she exhorts the bully boys on the unfriendly sidewalks before McGovern's:

> It's the old story I've told you many times before. Christ was a poor man, and He chose poor people to be His friends. He knows how hard we have to work to keep alive. He knows how strong and terrible our temptations are. . . . But let me tell you that it's you Christ waits for. You've sunk to the bottom, you know the bitterness and cruelty of life, and it's you Christ wants, to show the beauty and the glory and the light. When you and me who have fallen rise again, we're greater than our sins, we're bigger men and women than if we'd never sinned at all.

When Jim arrives in Hell's Kitchen, he tries to lure Nell back into a life of crime. She, in turn, tries to convert him. So Jim is on the horns of a sharp dilemma. He is conditioned to crime, but he still loves Nell. In a rage of frustration, he strikes her. Then, conscience-stricken, he stands on the outskirts of the crowd listening to Salvation Nell. Finally, he muscles his way forward to drop a coin in her tambourine. Big Jim Platt is a saved soul. . . .

Salvation Nell's theme of redemption through God was age-old, but the play gained impact from its sympathetic presentation of down-and-outs, drunkards, and whores. To see such types portrayed as human beings was for most an eye-opening experience. "In the closing scene of the play there was not a heart in the audience unmoved by its sincerity nor an eye that was not moistened by its tenderness," said one critic. Another saluted Sheldon as a playwright with a grip to him, while a third stated that under Sheldon's pink cheeks ran real red blood. Critic Ashton Stevens called *Salvation Nell* "the most daring play New York has ever seen. [It] not only dramatizes the Salvation Army, but it serves up Hell's Kitchen piping hot."

As the author of New York's most-discussed play the Golden Boy of Harvard became the Wonder Boy of Broadway. Sheldon enjoyed every moment of it. Still wonderfully stage-struck, he told an interviewer, "If anyone says, 'There goes an actor,' I always run to the window and look out." According to his biographer Eric Wollencott Barnes, "He ate up the life of the theatre as a hungry cat laps cream." Still, the twenty-one-year-old Wonder Boy took worldly success completely in stride. With his magnetism, Ned Sheldon had always been socially successful. Now he was merely operating in a new and glamorous locale—"a young lord in an atmosphere of champagne and flowers and the best restaurants." Girls hurled themselves at handsome Ned and one lady columnist assured her public that Sheldon's photographs did not begin to do him justice. "They show him passive," she explained, "but in person he is *active*, smiling, with hair tumbling and eyes alight." Yet where girls were concerned Sheldon seemed interested only in alluring Doris Keane, the actress for whom he eventually wrote the long-running play *Romance*. Miss Keane seemed enamored only of her career. With royalties pouring in, Sheldon took a beautiful Gramercy Park apartment, which he furnished in somewhat Fitchean splendor.

"Comfort tinged with theatricality," his biographer calls the striking décor. It featured black carpets, gun-metal mirrors, and French period furniture.

Having succeeded with a romantic play set against a realistic background, the young playwright (he had now reached the age of twenty-two) embarked on another. This bore a striking title—*The Nigger*. Alice Kauser, for one, did not like the idea. "The nigger problem is not one the American people wish to see on the boards," she said sourly, when he eagerly told her about it. Nonetheless, Sheldon persevered. He had never been South and apparently had no great interest in the plight of colored people—the inspiration for the play came from an article on the race question in a magazine. He got around his ignorance by concocting a highly charged plot on which he superimposed the Negro problem. *The Nigger* concerned Philip Morrow, a Southerner arrogant in his contempt for colored folk. In the first act Morrow, a local sheriff, finds himself arresting a Negro and (to his surprise) feeling sympathy for him. Yet he aspires to the governorship of his state and any softness toward Negroes would ruin his chances of election. "After all," his pretty fiancee soothes as the curtain falls, "it was only a nigger."

In act two, Morrow (played by Guy Bates Post) has been elected governor. Outside the gubernatorial mansion a race riot is in full swing. Inside, Morrow's enemies face him with evidence that Negro blood runs in his veins. He tells this to the girl, who draws back in horror. In what Sheldon apparently intended as proof that nigger-blood will out, he seizes her roughly, pins her arms, kisses her hard. She is saved from a worse fate by the sudden entrance of another person. The outraged girl runs from the stage.

In act three, she returns to beg Morrow's forgiveness. "I love you anyway," she says in effect, though nothing in her character to this point makes her capable of such nobility. He spurns her, saying that he plans to renounce his high office for work among his own people. As the curtain falls, he steps onto the balcony to inform his rioting constituents of his Negro blood and his future.

The Nigger was a super-sensation in 1909—and, indeed, might still be in certain localities today. As with *Sapho* and Shaw's *Mrs. Warren's Profession*, members of the audience stalked from the theatre in protest at the daring theme. But the majority responded enthusiastically. After the shocking love scene at the end of act two, the crowd rose cheering to its feet, giving Sheldon such an ovation that "he came forth with the timidity of a startled robin, clung frantically to the proscenium arch for an instant and bobbed out of sight again—when his cherubic face appeared one marveled that he could have written what we had just seen."

Part of the enthusiasm for *The Nigger* (though not all) came from the fact that it was the first worthwhile offering of an ambitious enterprise known as the New Theatre. Subsidized to the stupendous tune of $3,000,000 by millionaires like John Jacob Astor, August Belmont, Otto Kahn, Henry Clay Frick, William Vanderbilt, and others, the New Theatre was designed to save the classical drama in America, since the assorted millionaires saw on Broadway a deplorable trend toward the frivolous. One-third of all New Theatre productions were to be classics performed by a repertory company headed by E. H. Sothern and Julia Marlowe. For the project a colossus of a playhouse called the New Theatre (later the Century) was built on Central Park West. By the time *The Nigger* opened, the visionary New Theatre was sagging on the ropes. Sothern and Marlowe had inaugurated the enterprise with *Antony and Cleopatra*. The scenery for this was so massively cumbersome that it oppressed the actors, and an expectant audience went home disappointed. The next play was a lightweight comedy better suited to the tiny Punch and Judy Theatre on Broadway. This was followed by John Galsworthy's *Strife*, its English locale confusingly switched to Pennsylvania. So *The Nigger* was the first native play in the vaunted New Theatre repertory, and by far the most exciting.

Sheldon's third play also stemmed from magazines. It was *The Boss*, suggested by the muckraking exposés of Lincoln Steffens, Ida Tarbell, and Will Irwin. Though several novels had been devoted to analyzing the ruthless big-city political boss, the type had never been portrayed on the stage. Again young Ned Sheldon scored a *first*, but *The Boss* turned out to be the least striking of his early plays. For one thing, the plot hinged on the cliché situation of the moment: the girl the Boss loves offers him her body if he will end foreclosure on workers' homes. Behind this were hints of social unrest and some mild probing of the character of the Boss. But perhaps the opening of this play is important for a thoroughly irrelevant reason. The night before Sheldon stayed out late at a party. Next morning he rose early to greet his family, who arrived en masse from Chicago. By dinnertime he was weary. After dinner he went home, got into bed, and tumbled into dreamless sleep.

For perhaps the first time anywhere, a playwright slept blissfully through the opening night of his play!

One of the first to learn of an impending change in the theatrical atmosphere of Broadway was Charles Frohman.

In his hushed Gothic office above the Empire, Mr. Theatre sat cross-legged in favored Turkish fashion while an untried playwright named Eugene Walter read his play *Paid in Full*. For several reasons this added up to a provocative scene. One was Frohman's known partiality for importing foreign successes. Never did he undertake to produce a play by an untested American talent. At the same time, he was an avid reader of, and listener to, new plays. Almost any young playwright with proper connections could usually gain his ear.

The fact that the most important producer in America was indifferent to native talent provoked advance hostility on the part of playwrights like Eugene Walter. Yet Walter already had enough hostilities, without needing new ones. He was a broad-shouldered, rough-and-tumble character, with stints in news-paper city rooms of Cleveland, Detroit, New York, and Seattle behind him. But perhaps his longest stint had been in barrooms. In one New York bar, Walter had encountered the play-agent Arch Selwyn. After identifying himself as a tyro playwright, Walter talked with such flavor and zest that Selwyn came to believe him. Following attempts to make Walter create in New York City, Selwyn moved his problem playwright to the Long Island shore, where he wrote *Paid in Full*, a play about an em-bezzler who offers his young wife's fetching body to his employer in order to avoid prosecution.

Why did the prudish Mr. Theatre listen to the end of such a meaty play? Here indeed is one of the theatre's eternal mys-teries. But Frohman patiently heard the script through, then rose from his comfortable sofa to announce that it was not his sort of play. Employing his velvet manners to the utmost, he politely ended, "But I hope you will let me hear your next one."

The average playwright, brushed off in this way by Charles Frohman, might depart thankfully, cherishing the belief that the most influential producer in the country had expressed interest in his next effort. Not so rugged Eugene Walter. He flew into a towering rage. "Never," he bellowed. Then he advanced threat-eningly on the roly-poly producer. Pausing just short of Froh-man's actual person, he delivered himself of remarks casting aspersions on the producer's legitimacy. Then, to Frohman's horror, he hawked deep in his throat and spat vigorously on the expensive Persian rug. . . .

Eugene Walter, with his devotion to barrooms, was more typical of the new breed of playwrights than was Edward Sheldon. Indeed, Sheldon was something of a bridge between two types. On the surface of his polished personality he much resembled Clyde Fitch. These two were gentlemen, ever polite, radiating copious drawing-room charm—types, in short, who would never, never expectorate on a Persian rug. In addition, both worked like demons, as if driven by some intuition that the Fates held a massive misfortune in store for them, and wished to accomplish as much as possible before the hammer-blow struck. At his peak of fame and fortune Clyde Fitch was busy adapting foreign plays, a pursuit which would seem far beneath a playwright of his stature. On his part, Sheldon often labored over three scripts at once.

The other new playwrights springing up on Broadway had a greater inclination to mix robust pleasure with hard work. Eugene Walter, with his fondness for bars, spent more time lifting shot glasses than he did writing. Paul Armstrong and his collaborator Wilson Mizner were inspired wits and two-fisted practical jokers. Young men like Owen Davis, Channing Pollock, Jules Eckert Goodman, and George Middleton worked almost as hard as Fitch and Sheldon, yet led married lives with normal responsibilities. The aim of these new playwrights was to emphasize the play. "The play's the thing" was their working motto, and they sought to make the play itself important rather than merely a vehicle tailored to suit special acting talents. This difference was illuminated for George Middleton as he glanced over a script contrived by the veteran Paul Kester to clothe the talents of Lily Langtry. Middleton remarked the tepid quality of the climactic scene. Kester admitted that the script fell far short of potential impact. "Lily couldn't reach it," he explained. "This way she can."

The new playwrights were trying to make actors *reach*. They were also writing with flexibility and imagination. In the line of Ibsen and Shaw, they were switching the channel of playwriting from the well-constructed play which Shaw had contemptuously called (after Sardou) Sardoodledom. From the busy Road city of San Francisco Ambrose Bierce added his individual dash of bitters to this by defining a dramatist as one who adapts plays from the French.

The new playwrights were forced to abide by a few old rules. Seldom, for instance, was there an unhappy ending on a play. Yet instead of relying on the perfect constructions of Sardoodledom, playwrights were depending more on rugged contemporary themes. Some did this on a massive scale, among them William Vaughn Moody, whose *The Great Divide* showed the pressures where East meets West, not in the Orient but in the United States. Others found inspiration in the average man. Charles Klein, author of the popular *Lion and the Mouse*, advised, "Don't write about the man who goes up in a balloon because none of your audience knows how he feels, or gives a damn. Write about the fellow who's afraid of losing his job, or has lost it and is hungry, or who sits at the bedside of his sick child. Everybody knows how that man feels, and putting it into scenes they will recognize, scenes that hit home, is the secret of good authorship and a good income."

In aiding those ambitious to write melodrama Klein was more succinct. "Get your heroine in a corner," he recommended. "Beset her from all sides and when you make your audience want to climb over the footlights to rescue her, you've got a hit." Augustus Thomas heard a story of an Englishman pretending to be an American, and asked himself why a man would do this. The answer zoomed back at him: "A girl." So he got the germ of his successful *Earl of Pawtucket*. Producer Al Woods, a graduate of ten-twenty-thirty melodramas like *Nellie, the Beautiful Cloak Model*, passed along his own wisdom to playwrights. "The

plays that fail are those that make a single idea last all evening,"
he believed. "When the audience is thinking, 'There just can't
be another twist to this,' and a whole flock of new ones come
along, then a play is bound to be a hit."

The speed of some playwrights was phenomenal. At a tryout
of one of his plays Channing Pollock was told, "You'll have to
rewrite it." "Between now and next week?" he asked. "Between
now and the day after tomorrow," he was told. Pollock also held
a full-time job as a Broadway press agent. Nevertheless, by
working nights he finished a forty-eight-hour rewrite.

The Shubert brothers, reduced to two since the death of en-
terprising Sam Shubert in a railroad wreck, desperately needed
scripts for the fight against the powerful Syndicate. Where other
producers dallied for weeks and months over a script, the Shuberts gave fast opinions. For this reason they were favored by
playwrights. George Scarborough was a would-be author who
as a Secret Service agent had once investigated a white-slave
case. In five days he now wrote a script about a girl exposed to
the sinister persuasions of the madame of a high-toned bawdy
house. Just as awful pressures are being brought to bear, our
heroine is saved. Scarborough dubbed this moral cliff-hanger
The Lure and carried it to the Shubert office one morning. In
the afternoon he went back. His play had been accepted and he
was handed a contract and a check only six days after beginning
his script.

Scarborough was a lucky amateur; Paul Armstrong, the ultimate in professionalism. Broad-shouldered, with a ruddy face,
goatee, and a fondness for wide-brim black hats, Armstrong often
derived inspiration from the works of others. After reading a story
by Bret Harte, he retired to his hotel room and in ten days completed the hit play *Salomy Jane*. For this and other feats, he was
christened the Hair-Trigger Playwright. To Armstrong, anything he read was fodder. Sick in his hotel room, he was reduced

JOE WEBER and LEW FIELDS—Mike and Myer, onstage—were the funniest men of the turn-of-the-century era and Weber and Fields Music Hall the jolliest spot on the Great White Way until the incredible bust-up between the cut-ups. (*Above*) Fields (*left*) and Weber in a characteristic skit.

EDNA WALLACE HOPPER played Lady Holyrood in *Florodora*. Briefly the wife of much-married De Wolf Hopper, she mastered the intricacies of the stock market and died wealthy in 1959.

DE WOLF HOPPER was a massive fellow. A childhood bout of typhoid left him without a hair on his body; he was a lusty raconteur and both a man's man and the ladies' delight.

One critic declared that Mrs. Leslie Carter had all the subtlety of a lighthouse. She was the emotional star of the David Belasco stable until she married without consulting the Master. He never spoke to her again.

CHARLES FROHMAN, the Mr. Theatre of the time, was pudgy and conservative, polite and unobtrusive. A fundamental cheerfulness (he liked a laugh a day) enabled him to weather the vicissitudes of producing over twenty plays a season.

Elegant CLYDE FITCH once had five plays running on Broadway. He was a flamboyant dresser who might wear an orange tie with a purple velvet jacket. Yet where theatre was concerned Fitch showed no discord. He was an unerring craftsman.

The words *elfin* and *ethereal* were most often used to describe the charm of MAUDE ADAMS. Still, in photographs she comes through as a stunning and substantial girl-woman. Maude Adams was Peter Pan to a worshipful generation, but her own favorite role was the rooster in *Chantecler*.

MINNIE MADDERN FISKE was called the conscience of the American theatre for her long fight against the heartless Syndicate. Many today look back on her as the greatest actress this country has produced.

The curtain line in Eugene Walter's *The Easiest Way* was a shocking milestone in this country's drama. Here, weak-willed Laura seems agonized as her wealthy protector and her dearly beloved make a strange bargain. The players are (*left to right*) EDWARD H. ROBINSON, FRANCES STARR, JOSEPH KILGOUR.

E. H. SOTHERN and JULIA MARLOWE acted opposite each other for ten years before becoming man and wife. To them the theatre was Shakespeare, and every photograph handed out by Miss Marlowe bore a handwritten excerpt from the works of the Bard.

Vaudeville also had its stars—and NORA BAYES was billed as the Empress of the Two-a-Day. She seldom stepped into a gown costing less than two thousand dollars. Nora's hats, too, were the envy of contemporary females.

No skillfully carpentered play ever held as many heart throbs as the life of actor FRANK BACON, and the third act of his life was the finest. For Frank Bacon was the first star to walk out in the Actors' Strike of 1919. This made him one of the few actors, or perhaps the only one, ever to march down Broadway at the head of his own parade.

to browsing through the Bible. "What a book, Henry," he enthused to friend H. L. Mencken. "It's full of plots."

Armstrong's dependence on the printed word came to a brief stop after he met Wilson Mizner, a Brobdingnagian who had survived the Klondike Gold Rush. As a Great White Way fixture Mizner was known as the Beau Brummell of Nome and Broadway. He was fascinated by the underworld and a devout student of its raw jargon. His first playwriting effort was *The Only Law*, which stemmed from his line: "Being on the square with a pal is the only law we know." This was the first play to open in the year 1909 and the critic of the *New York World* found it vulgarly replete with "sluts, scoundrels, and boobies." NO GOOD SERVED BY YEAR'S FIRST PLAY, this review was headed. But Mizner stands forth as one of the great wits produced by this country. Once he said, "To my embarrassment, I was born in bed with a lady." He also uttered the famous, "Life's a tough proposition, and the first hundred years are the hardest." On another occasion he said, "Be nice to people on the way up because you'll meet them on the way down." Of play reviewers, he stated, "A drama critic is a person who surprises the playwright by informing him what he meant."

Meeting Paul Armstrong for the first time, Mizner listened to the Hair-Trigger Playwright complain of troubles with the Bret Harte heirs over the pilfering of *Salomy Jane*. Then Mizner told him, "If you steal from one author, it's plagiarism; if you steal from many, it's research." It was the beginning of a beautiful collaboration. Mizner was a superb storyteller, Armstrong a master craftsman. The two wrote *The Deep Purple*, based on Mizner's knowledge of the badger game. It was a success and Mizner characterized his new career as telling lies at two dollars a head. They collaborated on *The Greyhound* and other plays, and for one opening night Mizner imported his father from California. The old gentleman proved that his son's great wit was in part inherited. As the audience left the theatre someone said to him, "This is a very remarkable play." "It is indeed," the proud parent answered, "and the most remarkable thing about it is that it took two men to write it."

There is some doubt about the actual authorship of the play most frequently associated with the team of Armstrong and Mizner. This was *Alias Jimmy Valentine*, which, with its sound characterization and plausible central situation, established crime-melodrama as dramatic art. *Alias Jimmy Valentine* tells the story of a reformed safe cracker who betrays himself by using his old burglar tools to open the bank vault in which his fiancee's niece is trapped. As such, it derives unabashedly from O. Henry's *A Retrieved Redemption*. O. Henry was still alive and Armstrong—having learned his lesson with Bret Harte—paid him $500 for the idea. Armstrong then repaired to the office of Warden Fallon of the Tombs Prison to write the play. He always said that Mizner gave him no assistance on *Alias Jimmy Valentine*, claiming full credit himself. Yet a strong feature of the play was its pungent dialogue. The characters talked just like Mizner, leaving Broadway to wonder just how much Mizner had helped. Mizner, happily engaged in running a Times Square hotel, said nothing.

Some plays written by contemporary playwrights were clap-trap. In the course of an argument between father and daughter, one proffered these lines:

> Judith, you are throwing yourself away on a dreamer.
> Dreamers, my father, are the men who move the world!

These stilted words may have been as hard to write at the time as is the Tennessee Williams-Arthur Miller dialogue of today. But whether the craft came hard or easy, playwrights of the time met a multitude of problems. For one thing, they still rated only a trifle above the lowly actor in the esteem of producers. Even so spirited a figure as George Bernard Shaw was aware of the low estate in which dramatists were held. When *Man and Superman* was about to open in New York, the producer cabled that it ran too long. "Cut hell out of it," Shaw replied humbly. Years later, told that the length of *St. Joan* caused commuters to miss trains, his reaction was different. "Run later trains," he arrogantly ordered. In a day of inexpensive tryouts in Long Branch, Atlantic City, New London, Bridgeport, and even Brooklyn, playwrights complained that producers brought along rival writers who were ordered to doctor plays on the spot. In every possible way, the world seemed against authors. Said one, "Before the curtain goes up everybody knows you and says, 'Good Luck, old man.' At the end, nobody knows you."

Hard-working Channing Pollock encountered a brace of typical problems as he undertook to dramatize Frank Norris' *The Pit* for William A. Brady. The producer was not too impressed by the first draft. "Good," he wrote, "but *more love*. Too much financial stuff. Women not interested. *More love*. Act two good, but *more love*. Act three fine but *lacks love*."

Pollock dutifully injected love, then journeyed to New Haven for the tryout. Here he found the programs attributing authorship to William A. Brady and Channing Pollock. He tackled Brady, discovering that the rugged producer felt his recommendations of *more love* rated co-authorship. Ever a man to battle for his rights, Pollock talked him out of it. Wilton Lackaye was the star of *The Pit* and during rehearsals made a variety of constructive suggestions. When next Pollock saw a program he found that the authors were Wilton Lackaye and Channing Pollock. Again he clamored for justice. But Brady and (perhaps) Lackaye won out in the end. *The Pit* earned a profit of more than $500,000. As per agreement, Pollock received only an adapter's fee of $1900.

Even before tryouts, the playwright faced an ordeal in reading his play to producers who fidgeted, yawned, or went to sleep. When someone complained to England's Henry Arthur Jones of this last, he answered imperturbably, "Sleep is a form of criticism." One Broadway producer seemed to go to sleep before readings began. Arranging himself comfortably in a chair, he shut his eyes. "Have to visualize," he explained agreeably. Some playwrights were excellent readers, able to bring scripts to vibrant life. Once George Middleton found himself accused by a star's husband of reading "so damned well" that it had amounted to misrepresentation. George Ade, humorist-author of *The Sultan of Sulu, The College Widow*, and other monumental hits, worked out a personal formula for reading to indifferent producers. "Bring a pistol with you," he advised colleagues, "and place it close to the right hand, meanwhile murmuring casually to the producer, 'You're going to like this play.'" When reading a play to George M. Cohan in the latter's office at the corner of Broadway and Forty-second Street, Channing Pollock noted Cohan peering intently out a window. An annoyed Pollock stopped, at which Cohan swung around. "It doesn't seem possible," he said. "There isn't a single horse to be seen on Times Square."

Until 1909 few playwrights dared to place unhappy endings on their works. But now Eugene Walter, after scoring with *Paid in Full*, once more let himself be lured from Broadway bars and taken to the Long Island shore. On a refreshing diet of salt air, he wrote *The Easiest Way*. The rambunctious playwright did not offer this one to Charles Frohman. Rather, he gave it to David Belasco, who accepted it promptly. Belasco, however, soon demonstrated the total power of managers over authors by barring Walter from rehearsals of his own play. It happened because Walter objected to the casting of pretty, fragile Frances

Starr as the heroine. The playwright visualized a tougher girl as Laura Murdock, Broadway chorus girl and bit actress who, failing to scale heights in the theatre, allows herself to be supported by a Wall Street broker named Brockton—"a type to be seen nightly in the lobster palaces, in Churchill's and Rector's."

Brockton and Laura go on vacation in the Colorado mountains and, as the sun shines warmly on snow-capped peaks in fine David Belasco fashion, the girl tells her protector that she has fallen in love with a Denver newspaperman named Jack Madison. In the next scene Brockton and Madison sit, only the glow of cigars showing in the dusk, sealing a strange bargain. Wealthy Brockton will renounce Laura on the condition that, if she comes back to him, Madison immediately be told.

The key to *The Easiest Way* is, of course, the character of lovely Laura. She is a type known through the ages. Unfortunate and lacking in morals, rather than actively immoral, her weakness is revealed in the play's title. Faced by any crisis in life, Laura usually finds herself pursuing the easiest way. To her survival—rather than the morality involved—is what counts. This time she returns to New York determined to make her mark in the theatre, for Madison's sake as well as her own. She tries, but fails—in the words of a first-night review, "She beats her head against the Rialto's cruel wall of indifference." In the second of four acts she is down to her last dollar, living in a cheap theatrical boardinghouse. Inevitably, she phones Brockton and returns to the lavish apartment he offers.

In accordance with the bargain struck in Colorado, Brockton writes Madison, telling him that Laura has slipped back to the easy way. Laura steals the letter and burns it. Meanwhile, Madison, who has abandoned the trade of newspaperman, strikes it rich as a gentleman prospector. He arrives triumphantly in New York, where he and Laura tumble into each other's arms. They

are on the verge of departing for Colorado and holy wedlock
when Brockton's key clicks in the door—"no more effective moment has been devised in recent drama," declared a next-morning review.

So Laura is unmasked before her two men. Brockton learns
that she has destroyed his letter; Madison, that she has returned
to sin. "I know you don't think it can be explained," the forlorn
girl wails to Jack, "and maybe there isn't any explanation. I
couldn't help it. I was so poor, and I had to live. . . . I was hungry
and didn't have the clothes to keep me warm and I tried, *Oh,
John,* I tried so hard to do the other thing, the right thing, but I
couldn't."

She then threatens to shoot herself. But the men, fully aware
of her weaknesses, scoff at the idea. After they depart, Laura,
standing alone in the midst of luxury, summons her Negro maid
and utters words that constituted a milestone in the American
theatre:

> Open those trunks, take out those clothes, get me my prettiest
> dress. Hurry up! Get my hat, dress my body and paint up my
> face. It's all they've left of me. They've taken my soul away
> with them.
>
> Yassum, yassum!
>
> Doll me up, Annie.
>
> You goin' out, Miss Laura?
>
> Yes. I'm going to Rector's to make a hit, and to hell with the rest!

On the morning following this sensational fall-of-the-curtain
one critic asked, "Is it indecent, vile, corrupt, lascivious?" He
then went ahead to answer all four in the affirmative. The
Evening World's Charles Darnton was epigrammatic. "An evening of good acting and bad morals," he wrote. Yet the audience
sat spellbound throughout, making one charitable observer feel
that they left the theatre with a greater knowledge of life's problems. The characters in *The Easiest Way*—weak chorus girl,

ruthless broker, diamond-in-the-rough stage manager, predatory maid—have since become stereotypes in tens of thousands of plays, films, and TV dramas. But in 1909 such people had never been seen on a stage. Their stunning impact was increased by the fact that, in casting and directing Frances Starr, Belasco wrought a tender Laura. Here was no Sapho or Camille, rolling her eyes, beating her breast, or otherwise agonizing over the wages of sin. One could pass Laura Murdock in the street without realizing that she was a soiled Broadway butterfly. Instead, the reaction would be, "There's a pretty girl"—and this, perhaps, was the most shocking feature of *The Easiest Way*.

With such interesting pathways of sin illuminated, other playwrights rushed in to explore further. Next a short, swarthy, vital, ex-police reporter named Bayard Veiller made an appearance on the Broadway scene. He carried five playscripts tucked under an arm. Crosby Gaige, play-agenting partner of Arch Selwyn, discarded four of them as worthless. The fifth, called *Within the Law*, he dubbed a masterpiece of melodrama. Even so, it took two years and six dropped options (among the droppers were Charles Frohman and George M. Cohan) before *Within the Law* reached Broadway.

Within the Law took the Paul Armstrong formula of sound characterization and plausible situation, adding to it the ingredient of social criticism. For even more than unhappy Laura Murdock, the heroine of *Within the Law* was a victim of the times. She was Mary Turner, lovely department-store clerk unjustly accused of stealing. When led off to prison, she is first taken to the office of the president of the store. Her voice breaks and quivers as she sobs out for herself and other girls, "Why don't you give [us] enough to live on! Ten hours a day! Nine dollars a week! That's a *fact*!" Later she cries out bitterly, "That

wonderful twisted law, made for the rich . . . and they wonder
at crime!"

Mary Turner was the first major role played by Jane Cowl,
and delivered in her magnificent contralto these were wrenching words. After serving her sentence in prison, Mary becomes
the beautifully groomed leader of a gang of blackmailers and
con men who stay within the law. "Get it legally and get twice
as much," she instructs her boys. Her main purpose in life is
revenge on Gilder, the department-store owner who railroaded
her to jail. Mary marries his son and, as the final curtain falls,
she tells Gilder, "Four years ago you took away my name and
gave me a number. Now I've given up that number and I've got
your name."

On opening night a nervous Miss Cowl scrambled these all-
important lines saying, "Now I've given up that *name* and I've
got *your number*." A rapt audience never noticed. *Within the
Law* had the delicious odor of success from the moment its curtain rose. The opening added up to a magic premiere of which
Crosby Gaige (who had become coproducer) recalls:

> There is no human experience, so far as I know, that quite
> duplicates the opening night of a play destined to make dramatic
> history. The actors feel it, and the audience, by some more
> accurate sense, becomes aware of the fact and takes an emotional
> part in the performance. . . .
> From the moment the curtain went up on *Within the Law*
> until it fell to crashing applause on the climax of the third act,
> there was no question in anybody's mind that here was a hit of
> the first magnitude.

*   *

It is a rare stroke of justice that the most extraordinary
first night of the time—perhaps of *all* time—was furnished by
Clyde Fitch, whose eminence had been shaken by the advent
of Edward Sheldon, Eugene Walter, and others. Fitch had always chafed over the fact that so many thought him a male

milliner, capable only of contriving plays for and about women. Newspapers called him "exquisite" and accused him of living "a butterfly existence." Thus it became a challenge to the Great White Way's most famous playwright to compete at the same level with the rowdy newcomers.

Fitch cast about in his trained mind for the germ of a genuinely realistic play. Suddenly he had one—a drama exploring the corrupting influence of New York. It would be called *The City* and at the end of its tense second act a thoroughly corrupted character, told that he had unknowingly married his own sister, would shout, "You're a goddam liar." Never in Broadway history had the word "Goddam" echoed from the walls of a theatre, but Fitch was determined to use it nonetheless, together with the juicy fillip of incest.

When he finished his play Fitch was in a lather of high excitement. He invited a group of friends to the Other House in Katonah where, to provide the proper atmosphere, he lit a fire and turned out all lamps except two on the desk of his study. Outside, nature co-operated by providing a thunderstorm during the first part of his reading. After that wind and rain lashed the windows. At the end of the reading Fitch (in the words of Montrose J. Moses) was "shaking from head to foot—he had read with such violence that the veins in his temple stood out like cords."

Another playwright so enthusiastic over a script might devote all his time to preparing it. But Fitch was Fitch. Together with *The City* he was shepherding several other productions to the boards. He had also scheduled a motor tour of France and Italy. With *The City* set for fall production, he embarked for his beloved Europe. It was the summer of 1909. Fitch was forty-four years old, a man with new pride and satisfaction in his bearing. Posing fashionably at the rail of the SS *Lorraine*, he seemed the very figure of a fortunate and contented man. Yet he had one nagging worry—he suffered recurrent attacks of appendicitis. Like many others in the era, he dreaded an operation, for appendicitis operations were a number-one killer of the time.

Arriving in Europe, Fitch made business trips to London, Paris, and Heidelberg. He loved motoring and next set out on a far-flung tour of Italy and the Dolomites. Returning through eastern France, he got as far as Châlons-sur-Marne, where he was struck by an acute attack of appendicitis. He was three hours by fast drive from Paris, but decided to stop overnight on the chance that his agony would pass. He took rooms at a local inn, instructing his valet to apply hot-water bags and give him brandy. These orders could not have been worse. Cold compresses might have controlled the inflammation; hot compresses caused it to spread alarmingly. Soon the pain was unbearable and Fitch summoned the local physician, who insisted on an immediate operation. For three hours the operation appeared to have been successful. Then blood poisoning set in. On the morning of September 4, Broadway reeled under staggering news.

Clyde Fitch was dead!

The young actress Lucile Watson, already hired for *The City*, went to her doorstep and found the newspaper headlining Fitch's death. Beside it lay a postcard in the playwright's individual italicized scrawl. Others in New York had the same experience and the eerie atmosphere carried over into rehearsals of *The City*. The actors (Walter Hampden, Tully Marshall, Mary Nash, Miss Watson) had all worked for Fitch in the past and could sense what stage directions his mild voice would suggest, but never order. It seemed as if Fitch were still present, directing his own play.

No less than the actors, the audience on opening night seemed under Fitch's ghostly spell. The shouted "Goddam" provoked a pandemonium unprecedented in a Broadway theatre. A mixture of horror at the forbidden word, excitement over the pungent play, and mourning over the playwright's death drove the audience toward mass hysteria. Between the acts, men and women in evening clothes stood talking excitedly, while others senselessly waved hats and handkerchiefs. Some fainted, among them the drama critic for the New York *Sun*. At the end of the play, the emotionally exhausted actors responded to nineteen curtain calls, and at one point the confusion left the lighted stage momentarily bare. At this a terrible hush fell over the audience, for it seemed to many present that Clyde Fitch himself had slowly walked to the footlights, and was bending low in an appreciative bow. Now there was pandemonium, with hysterical screams and frantic cries of "I saw him! I saw him!"

So the lamented Clyde Fitch fully measured up to his challenge. He had proved that he could indeed write a man's play. *The City* was universally hailed as thoroughly masculine. Said one review: "It seems tame to say the play is strong, for its strongest scene is tremendous. The play is as strong as a raging bull."

8: THREE ACTRESSES

Through the years the powerful Syndicate flourished, riding roughshod over scattered opposition, tolerantly permitting (at first) the existence of the brothers Shubert, moving stars and plays like figures on a giant chess board, callously discarding actors who seemed to be slipping, blatantly offering favors to those on the rise. Newspaper editorials, magazine articles, lectures, and sermons inveighed against the power of the Syndicate —or the Trust, as others called it. *Collier's* and the *New York World* exposed its machinations. Drama critics dared to risk libel laws. William Winter dubbed it The Incubus. On another occasion he called it "a fang of commercialism." The *Dramatic Mirror* used such picturesque phrases of castigation as "theatrical throttlers," "insolent jobbers," "crooked entrepreneurs," "greedy, narrow-minded tricksters." As if determined to live up to these charges, Abraham Lincoln Erlanger began the procedure (later followed by the Shuberts) of banning from Syndicate theatres any writers he did not like.

In his fiendish way Erlanger still harassed all those he could not obliterate. David Belasco was again a prime enemy and the Syndicate labored endlessly to damage him. Belasco was co-author of, or collaborator on, nearly every play he produced. Sometimes the origins of his plots were extremely obscure, and

with each Belasco opening over the years the Syndicate solemnly
produced an unknown author to sue the Bishop of Broadway for
plagiarism. The cases always got to court, for Belasco loved
litigation almost as much as he adored the theatre. Once—to
clinch a case as few have been clinched—Belasco invited judge
and jury to watch the play he had produced, followed by a performance (with the same cast) of the script he was accused of
stealing. This double bill began at eleven A.M. and resulted in
glorious vindication for Belasco. William Winter, who was
present, described the second play as "the veriest farrago of
impalliable trash."

Erlanger piously continued to claim that he and his associates
merely leased theatres. Yet his hold was as tight as any owner's
could be. To associates he still talked of controlling all the theatres
in the United States and as many elsewhere as his life span allowed. In hindsight, it is apparent that Erlanger (much in the
manner of dictators of a later day) was presiding over his own
doom. For if the Syndicate held a cancer in its body, it was Erlanger himself. Irascible, undiplomatic, and inartistic, he acted
as if he had been set upon this earth to antagonize his fellow man.

As soon as his methods became widely known a Broadway wit
dubbed him Dishonest Abe. Still, no man is totally without
friends and—it must be recorded in fairness—a few people liked
Erlanger. Harry B. Smith, librettist of *Robin Hood* and the *Ziegfeld Follies,* was an esteemed gentleman whose off-theatre hours
were spent collecting first editions. He was closely associated
with Erlanger and appears on the record as saying, "I know he
was widely disliked, but I must say he never did a single thing
to make me join his detractors." James Weldon and J. Rosamond
Johnson, Negro brothers from Tampa who wrote the lively ragtime tune "Under the Bamboo Tree," worked for Erlanger when
he produced a series of musicals. The two young men found
him a hard taskmaster, but not unbearable. As long as no one

contradicted him, Erlanger (they found) could be tolerated.

Yet for each friend, Dishonest Abe seemed to have a thousand foes. Some resented the fact that he had no real love of the theatre—of Syndicate directors only Charles Frohman did. Erlanger was obsessed by the accumulation of theatrical real estate and his success in this field blinded him to the fact that the Syndicate was slowly strangling on its own power. Once Klaw and Erlanger gained control of theatres it was necessary for them to keep the theatres filled. At the same time their ruthlessness was destroying a large part of the creativity which led to a flourishing theatre. As playwright Owen Davis observed: "They performed miracles in building up a really imposing structure, but after it was built they never had the slightest idea what to do with it."

This, though, may be a simplification. Klaw and Erlanger had an idea what to do with the theatres they gained, but never a real *interest* in doing it. This gave an edge to the brothers Shubert in their David-Goliath battle with the Syndicate. For unlike Klaw and Erlanger, the Shuberts were—if not precisely devoted to the theatre—at least highly theatre-wise. The brothers (especially Lee) read scripts, cast them cannily, and personally wet-nursed plays into Shubert theatres. Yet the brothers, who liked to pose as opponents-to-the-death of the Syndicate, never really played that shining role to the hilt. Much fancy footwork is involved in imposing a trust on a widespread industry, and this can be equally true of fighting a trust. At times the Shuberts and the Syndicate behaved like spitting enemies, hurling accusations, seeking legal action, and in every way acting like implacable foes. Next, the two appeared to be working hand in glove, exchanging theatres, productions, and even actors with the utmost amiability.

Of all those who fought the Syndicate, two ladies seemed to

do it with the greatest spirit. One was the great Sarah Bernhardt, who had made her first American tour in 1880. Twenty years later she returned, minus one leg and with the coffin in which she expected to be buried, for the first of a long series of farewell tours. In 1906 she was brought over by the Shuberts, who at the moment were truly at odds with Erlanger. Informed that because of the strength of the Syndicate she could not play in top theatres around the country, Bernhardt merely batted expressive eyes. This was all right, she stated, so long as the public was able to see her. According to romantic theatrical legend, Bernhardt toured the South playing under a tent which she glowingly called "My canvas temple." Channing Pollock, who was her press agent on tour, refutes this. He swears that only in Dallas was it necessary to use a tent and that Bernhardt much enjoyed the experience of playing amidst a tanbark circus atmosphere. In addition, she grossed $11,000 that night. The Divine Sarah loved money as much as she loved applause. "She spoke very little English," Lee Shubert has recalled, "but she always understood you when you talked about money."

More than Sarah Bernhardt, New Orleans-born Minnie Maddern Fiske was the symbol of opposition to the Trust. This determined lady steadfastly refused to truckle before the greedy incubus. As a result she was driven to performing under rugged conditions. Not only did Mrs. Fiske play in tents, but also in skating rinks, Masonic halls, churches, abandoned opera houses, and decrepit theatres in Negro districts—in practically any kind of auditorium with seats. Such moments as her New York opening of *Salvation Nell* came when she caught the Syndicate napping and was able to slip quickly into a Broadway playhouse —in this case the Hackett. For thirteen years she battled gallantly, the programs of her performances featuring the defiant line, "Mrs. Fiske does not play in theatres controlled by the Syndicate."

Warfare between the Syndicate and Mrs. Fiske was ferocious, with no holds barred. One of the triumphs of her long career came with the New York premiere of *Becky Sharp*, when the audience clapped and clamored through uncounted curtain calls. Within a week the Syndicate rudely ordered her to vacate the premises where she had scored such a hit. Nor could she find another playhouse in New York City. In a move probably without precedent in the theatre, Mrs. Fiske was obliged to take a popular success on tour two weeks after its opening.

This was only the beginning of Erlanger's cruelty to Mrs. Fiske. Next the Syndicate unveiled its own *Becky Sharp*, almost identical with Mrs. Fiske's Langston Mitchell version. Hauled into court, the Syndicate claimed that its play was the work of an author recently deceased. The case collapsed when the man's widow testified (for Mrs. Fiske) that her late husband had never written such a play. So the Syndicate lost, but got even by circulating documents which allegedly proved that Mrs. Fiske, then thirty-nine, was actually over sixty. One evening the star and her husband, Harrison Grey Fiske, took a stroll down Broadway. Suddenly the squat, stepped-on figure of Abraham Lincoln Erlanger approached from the opposite direction. Catching sight of the redheaded Mrs. Fiske, he walked close to her to hiss an unprintable word. Harrison Grey Fiske handed hat, stick, and gloves to his wife. Then he knocked Abraham Lincoln Erlanger down.

Mrs. Fiske's war with the Syndicate was not for herself alone. It is safe to say that the time inevitably would have come when this gifted and independent lady would refuse to play Syndicate theatres. But the process was hastened by Syndicate efforts to force into retirement stars who were no longer potent drawing cards. Modjeska and Fanny Davenport were two the Syndicate elbowed out of the way, and Mrs. Fiske's compassionate heart bled. Her husband was editor and publisher of *The Dramatic*

Mirror, which set out to castigate the Trust in every issue. In retaliation, the Syndicate posted notice in all its theatres ordering the actors to boycott *The Dramatic Mirror*. HAVE NEVER READ A DRAMATIC NEWSPAPER BUT WILL READ MIRROR REGULARLY HEREAFTER, Maurice Barrymore wired Erlanger after reading this ukase. In time, *The Dramatic Mirror* printed agreements between Syndicate members which were supposed to be secret. With this, Erlanger sent word to *The Dramatic Mirror* office, "We will drive Mrs. Fiske out of the theatre!"

For her continuing opposition to the Trust (as she called it) Mrs. Fiske has been called the conscience of the American theatre. She has also been honored (because of numerous appearances in small towns when the Syndicate barred her from cities) as the actress who brought the drama closest to the greatest number of contemporary Americans.

But with these high tributes, a greater one accrues to Minnie Maddern Fiske. For many American playgoers—a dwindling number who saw her, a growing number who have only read about her—consider her the greatest actress this country has ever produced. In his time, Alexander Woollcott, who appeared on the Broadway scene early in the century, became the High Panjandrum of the Mrs. Fiske cult, but there were others before him and many since. Onstage Mrs. Fiske was inclined to flounce and (in later years) jitter, rather than rely on the deep emotional magnetism of a Bernhardt. Yet in her own way she was an endlessly vivid personality. "A flame, glorious, gorgeous, and always individual—there was no one like her," an ardent fan recalls. Edith Wharton paid tribute to her "marvelous skill in producing effects with the smallest expenditure of voice and gesture . . . the audience vibrates to every one of her touches." Ashton Stevens snapped, "*Dull* people do not like Mrs. Fiske's acting." The redoubtable Chicago critic Amy Leslie invoked "the sun of her great art." But the greatest tribute rendered Mrs. Fiske is an intangible one. It seems that in the audience of each of her performances—and in her lifetime she probably gave more than any other star—there was at least one person (often more) who left the theatre believing Minnie Maddern Fiske to be the greatest actress of all time.

Mrs. Fiske's unique talent burned brightly from childhood, enabling her to escape many of the vicissitudes suffered by young actors. She was born Marie Augusta Davey in New Orleans. The year was 1863, her parents actor Tom Davey and actress Lizzie Maddern Davey. Tom Davey's temperament seems to have resembled that of Maude Adams' errant father. Lizzie Maddern, however, had none of the stamina of Annie Adams. Frail and lovely, she seemed all soul, no body. Abandoned by quixotic Tom, she took young Minnie—the name Minnie Maddern was chosen as a suitable stage name—on tour. Inevitably the redheaded child appeared in plays. At three she brightly performed her first Shakespearean part. At six her talents were much in demand, with one star offering her a part in New York City while another countered by promising feature billing as LITTLE MINNIE MADDERN. Minnie was ten when her fragile mother died and for a time Helena Modjeska took the carrot-top child under her wing. But even as a child Minnie distrusted the heavy, emotional Modjeska-type acting. She believed that actors should speak much as they did in everyday life. She also thought that many lines spoken onstage were stilted and unreal. One reason for the rapid, slurred diction which later bothered her admirers was that as a developing actress she liked to edit lines on stage. She spoke the revised ones fast, hoping to get them out before the prompter corrected her.

Minnie Maddern's youthful glories were her electric blue eyes and a stunning sheen of bright red hair, under which lay a delicate broad-jawed, vivacious, Irish-bright face. The eyes seemed able to switch with her moods, turning from blue to violet, bronze to opalescent green. By the age of seventeen the vivid girl was the toast of New York, appearing in a comedy called *Fogg's Ferry* where she was called "a little delicate wisp of girlhood, all luminous intensity, verve and spirit, fine and sheer as a mist of lace."

Even then, some member of each Minnie Maddern audience appeared to become smitten for life with the magic of her personality, and at one performance of *Fogg's Ferry* it was Harrison Grey Fiske, offspring of wealthy parents, so precociously stage-struck that in his teens he was editor of *The Dramatic Mirror*. Another who shortly succumbed to buoyant Minnie was the veteran tragedian Lawrence Barrett. He watched *Fogg's Ferry*, then sent her a printed volume of *A Doll's House* by an obscure Norwegian named Ibsen. The seventeen-year-old girl tried to read it, but found it undramatic. She filed it away in a trunk.

When *Fogg's Ferry* went on tour it took a pit orchestra along. Industriously beating the snare drums in this was a colorful young man named Legrand White. Son of a wealthy Brooklyn family which manufactured pianos, he may not have been a black sheep, but he displayed a few black stripes. Having seen *Fogg's Ferry* as a member of the audience, he too fell in love with Minnie. Using both charm and inherited musical ability, he got a job in the orchestra. He next used his social grace to meet the sparkling young star. He told her he loved her, and of a play he planned to produce on the Great White Way. When, at the finish of the tour, Legrand White returned to Brooklyn, he brought with him a redheaded bride.

The marriage lasted only through the single play, which White actually did produce. Then Minnie left him—frequent quarrels were the given cause—to star in a play called *Caprice*, in which she hauntingly introduced the song "In the Gloaming."

At the close of this, she went to visit relatives in Larchmont, New York. Minnie was now twenty-three, and as a child of the theatre had never in all those years passed a summer in the country. Never had she learned to swim or ride, or worn out-of-doors attire. Discovering all this made a pleasant interlude. She next returned to acting in *In Spite of All*, produced by Charles Frohman. During this she was introduced to Harrison Grey Fiske, also still in his twenties. The following summer she returned to Larchmont. Fiske, who lived on an estate nearby, began an ardent courtship. Minnie postponed her momentous decision through a play called *Featherbrain*. In 1890 she and Fiske married.

For the next four years she lived the life of a woman of wealth. Certain vagaries in her character had persuaded her that she would be a poor mother, and she attempted no children. Time hung heavy. Minnie tried self-improvement reading, since as a theatre-child she had never attended school. She also wrote plays. Asked later what she had done during this period of domesticity, she smiled and said, "I got older."

When Lawrence Barrett died his obituaries reported heartbreak because of his inability to interest an American actress in the plays of Ibsen. Mrs. Fiske went to her trunk for the copy of *A Doll's House*. This time she discovered its depth. She began to study and in 1894 emerged from retirement to perform the play at a benefit matinee at the Empire. This was the second performance of an Ibsen play in the United States, and the first to stress the playwright's compassion and humor. The Empire performance was much praised, but if New York had matured to Ibsen the remainder of the country had not. Mrs. Fiske took *A Doll's House* to Pittsburgh, where audiences remained seated after the famous slam-of-the-door that ends the play. Despite blinking of house lights, people patiently waited for Nora to return and provide the traditional happy ending.

So Mrs. Fiske abandoned Ibsen but not the comeback trail.

Sprightly Minnie Maddern had become thoughtful Mrs. Fiske, and her second career began with a dramatization of the Thomas Hardy novel, *Tess of the D'Urbervilles*. Mrs. Fiske's friends and advisers were appalled at her choice of Tess, a girl who kills her illegitimate child and dies on the gallows. But (like Hardy) Mrs. Fiske saw Tess a pure soul, more sinned against than sinning. In her performance, this purity was visible. Mrs. Fiske, now thirty-two years old, had failed to keep Dion Boucicault's three rules for actresses: (1) Keep your figure; (2) Keep your figure; (3) Keep your figure. Already she was inclining toward future dumpiness. Yet she managed to appear young onstage. Of her as Tess a critic wrote: "Such a pretty star she is! Such a winsome, wistfully sweet, unaffected little lady. No wonder that weird, eerie, lovely little face catches the heart. . . ."

A second peak in her career was provided by *Becky Sharp*, adapted from Thackeray's *Vanity Fair*. With this, she commenced her struggle-to-the-death with the Syndicate. The first round went to Abraham Lincoln Erlanger, when *Becky* was forced out of its theatre. The indomitable lady took *Becky Sharp* on the Road, where she largely remained for over a decade. Mrs. Fiske's years of touring have been called one-night stands, in four-act plays, in fifth-rate theatres. Over the Road years she played not only *Tess* and *Becky*, but *Divorçons*, *Leah Kleschna*, *The New York Idea*, *The High Road*, *Salvation Nell*, and a host of others. Yet there were heart-warming compensations. Once in St. Louis she succeeded in renting the Grand Opera House, an ancient and almost-forgotten edifice. At her opening, the managers of all the flashy Syndicate-operated theatres in St. Louis left their posts to see her. The next morning a St. Louis paper, commenting on the decrepit theatre, said, "For genius all places are temples." Another commented, "Wherever Mrs. Fiske sits is the head of the table."

In California, with Los Angeles and San Francisco closed to
her, she appeared in towns like San Jose, while the citizens of
big cities organized Mrs. Fiske Anti-Trust Excursions to see her.
In her years of unceasing battle, she played more one-night
stands in tiny towns than any other American actress before or
since. Once, as her company train sped by a three-house hamlet,
an actor said, "We ought to stop the train and apologize for not
playing there." Mrs. Fiske was able to see the humor of this. Any
building with seats and a stage was satisfactory. At the same
time she enjoyed several victories over the Syndicate. One was
the Hackett Theatre run of *Salvation Nell*. At another point
her husband heard through the Broadway grapevine that the
Manhattan Theatre, on the site of the current Gimbel's, was
up for lease. Obsessed with plans of country-wide expansion, the
Syndicate had again failed to hear of this opportunity in its own
backyard. Fiske quickly leased the Manhattan, redecorating it
splendidly. Now Mrs. Fiske had a New York showcase. It was
at her Manhattan opening—in an unfortunate play called *Miranda
of the Balcony*—that theatre programs as we know them were
first handed to an audience.

Becky Sharp was Mrs. Fiske's most successful play, earning
for her profits of $90,000 in a single year. Yet being the con-
science of the American theatre proved an expensive business.
Each of the abandoned theatres, grange halls, and skating rinks
required costly alteration. When David Belasco opened his *An-
drea* in Washington, D.C., despite Syndicate efforts to stop
him, he found that the adventure into independence ran to an
extra $25,000. Through the years of her tussle with the Syndi-
cate Mrs. Fiske was forced to pay comparable sums on many
of the odd auditoriums she used. In addition, she shelled out
heavily to transport scenery and actors over long jumps. In the
years of her greatest earning power, she turned most of the prof-

its back into her one-woman fight against the Trust. Spearheading opposition to the Syndicate also took a physical toll. As an actress-manager piloting big companies around the country, she encountered far more than her share of vicissitudes, most of them engendered by the Syndicate. Yet she never gave in. Rather, she straightened her back and said, "It must be shouldered."

And it was. . . .

Theatre problems were not the only ones to bedevil the conscience of the American theatre. Harrison Grey Fiske continued a steadfast admirer of star Minnie Maddern Fiske. He directed her plays (though many thought she did most of it herself) and guided her tangled affairs from the safety of New York. But slowly it became apparent that, much as he admired his wife on the stage, Harrison Fiske would ever cast eyes on a succession of younger and prettier girls. Mr. and Mrs. Fiske tried hard to continue a relationship by which both focused on the better qualities in the other. Still, says her biographer Archie Binns, Mrs. Fiske's acceptance of her husband as a womanizer "carried her farther and farther away from home and hearth—she had nowhere to go but on."

Under such goads, Mrs. Fiske became a remarkable person— even more of a woman, it might be said, than an actress. Few hearts have pounded so hard for the underdog—or for dumb animals. Mrs. Fiske was fanatically devoted to animals and could not bear to see a cat or a dog in misery. She traveled with a wild assortment of rescued dogs, the number increasing with each stop. She berated restaurant owners who showed crawling lobsters in windows and with her own umbrella punished drivers who beat horses. Her wide travels allowed her to discover instances of cruelty to animals unnoted by ordinary citizens. She crusaded for humane cattle cars, so that animals on the way to slaughterhouses did not freeze in winter and bake in summer. She started a campaign against the branding of cattle on the range. She fought the trapping of wild animals, and when near Juarez or Tia Juana, leaped the border to pass out handbills against bull-fighting. At home, she fought rodeos with the same fury.

Mrs. Fiske was a pioneer anti-vivisectionist and it is said that she was a contributing member to every humane society in the world. She founded her own National Humane Society which, together with all else, established drinking fountains for horses. She was arrested for dognapping after hustling a limping dog to a vet. Again she heard of an armless man noted for his ability to shoot pigeons. She had him arrested before discovering the pigeons were clay. She assailed President Theodore Roosevelt for his African hunting safaris, and in cold weather risked illness by occupying top-floor hotel rooms with windows wide open for birds to fly in to be fed. Her most memorable crusade, however, was on behalf of the snowy heron, or egret, source of the waving feathers which topped women's hats. "No power on earth can save the egret from extinction at the hands of plume hunters," an ornithologist mourned in 1910. Minnie Maddern Fiske could —and did. She organized boycotts of stores selling egret-topped chapeaux and so shamed the female population that no woman in America dared wear an egret plume.

At the same time she managed to be considered America's greatest actress by most who saw her. Bayard Veiller, one of them, said, "If you were for her, you were ready to wage bloody war on her behalf." This is the more remarkable because even her most fervent fans had to admit that Mrs. Fiske's diction was slovenly and that often she was unintelligible onstage. "Mrs. Fiske represents the triumph of mind over mutter," a contemporary witticism had it. Yet hers was always a magic, captivating voice. Many writers tried to capture its curious appeal, the one who did best being the versifier Franklin P. Adams, who wrote:

> Staccato, hurried, nervous, brisk,
>   Cascading, intermittent, choppy.
> The brittle voice of Mrs. Fiske
>   Shall serve me now as copy.
>
> Time was, when first that voice I heard,
>   Despite my close and tense endeavor,
> When many an important word
>   Was lost and gone forever
> Though unlike others at the play,
> I never whispered: *"What'd she say?"*
>
> Some words she runstogetherso;
>   Some others are distinctly stated
> Somecometoofast and s o m e t o o s l o w
>   And some are syncopated
> And yet no voice—I am sincere—
> Exists that I prefer to hear. . . .

Not only was Mrs. Fiske a superb actress herself, but she seemed able to inspire the best in those who played with her. Good actors like Maurice Barrymore, Tyrone Power, Sr., and John Mason rose to heights of greatness supporting her. In part, this may have been because she was so immensely proud of her calling. "Please uphold the dignity of the company at all times," read a notice posted on the callboard of theatres she occupied. Yet she believed actors should behave like ordinary folk outside the theatre. Members of the cast were asked not to speak to her on the street, for she did not wish attention called to herself. She was famous for wearing thick veils and seldom stepped forth without being shrouded in one or more. At the same time, she was a pioneer female smoker of cigarettes in public. With her this was like the rising and falling of a theatre curtain as she lifted veils to take a puff, dropped them quickly until the next. Maxine Elliott, also a trail-blazing female smoker, did it boldly, omitting the veil and blowing smoke freely at the world.

Mrs. Fiske carried her modesty onstage. In a profession where vanity easily becomes ego, with ego rising to monomania, she never seemed especially concerned with herself. If others about her burst into temperament, she said brightly, "Dear, dear, how seriously we take ourselves!" She was, in fact, so un-actressy that she did not appreciate applause during a performance. "The actor who is applauded has only himself to blame," she declared. According to George Arliss, a mainstay in many of her productions, she rose to superb heights in flashes—pregnant silences, sudden exclamations, quick utterances. With these she might have kept audiences in a state of perpetual excitement, but she preferred unit playing, the subordination of the actor's gifts to the group performance. She enforced this rule rigidly on herself. At one rehearsal Arliss asked in amazement, "Are you going to say all that with your back to the audience?" "Yes, I am," Mrs. Fiske replied. "I want people to see your face."

There was method to this, for more than any actress who ever lived, Mrs. Fiske was able to dominate a stage by doing absolutely nothing. Other actresses might fear to turn backs or stand still, but not Mrs. Fiske. In *Salvation Nell* she sat for ten minutes on the barroom floor cradling Jim Platt's head. She said no words, nor did she move, yet every eye in the house stayed riveted on her. "Oh, to be able to do *nothing* like that," the singer Mary Garden breathed.

One of the first indications that the power of the Syndicate had reached a crest and begun to recede came in 1911 when Abraham Lincoln Erlanger wired Mrs. Fiske inviting her to play Syndicate theatres. The telegram was handed her backstage at the Lyric Theatre in Cincinnati and what emotions coursed through her as she read its contents are not known. It is safe to say, though, that tingles of triumph flooded her dumpy frame. She was forty-seven, and looked more like a schoolmarm than a flaming star of the drama. Yet she was physically attractive, always managing to look younger onstage. A new play, *Mrs. Bumpstead-Leigh*, had cast her as a diamond-in-the-rough mother whose snobbish daughters are ashamed of her. In the end, of course, Mother knows best. It was a hit and had taken a place in her popular repertory.

If Mrs. Fiske suffered criticism, it was because she seldom appeared in plays which measured up to her stature. In this, the bouncy *Mrs. Bumpstead-Leigh* was a prime offender. The actress responded by citing her lack of success with Ibsen—in all, she played *A Doll's House, Hedda Gabler, Rosmersholm*, and *Pillars of Society*—when fiery Alla Nazimova had fared better with public and critics. Still, the lament runs through her correspondence—she cannot find suitable vehicles. Mrs. Fiske might have been better off in an era when plays were tailored for stars. But by her own forthrightness she had done much to end this practice. "I detest the star-play," she said once, "with everything distorted to make a part for one actor. If the theme is interesting, the story told dramatically, I do not care if the part that suits me has two lines or two hundred." It was a refreshing statement from a star, but as policy it may have harmed her.

Mrs. Fiske saw herself only as an actress. "An actress must give up everything. All one's strength must be saved for the night's performance; social life is foresworn and one becomes a hermit, a crank, and boorish in everything." This was somewhat distorted, for Mrs. Fiske never became a hermit. Her good works for dumb animals kept her active outside the theatre and while on tour luncheons and dinners were constantly given in her honor. Nor did she turn into a boor or a crank. Her infectious, redheaded humor stayed with her. In the 1920's she rehearsed one new play through a long night. At six a.m. she peered out into the gray, stagnant auditorium. "This is the hour when lifted faces fall," she said lightly.

"God did not destine Mrs. Fiske ever to be an ex-actress," the devoted Ashton Stevens wrote. She never was. However, her continuing career was dictated as much by necessity as by desire. Harrison Grey Fiske continued as manager of his wife's affairs, performing in a manner that ran an unsteady course between the brilliant and the disastrous. In the end, disaster won, and his mistakes lost the money which might have kept the conscience of the American theatre from ending close to poverty.

When death reached Mrs. Fiske—in 1932, at the age of sixty-nine—she all but expired on the boards of a stage. The cause of her death was diagnosed as delayed fatigue.

Much of the spirit of the early winsome Minnie Maddern was reincarnated in the younger actress Laurette Taylor, who in 1912 scored a smashing success in *Peg o' My Heart*.

Born Loretta Cooney in Harlem, when this was a tree-shaded if somewhat impoverished neighborhood, she got on the stage by the amateur-night route, billed as "La Belle Laurette." At sweet sixteen Laurette was a fetching morsel with red-gold hair, pert moonface, Irish-merry eyes, and what in time would be described as a Tom Sawyer grin. At precisely this age she was spotted backstage by thirty-six-year-old, twice-married Charles Alonzo Taylor, a playwright fondly known around the Road as the Master of Melodrama. Swept off his solid feet by the sight of so cute a girl, Taylor launched into a whirlwind court-ship. Shortly the two were married and the Master of Melodrama introduced his bride as "a child I rescued from the wolves of Broadway." He also wrote for her a play called *The Child Bride*, but after this he lapsed back to blood-and-thunder melodrama. This caused the first rift in the marriage, for impish Laurette starred in her husband's plays and could not deliver his stilted lines seriously. She giggled when uttering the meatiest and nightly her husband's fury fell on her head.

Eventually the Taylors settled in Seattle, which in Charles
Alonzo's opinion needed a repertory of rip-roaring melodrama.
It was a sad decision, for public taste everywhere was growing
away from melodrama. During this unhappy period the Taylors
had two children. Laurette, who used to beg her Maker, "Deliver
me from being a personality, let me be an actress," persuaded
her husband to allow her to play Camille and other emotional
parts. These gave her confidence. When the marriage ended,
Laurette with the two children took off in the direction of the
nirvana known as Broadway. There she rapidly appeared in five
plays, during which her natural brightness of outlook was chan-
neled into light comedy, the kind that often hides a breaking
heart. Yet under this burned a gemlike flame visible to the dis-
cerning. Of her acting, critic Louis Sherwin wrote:

> People talk of *sudden rise—luck—personality*. Bosh! This woman
> has worked and striven as few persons on the stage have had to
> work . . . for years she struggled in the most obscure branch of
> her profession, playing vile parts in cheap melodramas, learning
> her trade in the most unpromising surroundings. . . . Personality
> she has—but it is a personality which is an outward and visible
> manifestation of brains, character, and temperament.

Laurette did not truly find herself until she met and married
J. Hartley Manners, an English playwright who did his writing
between midnight and five a.m. For his bubbling bride, Manners
wrote *Peg o' My Heart*, the saga of a hoydenish colleen dumped
by the codicil of a will into the center of an aristocratic English
family. When Manners read aloud the first draft, Miss Taylor
cried out, "Hartley, it's awful!" But it was not. *Peg* was a stupendous success. In New York it ran for 604 performances,
neatly smashing the record established by Maude Adams in
What Every Woman Knows. While the Broadway troupe played
to capacity, four Road companies toured the hinterlands and

from these alone the fortunate author cleared an incredible
$10,000 a week.

In the midst of success Laurette Taylor felt trapped by her
own play. "I don't want to hear about it again until I'm eighty,"
she stated after the final performance. This protest against the
awful monotony of hit-show acting was a familiar one during
the period when the legitimate theatre was practically the nation's only entertainment. At the end of a successful Broadway
run, actors found the Road clamored to see original Broadway
casts, thus adding to the actor's burden of monotony. When
Peter Ibbetson toured the country John Barrymore, not so bibulous as he later became, was driven to collecting specimens of
antique yellow glass to keep himself from madness. Constance
Collier, his co-star, was similarly distracted and annoyed Barrymore by trying to reach local antique shops first. Otis Skinner,
chained to the spectacular *Kismet* (produced by Harrison Grey
Fiske), wrote "Toward the end of the run the part began to get
on my nerves. The work became so mechanical through repeti-
tion that the words sometimes seem almost meaningless to me. I
began to have a sense of separation from my performance. Terror
lest I forget my lines would visit me."

Laurette Taylor went onward to star in *Humoresque* and
other plays, but she remained Peg to a whole generation. No
role took its place, for—no less than Mrs. Fiske—she had difficulty
in finding plays worthy of her genius. Hartley Manners continued to provide vehicles for her and altogether took such splendid care of his wife that after his death she said, "When Hartley
was alive I was kept like a very fine race horse." But Hartley
Manners' plays, though clever, never measured up to Laurette
Taylor. "Alas, poor Hartley, only the audiences like his plays,"
Ethel Barrymore concluded. Laurette knew this and in one
phrase summed up her husband's difficulty—and hers. "Hartley,"

she said, "writes like a man with a knowledge of inherited silverware."

Minnie Maddern Fiske and Laurette Taylor, thrashing about in quest of suitable plays, needed but to look a short distance to find an actress who had deftly solved the problem. Her name was Julia Marlowe, and partisans considered her a greater actress than Mrs. Fiske. True or not, the stately Miss Marlowe apparently enjoyed a more satisfying career. She did so by falling in love with the works of William Shakespeare at the tender age of fifteen. After that she never ceased to worship the Bard. Through a long life (she died at eighty-five), Julia Marlowe spent time poring over Shakespeare and annotating her theatre prompt books. For her to give a performance of Shakespeare was never a chore. Rather, it was bliss. "I steep myself in the joy of it," she said. "I would I could play Shakespeare forever."

The lady was unusual in other respects. Though she idolized Shakespeare, displaying intolerance of nearly every other playwright, she was nonetheless a person of humor, friendliness, and (it would seem) compassion. Her queenly charm was so lavish that she seemed to pass it around like dessert. Her voice, called the finest of any on the American or English stage, was best described as *golden*. Her words were always well chosen and she abominated slang, dismissing it regally as "the vernacular." Even in her inner thoughts Miss Marlowe employed noble phrases. Said she: "I always insist that every thought, whether I voice it or not, shall be well rounded and couched not only in language clear to me, but in the best words I can find."

Still, the most remarkable fact about Julia Marlowe is that she stepped from humble, non-theatrical beginnings directly into stardom. She did not do this by a stroke of good fortune, but because she desired it that way. Gazing back on herself as an aspiring actress, she once said, "I had no idea of considering minor parts—I was determined to begin at the top of the ladder."

Julia Marlowe was a stage name—Julia being a name she had always liked, Marlowe borrowed from Shakespeare's contemporary. As Sarah Frances Frost, she was brought to this country from England in 1870. She grew up in Cincinnati, where her father (like those of Maude Adams and Minnie Maddern) played little part in her development. Her mother became the stern proprietor of a cheap but respectable hotel. Julia's was, she said later, a childhood sordid and hard. To make matters worse she was what now would be called a gifted child. In school she learned faster than her classmates. Outside the classroom, their games seemed silly. She reached the age of fourteen without seeing a stage play or giving thought to the theatre. Yet the high IQ made her restless, and her mother's complaints of poverty brought the idea of getting a job. Choosing at random, she answered an advertisement for a touring company called the *Children's Pinafore*. If her mother agreed, she was told, the job was hers. Her mother was a steely woman, but the child could be steely too. "I'm going," she announced—and went.

The tour of *Children's Pinafore* was short, but as a happy result Julia was accepted in Cincinnati as a full-fledged member of the theatrical profession. She could wander at will in backstage regions of theatres and from the wings of the Grand Opera House saw her first performance of Shakespeare. No record states that lightning struck the theatre at this moment, but it could have. The fifteen-year-old girl discovered utter fulfillment in what she heard. Dashing home, she badgered her mother into buying a cheap set of Shakespeare. At the Opera House, the girl had watched the emoting of Lawrence Barrett and John McCullough. Reading the words these titans had uttered, she decided her own interpretation of certain scenes would be differ-

ent. So began her ever-fresh and stimulating approach to Shakespeare. Julia (or Sarah) was the kind of girl who appeared shy
offstage, but blossomed on. Possibly she also bloomed backstage,
for now Miss Ada Dow, sister of the Opera House owner, began
to notice her. Miss Dow, a character actress herself, was struck
first by the girl's beauty, then by her brains. She decided that
the unusual girl was a winner, and set out to help her win.

Miss Dow—who rapidly became Aunt Ada to the girl—did this
at first by getting acting jobs for them both in the touring Shakespearean repertory of Josephine Reilly. Julia's parts were minor
and she did not appear prepossessing to the company. "A pallid
young person, who usually sat by herself with nose in a book,"
one recalls. "She had big, bright eyes, a high and wide forehead,
and a suggestion of anemia." Yet if her parts were minor, the
girl made a major project of watching Josephine Reilly in action.
"I stood in the wings tonight and watched the Potion Scene,"
she told Miss Dow, after a performance of *Romeo and Juliet*. "I
don't think that's the way to play it, or anything like the way."
Impressed instead of annoyed by such precocity, Miss Dow
urged the girl to continue finding fault.

After the Josephine Reilly engagement, the intrepid pair went
to New York City, where Miss Dow rented a small apartment on
West Thirty-sixth Street, the contemporary heart of the theatre
district. So began one of the oddest regimes in show-business
history. Nearly eighteen, Julia was turning into a beauty, with
cleft chin, cascading black hair, brooding dark eyes, and strong
features. She had no interest in social life, or in enjoying herself
as the wide world understands it. "She was without a friend and
almost without an acquaintance," states one account. At eight
every morning the girl rose, downed a swift breakfast, took a
horsecar to Central Park, where she walked vigorously until
noon. This, though, was mental exercise rather than physical.
During the walks she concentrated on Shakespeare roles—"Her

method was to repeat to herself her part with all its cues, and then go over it line by line as she would say it on a stage, turning it to and fro, weighing the words. . . ."

Returning to Thirty-sixth Street, she ate lunch, then studied Shakespeare through the afternoon with Miss Dow. It was Aunt Ada's policy never to instruct, but rather to stimulate the girl into her own interpretations. "Be yourself, never imitate," she drilled. At the finish of these skull sessions, Julia picked up a fencing foil to lunge ferociously at the wall, first with the right arm, then the left, so that one side of her body would not be overdeveloped. After dinner, she and Miss Dow sometimes went to the theatre. More often they stayed home to study diction and entymology. "No art is more exacting than the dramatic art," Julia Marlowe liked to remark later on.

The theatre of these years boasted a forgotten institution known as the Trial Matinee. An aspiring actor or actress with sufficient funds could hire a major theatre on a non-matinee afternoon, assemble a cast, and put on a play. Critics were invited to these informal performances and—amazingly enough!—they came. Miss Dow was far from rich, but with help from Julia's mother she hired a theatre and announced a Trial Matinee of Julia Marlowe in *Ingomar*, an adaptation from the German then rated nearly as high as Shakespeare. Julia was nineteen, her theatrical experience being the *Children's Pinafore* and Josephine Reilly companies. The manager of the rented theatre, astounded at her youth and lack of training, asked, "Will your voice carry?" "It can carry the whole theatre—and it will," the girl answered serenely. Nor was she nervous at the prospect of her sudden Broadway debut. Indeed, Julia Marlowe resembled John Drew in that she was forever spared the agony of opening-night nerves. Of *Ingomar*, she later said, "I was never frightened before an audience, that time or any time. I have never known stage fright, or any sensation of it."

Ingomar was a success and—to make a story that surpasses belief—several New York critics hurdled the footlights to congratulate the young actress. Said *The New York Times*: "Julia Marlowe—remember the name, you will hear of it again!" Another critic cited her priceless voice, going on to rhapsodize over her "loose black hair, pale face, rich full mouth, wise eyes, provocative eyes." Emboldened by such notices, Julia (she had picked the name Julia Marlowe for this debut) took *Ingomar* on a tour of New England.

Excellent though the New York notices were, her renown had not penetrated far enough and this early tour was a failure. But in the course of it she demonstrated an ability to inspire passionate loyalties. The journalist Charles Edward Russell, who in time became her adviser and biographer, was already a devoted slave, having seen her in the Reilly company. Now a ladies' maid saw *Ingomar* and immediately abandoned her wealthy employer to serve Miss Marlowe. A theatre doorman to whom the radiant girl threw a smile began compiling a scrapbook of her notices, continuing until his death thirty years later. After a Julia Marlowe performance in Philadelphia a local millionaire ordered the town painted with signs which said COME TO THE CHESTNUT STREET THEATRE AND SEE JULIA MARLOWE THE GREAT! Miss Marlowe was horrified at such vulgarity and ordered the signs painted out. A gambler with the suitable name of Jack Oakhurst went on record as saying that the beauty of a Marlowe performance made him abandon cards forever. Later, Miss Marlowe contracted typhoid fever and to save her life it was considered necessary to lance her swollen cheeks. In the operating room the doctor bent over her, then straightened to hurl his instruments to the floor. "I cannot do it," he moaned. "I have seen her play. If this girl's cheeks are lanced she will never be able to act again. I cannot do it!"

Following *Ingomar*, Miss Marlowe set her sights on Juliet.

She knew the part and as always had developed original concepts. The Marlowe Juliet would be restrained, a girl whose character grows with love. On the opening night the most delighted person in the audience was the Great Agnostic, Colonel Robert Ingersoll. His only God was Shakespeare, and he sat through the first act in what has been called a state of rapturous ecstasy. During the intermission the doughty Colonel encountered critic William Winter, whose enthusiasm was not so great. Ingersoll berated him loudly, a fact which turned Winter against Julia Marlowe for years to come. At the final curtain Ingersoll ran backstage to dub the actress the Shakespearean's Juliet. He sat up till dawn writing letters to dedicated Shakespeareans across the country telling of the miracle he had seen. From then on he was Julia Marlowe's most ardent admirer, aiding her career with his own great prestige. He also counseled her, advising (among many other things) that she read one beautiful poem and think one unselfish thought a day.

With *Romeo and Juliet*, the twenty-year-old girl became Broadway's newest star. This resulted in curious episodes, for on the Great White Way a star was a star, whether Shakespearean or otherwise. Almost immediately Miss Marlowe was offered the leading feminine role in Sardou's *Theadore*. Every actress along Broadway wanted this part, but Miss Marlowe spurned it. "I couldn't play it," she stated. "I want to play only noble things and good women." Next, Charles Frohman and William Gillette came to call. They wanted her for the leading role in Gillette's *A Legal Wreck*. Again Julia refused.

"Oh, no," she said. "I want to play nothing but Shakespeare."

"But people don't want more Shakespeare," Frohman told her.

"Maybe they will want it as I play it," she replied.

She had a point. For as her deep study of Shakespeare—it could hardly be deeper—went on, her fresh approach delighted Shakespeareans. She continued the long walks through Central Park, during which she pondered every syllable. Her prompt books grew to majestic size, interlined with comments and ideas. "She bathed her soul in Juliet's being," one newspaper said. Her approach to other roles was as complete. Of her Viola, a writer said: "Nobody I ever saw on or offstage could put into two words the challenge and the retreat, the winsomeness, the temptation and the clean innocence that Julia Marlowe, as she sat on the log near Orlando, put into the words *Woo me.*"

Yet Julia Marlowe was human. She married her leading man, Robert Taber, whose mild acting talents kept static while hers soared. Aunt Ada Dow married, becoming the bride of an elderly actor. Possibly because of Taber's influence, Julia Marlowe temporarily mellowed in her opposition to living dramatists and popular plays, accepting the lead in Clyde Fitch's *Barbara Frietchie*. In no way did the line "Shoot if you must this old gray head" apply to luscious Julia, and her young, lovely Barbara aroused protests from a multitude of Whittier fans.

The best-selling novel of the time was *When Knighthood Was in Flower* and next Miss Marlowe was approached to play the part of Mary Tudor, kid sister of lusty Henry VIII. She agreed, provided Paul Kester, master of the tailor-made play, did the adaptation. Mary Tudor was pure hoyden—"pert, saucy, ready of wit, brisk of action, fascinatingly unconventional." In one scene she demolishes a room in a girlish tantrum. Julia Marlowe's past roles had all stressed dignity, but as saucy Mary she was a veritable laugh riot. "If this is what they want, this is what they shall get," her attitude seemed to say and she hurled herself at the part with gusto. The result was an evening of love and laughter.

From *Knighthood*, Miss Marlowe made a personal profit of $50,000 in the first year, and enough from the second to make her financially independent for life. But her reactions to this

were those of the Shakespearean's Juliet. Of the opening night,
when some twenty-five curtain calls assured her of fortune, she
recalls, "My whole body throbbed with a sense of victory. I
saw my dear object accomplished—my return to Shakespeare's
heroines. Freedom was mine." At the end of the play's run the
Shubert brothers appeared, dangling a weekly salary of $2,500
if she would appear in one of their productions. "I would not
do it for any money," she declared. "I am going back to play
Shakespeare for the people."

Julia Marlowe—it may be presumed—saw herself as America's
Ellen Terry. But to become as great as Terry she needed a permanent leading man, another Sir Henry Irving. Robert Taber,
her husband, had vanished and she cast about until her eyes fell
on E. H. Sothern. Son of a famous actor, he too had a consuming
passion for Shakespeare. His *Hamlet* (played at the age of forty)
had been a muted triumph in New York and an unexpected
disaster on the Road, where a theatre fire destroyed both scenery
and costumes. Like Miss Marlowe, his popular successes had
enabled him to persevere with Shakespeare. His *If I Were King*
was almost as great a box-office draw as *When Knighthood Was
in Flower*.

Onstage, Sothern was a nervous actor, thrown off by the
slightest change. He liked every chair to be in the identical spot
every night, and each bit of business had to stay rigidly the same.
To achieve this he rehearsed endlessly, until someone said, "He
would rather rehearse than act, and much rather rehearse than
eat." Maude Adams puts it more delicately: "He took the
theatre so seriously that one felt he had a stake in the universe."
Yet Sothern's dogged rehearsing paid off. His performances—if
not those of his tired cast—were concentrated and moving. Over
all his productions, it was said, lay a scholar's thought.

Pondering this, Miss Marlowe decided, "Mr. Southern believes

with all his mind and all his soul that acting is in every way as
worthy as any other art, as valuable to mankind, as much of an
ethical agent, and he may be said to devote himself with fervor
to the exposition of this faith." Such high-flown verbiage in-
dicated approval, and after delicate overtures the two combined
to star in three plays in as many years, with a fortunate Charles
Frohman as producer. Their first endeavor was *Romeo and
Juliet*, the second *Much Ado About Nothing*, the third *Hamlet*,
where Miss Marlowe's Ophelia moved audiences to sobs. The
unfortunate events at the New Theatre, where *Antony and
Cleopatra* was a colossal failure, did nothing to blemish the partnership. As an acting team Sothern and Marlowe were superb,
but offstage Miss Marlowe was the bane of journalists. She would
allow interviews only on the subject of Shakespeare, on whom
she had become a prodigious authority. One editor tried to lure
her into personal chitchat by saying, "We syndicate our articles
—what you say today will be printed in one hundred and seventeen papers tomorrow." "That," Miss Marlowe replied coldly,
"is one hundred and seventeen reasons for not doing it."

Sothern and Marlowe put so much hard work into acting that
little energy remained for temperament. Outside the theatre the
two labored endlessly on period research, and it was said they
would walk ten miles to view a painting which might help them.
Miss Marlowe still did her best thinking on long walks, during
which she also believed in extra-deep breathing. She liked to
skate and swim, and for reading preferred poetry and essays.
Both were aware of the value of money, but preferred to spend
it lavishly on productions rather than on themselves.

When the two had appeared together as stars for over a decade
theatregoers thought of them as one. Yet they were not yet man
and wife. Finally—as if they had been rehearsing over the ten
years—they got married. It made little difference to the public,
but it did make a change in their lives. Instead of traveling in

two elegant private cars, they started the practice of inhabiting houses while on the Road. An emissary traveling ahead rented the finest mansion obtainable for the period of two weeks. So Miss Marlowe was able to indulge a passion for cooking which had lain dormant all her life, while Sothern could toast his toes before his own hearth.

Gradually the Sothern and Marlowe repertory opened up to include *If I Were King* and *Richelieu*, two of Sothern's great successes. But for the most part the focus stayed on Shakespeare. Finally, they reached *Macbeth*, in which Miss Marlowe played Lady Macbeth as a physically desirable woman. In a sense, the *Macbeth* production capped the Sothern and Marlowe careers. It cost $25,000, a large sum in pre-World War I days. For the proper background, the two ransacked every possible library, reading histories, commentaries, and essays, while also studying paintings and old prints. *Macbeth* was a solid success—a term which might be applied equally well to the Sothern and Marlowe marriage. During summer layoffs, the couple traveled to Egypt and other far places. Always they manifested deep affection for one another. Once a friend asked Sothern, who seemed to have no hobbies, what he did during the long days of vacations.

"Oh, I just sit and look at Julia," he said.

9: VAUDEVILLE

During the year 1912 a man named Adolph Zukor stepped forward to announce formation of a company to be known as Famous Players.

Famous Players would produce motion pictures—or flickers, flicks, or flickering flickers, as they were commonly called. Zukor was an experienced man in this new medium. He had been in partnership with Marcus Loew in the penny arcades and nickelodeons where the flickers first made a debut. But to date his work in motion pictures, though rewarding, had left him feeling vaguely dissatisfied. Like Charles Frohman, Zukor was a believer in the star system. So far films had produced no stars, nor had the burgeoning art attempted to. The movie studios in and around New York City had been used by Broadway leading men like John Barrymore and Robert Edeson—and ingenues like Mary Pickford and Mary Miles Minter—chiefly as a means of earning extra income. By day they had emoted before the cameras of studios like the Biograph on Twenty-third Street. By night they gave their all on a Broadway stage.

Famous Players had plans for changing this debonair attitude toward the flickering flicks. With Daniel Frohman, brother of Charles, Zukor had established it to tempt top stars into acting in films. They had already been lucky at this. They had signed

Sarah Bernhardt to film *Queen Elizabeth* and James O'Neill for his tried and true *Count of Monte Cristo*. Soon they would annex James K. Hackett for *The Prisoner of Zenda*, Mrs. Fiske for *Tess of the D'Urbervilles*, opera star Geraldine Farrar for *Carmen*, and becurled Mary Pickford, to be lifted to stardom in *A Good Little Devil*.

Famous Players constituted the first attempt to divorce the motion-picture industry from the legitimate stage. The unique type of stardom it offered would allow stars to be seen in many places at once. Further, Mr. Zukor's films would no longer be made on Broadway's outskirts, but across the country in an un-known suburb of Los Angeles called Hollywood. So this raid by Famous Players on the legitimate drama was the first overt act by an industry which up to now had seemed a harmless offshoot of the theatre.

The Great White Way did not seem overly concerned by it; the possibility that movies might seriously cut into stage profits or popularity seemed remote. The best Broadway opinion said that films would merely fill the void left by the disappearance of the lurid ten-twenty-thirty (so named for seat prices) melodramas typified by the masterpieces of Charles Alonzo Taylor. Least of all did movies appear a threat to the towering world of vaude-ville or variety. Here, if dollars and cents were carefully counted, was a field even more prosperous than the legitimate and musical theatres. The man who controlled a vaudeville chain, or only one variety house, was accounted the most fortunate in show business. As Abel Green and Joe Laurie, Jr., point out in the book *Show Biz*, the legitimate-theatre producer was forced to shell out large sums for the purchase of scripts, salaries for actors, staff, and stagehands, and for costumes, scenery, advertising, and other items. The vaudeville impresario, on the other hand, fur-nished theatre, stagehands, box office, orchestra, and salaries. The entertainers themselves brought the rest—wardrobes, sketches, musical arrangements, backdrops, and (presumably) talent.

In the era of the Wonderful World of Vaudeville, the owner of a variety theatre did little more than sit back and reap rewards. When a small Midwest impresario died leaving $7,000,000, no one in the industry was particularly surprised.

The Wonderful World of Vaudeville! Across the United States stretched more than 2000 vaudeville houses. Big cities boasted vaudeville's big-time—two-shows-a-day, in showcase theatres of such chains as Poli, Pantages, and Proctor. Smaller-time vaudeville ran cheerfully from the three-a-day to the six-a-day. Indeed, there were so many gradations in the field that, on being offered a contract, one performer reputedly asked, "What is it—small-time, medium small-time, big small-time, little big-time, medium big-time, or big-time?" On each level the paying public was treated to a splendid assortment of acts, with shows changed in midweek to offer another splendid assortment. European acts flocked to this country. Usually these were acts which did not rely on chatter—acrobats, contortionists, toe dancers, jugglers, adagio dancers, weight lifters, balancing acts. But their number swelled the acts already available so that, as in the theatre, there were always more actors than jobs.

The arrangement of a successful vaudeville bill was something of an art. It reached its peak in 1913 with the opening of the hallowed Palace on Broadway. But in each cross-country theatre the manager was the little czar of his own domain, free to shuffle acts to suit himself. He could also—to the fury of entertainers— edit material for humor and good taste. Still, it was a manager's responsibility to make money for his owner-chain and no one dared dispute his knowledge of a local audience.

Usually the manager opened his bill with what the trade called a dumb act—the act which did not talk. If composed of human beings, this might be acrobats, jugglers, bicycle riders,

or tightrope walkers. Acrobats were the most usual of this group
and with them (as with almost all other vaudevillians) the
mark of success was the glittering diamond—a large ring if the
performer was highly prosperous, a stickpin if less so. (The
diamond was hocked when funds ran low.) One English vaudevillian returned home to report to his countrymen that the acrobats in America wore the filthiest underwear and the largest
diamonds he had ever seen.

Or the opening act might be an animal act, ranging from ele-
phants to monkeys, with trained horses, bears, dogs, cats, snakes,
seals, or almost anything else in between. (Rhinelander's Pigs
was a cherished turn.) Some animal acts performed uncannily,
but offstage matters were not happy. The glamorous young
dancing couple, Irene and Vernon Castle, making two-a-day appearances after 1912, were horrified at the cruelty with which
stage animals were treated. They began buying all they saw
abused. The result was a sizable menagerie, which at one point
included a trained bear they saw knocked cold by a trainer's
baseball bat.

After the acrobats came a ventriloquist, monologist, boy-and-
girl dance team, or a song-and-dance man, slapping out rhythms
to the old soft-shoe. After this might come a magician or an
illusionist, a comedy team with fast patter, or perhaps blackface
comedians, a sister act, or even a tank (swimming) act, or
dancers, ballet or tap. Next might come an elaborate act like
Singer's Midgets or Karno's Night in an English Music Hall,
featuring Charlie Chaplin. With each step toward the top of
the bill, quality supposedly increased. Then, at the top came
the star act. THE STAR! It is safe to say that at one time the star
had been in a bottom place on the bill, perhaps starting in the
lowly second spot, following the dumb act. By hard work and
talent he or she worked upward to the most envied spot of all.
Many top attractions—in the classic phrase—spent fifty years

polishing twelve minutes. By the time the twelve minutes hit the top of the bill, it was superb. The headliners of vaudeville could sweep out and take instant command of an audience as could no other performers.

One headliner during the early Golden Years might be Eddie Leonard, graduate of the minstrel shows, singing "Ida," "Roll Them Roly-Poly Eyes," or "Playmates." It might be the English Vesta Victoria, singing "Waiting at the Church." It might be homely Marie Dressler, singing "Heaven Will Protect the Working Girl." It might be Pat Rooney, doing his famous clog dance to "She's the Daughter of Rosie O'Grady." It might even be Harry Houdini, the first dumb act ever to reach top rung. Houdini, beginning in Midwest medicine shows, was an escape artist who allowed himself to be snapped into handcuffs, strapped into strait jackets, and buried alive. From each he extricated himself to long o-o-o-ohs and a-a-a-ahs from crowds.

Atop the bill might be another dumb act that scaled the heights —Annette Kellerman in her exhibition of diving and glass-tank swimming. Miss Kellerman clothed her superb figure in a one-piece bathing suit and succeeded in shocking the nation. Yet every great act invites imitation. Almost as famous as Annette Kellerman was Enoch the Fish Man. He too dived and swam about in a glass tank. Underwater, Enoch placed a pail over his head and sang an audible song. After that he played a trombone solo.

There were also top headline sketches. Smith and Dale's "Dr. Kronkheit" was one. Mr. and Mrs. Sidney Drew, uncle and aunt of the Barrymores, toured regularly in the hilarious skit "Billy's Tombstone." "Fun in a Gym" was another popular act, while others rejoiced in such titles as "Pest House," "Flinder's Flats," and "Tell Them What I Did to Philadelphia Jack O'Brien." The Lunatic Bakers was a dumb act in which the mute bakers dashed insanely in and out of ovens. Top legitimate stars appeared in vaudeville dramatic sketches. Sarah Bernhardt, after her many farewells to the legitimate drama, turned to the two-a-day for so many more that someone said, "Much adieu about nothing." Bernhardt's favorite sketch—if so peerless a moment can be called a sketch—was the death of Camille. Here the Gallic star vastly increased realism by smearing the underpart of the bedsheet with white make-up. Every time she wiped her face it grew paler.

In New York City, the pinnacle of vaudeville (until 1913 and the Palace) was Hammerstein's Victoria, on the corner of Broadway and Forty-second Street. This was run by Willie Hammerstein, son of impresario Oscar. Willie Hammerstein was a treasured figure in the entertainment world. Daily he sat in an upholstered chair in the lobby of his crossroads-of-the-world theatre, transacting business while lending an ear to the gagsters who made a career of keeping him amused. Willie Hammerstein introduced Freak and Stunt Acts to vaudeville. A typical Stunt Act was The Twelve Speed Mechanics, who assembled a Ford onstage in two minutes flat. The Freak Act was a person who had just headlined in the newspapers. Hammerstein's top success in this field came with Evelyn Nesbit Thaw, whose millionaire husband shot the architect Stanford White. Hammerstein (he had already scored with Nan Patterson, who shot her lover in a hansom cab) offered Miss Nesbit $3500 a week before discovering that American newspapers were weary of her and would no longer print her name. But this was a period when newspapers gobbled up all news from abroad. Hammerstein calmly sent Miss Nesbit to London, telling his English representative to cable American papers about her great success there. When Evelyn returned, the public flocked to see her at Hammerstein's Victoria.

On Sixth Avenue, two blocks from the Victoria lay the vaunted Hippodrome, the block-wide edifice which specialized in panoramas, extravaganzas, and (at times) straight vaudeville. Annette Kellerman seemed most at home in the vast Hippodrome, and in time her water-motif was carried over into the famous finale where a line of beautiful girls slowly descended steps to disappear into the depths of a watery pool.

With vaudeville far-flung and prosperous, it too—in an era of trusts—cried out for the heavy hand which would try to weld it into a profitable and soul-less whole.

The man striving to achieve this as the world whirled into 1912 was Edward F. Albee, a frosty man from Maine who was the partner of an equally chill New Englander named Benjamin F. Keith in the famed Keith-Albee circuit. Keith had made the two all-important contributions which turned vaudeville into an integral part of the national amusement scene. He began in Boston as operator of a small theatre featuring a permanent exhibition of freaks and (on a stage in the rear) such variety acts as Jerry and Helen Cohan and scenes (pirated) from Gilbert and Sullivan. Keith noticed that many potential customers walked up to the box office to inquire the time of the next performance. Told it was half an hour or so hence, the patrons drifted away. His New England mind snapped into high gear and he conceived the idea of a continuous show, one performance quickly following another. In the world of vaudeville Keith was known for years as "the continuous man from Boston."

Keith's second stroke of genius stemmed from piety. A devout churchgoer, he mortally feared that his shows would give offense to churches and religious groups. For a time he stationed a Sunday-school teacher in the rear of his theater to censor any *damns* or *hells* dropped by uncouth performers. Keith's insistence on high moral tone impressed Boston, and when he decided to build the ornate Colonial Theatre, funds were loaned him by the Catholic diocese. After this enormous vote of confidence, Keith widely touted the morality of his shows. Other impresarios, noting his success, began doing the same. Across the country, vaudeville became known as clean, family-type entertainment. A man could take his entire brood to a vaudeville show, and nothing would give moral offense. Instead, there would be songs, dances, funny sayings, animal acts, and acrobats. So began the Golden Age which lasted until approximately 1920 when vaudeville, staggering from the impact of films, began to get raw.

Having done so much, Keith willingly disappeared forever into the background—the dividends on his two inspirations were vast—while his assistant E. F. Albee took over. Albee, who had been hired as a trouble shooter, immediately decided to expand to Philadelphia. There he built a beautiful Keith-Albee theatre in which to display Keith's clean, continuous entertainment. Next he moved on to New York. In both cities, his theatres were an immediate success, bringing the inebriating idea of a Keith-Albee chain covering the United States. The backbone of this would be fine new Keith-Albee theatres in major cities. At the same time opposition chains would be bought out so that eventually Keith-Albee would gain control of every variety showcase in the land.

Opposition to this scheme appeared formidable for, unlike the helter-skelter legitimate theatre, vaudeville houses were controlled by efficient chains operating in well-defined territories. Or would organized opposition simplify the task? Albee decided that in the long run established chains might be easier to swallow. Facing him, as owners of these chains, were men whose names still strike a chord, since they are to be found on theatres in some cities, as are the names Keith and Albee. Prominent among them were Percy Williams (*his* name decorates the Actors' Home at Islip, Long Island, to which worthy cause he left his large estate); F. F. Proctor, another New Englander, who incurred Keith-Albee hatred by stealing the continuous idea and using it first in New York City; Sylvester J. Poli, a great figure in Connecticut and New England; Martin Beck, owner of sixteen to eighteen theatres in a Chicago-to-West-Coast Orpheum circuit; and Alexander Pantages, King of the Far West.

Like Abraham Lincoln Erlanger, Albee firmly believed that every man had his price. Little happened during his campaign of acquisition to refute this notion. Soon a chain of Albee theatres ran across the Eastern part of the country. Linked with this were the theatres Albee had succeeded in buying. He had little difficulty in gaining the F. F. Proctor chain of eleven theatres in New York. Proctor was an odd man—vaudeville seemed to breed such—who started out as a foot juggler in six-a-day vaudeville. Over the years, he fought his way to the eminence of theatre owner. As one, he had no use for his performers. The smell of greasepaint made him ill. He seldom went near his theaters, and never set foot backstage. Such a man, facing a raging tiger like E. F. Albee, might be expected to sell out at a profit. He did.

Percy Williams came next. Despite the effete name, he was a rugged chap who got into show biz by managing prizefighter Bob Fitzsimmons. Williams determined to keep his theatre chain and as a first step announced the signing of the celebrated English beauty Lily Langtry. The Jersey Lily was in England and Williams reported that on arrival she would appear exclusively in his theatres. Albee believed females could be bought no less than males. His English representatives visited the Jersey Lily, offering her an irresistible sum to come to this country three weeks ahead of time. During those weeks she appeared in Albee theatres. Such ruthless tactics caused Percy Williams to reconsider. He first joined the Albee organization in a capacity which gave him slight control of his own theatres. Then, in 1912, he sold out for $6,000,000.

Sylvester Poli in Connecticut . . . Martin Beck in Chicago . . . Alexander Pantages on the West Coast . . . these and a few others eluded the Albee grip. Martin Beck was a particularly wily opponent, who in a few years would dare build the Palace Theatre on Broadway, the heart of Albee territory. But Albee would secretly buy into this showcase of vaudeville. On the day his beautiful Palace opened, Beck discovered he owned only twenty-five per cent of the theatre!

For a time, the battle of vaudeville worked to the advantage of the paying public. In order to strengthen themselves, the wrestling chains booked the best possible acts, offering them at low box-office prices. The struggle also aided performers, if they were good. "Salaries became fantastic, with competition rising so high," Joe Laurie, Jr., writes.

Through the Hippodrome, the Victoria, and (in time) the Palace—as well as the country's thousands of other vaudeville theatres—trooped an endless parade of acts. There were male singers like The Empire City Quartette, first to sing a bum-bum-bum counterpoint; single acts like cute Cissie Loftus, who got $2000 a week for her impersonations; singing, dancing, scrubbed little Elsie Janis; Leo Carillo who (believe it or not!) specialized in Chinese dialect stories; two-man acts like Gallagher and Shean, Clark and McCullough (whose Clark became the great Bobby), Montgomery and Stone, Willie and Eugene Howard, Savoy and Brennan (Savoy a female impersonator, Brennan his straight man, or feeder of lines). Mahoney Brothers and Daisy (Daisy, a dog); Duffy and Sweeney; Cantor and Lee (with Cantor turning into the immortal Eddie), Wynn and Russon, with Wynn becoming Ed Wynn, the Perfect Fool.

Magicians . . . Illusionists . . . Card Men . . . Hypnotists . . . Ventriloquists. The greatest in this field remained Houdini, but Thurston, Keller, and a host of others excelled in the suave art of the magician. There was even a Mad Magician. His name was Frank De Koven, and he specialized in madness rather than legerdemain. He would get two men up from the audience, hand each a block of ice, urge them to shake hands.

Blackface Acts! McIntyre and Heath, Lew Dockstader, Frank Tinney. Williams and Walker, the former a light-skinned Bert Williams, one of the greatest performers America has ever produced. He became the first Negro to headline in vaudeville, then appeared in the *Follies* and other top shows. Williams (*I ain't never done nothin' to no-bod-eee*) was so good that a country not disposed to acknowledge the skills of Negroes called him great. This produced in Williams a kind of controlled bitterness. As a vaudeville headliner, he stayed in the best hotels in each town, but he was forced to ride to his floor in the freight elevator. One day as he gave his vaudeville monologue a stagehand pointed from the wings and said, "There's a good nigger, he knows his place." Williams made his exit to thundering applause and as he passed the stagehand said, "Yes, a good nigger, knows his place, going there now, dressing room ONE!"

Family Acts! The Four Cohans . . . May Wirth and Family, fabulous equestrians . . . Eddie Foy and the Seven Little Foys ("If we lived in Flatbush, it would be a city") . . . The Three Keatons, with child Buster tossed about as The Human Mop . . . Pat Rooney, Marion Bent, and Pat Rooney, Jr. . . . Hyams and McIntyre, with beautiful daughter Leila . . . Keno and Green, with beautiful Mitzi . . . The Marx Brothers . . . and the unrelated brats of Gus Edwards' School Days, Walter Winchell, Georgie Jessel, Eddie Cantor, and Georgie Price.

Sister Acts! The dazzling Dolly Sisters, the clever Duncan Sisters, the glamorous Courtney Sisters, and the Cherry Sisters, who capitalized on their awfulness by appearing behind a wire screen at which audiences hurled vegetables.

Glamour Acts! It is hard in our sophisticated day to comprehend the effulgent appeal of the greatest of these—Julian Eltinge, female impersonator. For thirty years, Eltinge drew salaries

hovering above or below $3000 a week. He achieved the apogee
of Broadway fame with a theatre bearing his name. His success
aided the career of the important Broadway producer Al Woods.
Exquisitely gowned, waving a peacock fan, Julian Eltinge gracefully pirouetted about the stage, doing an Incense Dance or what
was described as a beautiful Salome. He was (by all counts) in-
offensive. "Eltinge's act is extremely high class," *Variety* testified. Says Joe Laurie: "His make-up, wardrobe, dancing, artistic
ability, and songs were never offensive; it was true art."

Eltinge made and lost fortunes, took several round-the-world
tours. In time he added weight, so that he looked heavy even for
a middle-aged female. The great vaudeville public continued
to adore him, remaining convinced of his complete masculinity.
In part, this can be attributed to the naïveté of the times, but
also important was a publicity stunt which launched Julian Eltinge's big-time career. His press agent hired a group of longshoremen to stand in a Ninth Avenue bar. When Eltinge swished
in, they fell upon him. The female impersonator beat them all to
a pulp. Newspapers of the day were extremely gullible and gave
this extraordinary feat country-wide attention. So the nation accepted Eltinge as a hairy-chested he-man, with no more than a
strange method of earning a living. The longshoremen, of course,
were well paid to take a phony beating.

Single Women! The most dazzling act on any bill was the
Single Woman, the personality-plus gal who swept onstage in a
gown worth at least a thousand simoleons. She appeared to up-
beat music and kept the mood of her act that way, rendering
ballads, ragtime, and at late-evening shows an occasional risqué
song—all interspersed with bright patter.

Greatest of all was Nora Bayes, cherished particularly for her
poignant rendition of "Shine On, Harvest Moon." "Nora was
heart, all heart, her act was full of heart," an old-timer recalls.
She strode up and down a stage, putting over songs, clowning,

swinging hips, pausing center stage (full spotlight) to deliver a sentimental recitative. In everything she did Nora was a lady (she once walked out of a *Follies* because Flo Ziegfeld ordered her to wear tights). Confident and friendly, the heart so warmly apparent in her songs was balanced offstage by a sense of humor. "The greatest thing in the world is a laugh," she liked to say— and seems to have meant it.

Nora Bayes worked while holding a silk handkerchief (the best silk money could buy). Her voice was a husky contralto, throbbing with personality "She sold songs, where others just sang them," an admirer has stated. Nora was born Leonora Goldberg in Chicago, got her start at amateur nights. On the vaudeville stage as a child singer her first hit was "Down Where the Wurtzburger Flows." Next came "Has Anybody Here Seen Kelly, K-E-double-L-Y?" When rendering an Irish song she seemed like a bouncy refugee from Tipperary. Realizing this, she changed her name to Nora Bayes, and sang her way upward to billing as The Empress of the Two-a-Day.

The first husband of the girl who loved to laugh was an undertaker. Her second was personable Jack Norworth, author (with Al Von Tilzer) of "Take Me Out to the Ball Game," as well as her partner in the headline act of Bayes and Norworth. While the two appeared together he wrote "Shine On, Harvest Moon," with Nora supplying enough assistance on the lyrics to be listed co-author. As Bayes and Norworth, the two got $2500 a week, with Nora doing "Shine On" and other songs while Jack did magic tricks to music and tossed in a bit of soft-shoe. "Their duets, their teamwork in those days was the talk of show business," recalls Eddie Cantor. "They actually laughed as they sang." When the marriage blew up, so did the act. Miss Bayes went on to marry three more times, and to reach $3000 a week as the top class act of the time. Her name also became a synonym for extravagance—Nora did everything with a marvelous flair.

She traveled in a private car like any top star of the legit. In hotels she was never content to occupy a suite, but took half a floor, or a whole one. Her entourage included a husband (when she had one), three adopted children (whom she adored), an accompanist (at one time youthful George Gershwin), the accompanist's wife and children (if any), plus numerous Goldberg relatives and Broadway hangers-on.

Single Women! Nora's main rival was Eva Tanguay, who for some years was the highest-paid single act in vaudeville. Little Eva started as a lovely, high-spirited chorus girl in a forgotten New York show. Her backstage clowning attracted the attention of the stage manager, and when a headliner fell ill, Eva was pushed onstage as a substitute. Eva's sisters of the chorus did not approve of this, and offered disparaging cracks as she sang. Later, the envious girls pelted her with rolls from a nearby restaurant. Eva took it as long as she could, then commenced an onstage hair-pulling fracas. Unlike the Julian Eltinge brawl, this was the real thing—and again newspapers paid resounding attention. From then on, it has been said, Eva Tanguay was seldom out of the news. She was the most fiercely competitive of performers in a profession where self-centered ambition is a must. Nor was her ambition restricted to backstage maneuvering. Onstage, the girl who could easily get by on looks and personality seemed to try to knock herself out at each performance. Not until the subsequent frenzies of Betty Hutton would anything approaching her gyrations be seen. Eva Tanguay's most successful song was "I Don't Care." Least of all, she seemed to care about herself.

Nora Bayes and Eva Tanguay waged tireless rivalry in the matter of dress. Neither appeared onstage (or off) in a gown costing less than $500. Often it was $2000. A result of this free-wheeling expenditure was that Nora always looked superb, while Eva could frequently be accused of bad taste. One costume she wore was composed of dollar bills stitched together. With other of Eva's excesses, this caused the neophyte drama critic Heywood Broun to address a column to her. SOMETHING ABOUT WHICH EVA TANGUAY SHOULD BE MADE TO CARE, it was headed. Dynamic Eva was not one to take abuse quietly, and she retaliated with a full-page ad in *Variety*. Everything this girl did had a special twist and the *Variety* ad was in rhymed prose. If nothing else, it gives an insight into the mind-processes of a woman who scratched her way up on the variety stage:

> Have you ever noticed when a woman succeeds how they attack her until her character bleeds? They snap at her heels like mongrels unfed, just because she has escaped being dropped into FAILURE's big web. They don't give her credit for talent or art. They don't discount a very hard start. They don't give her credit for heartaches or pains; how she grimly held tight to the reins when the road ahead was rocky and drear; how smiling she met every discouraging sneer. . . .

Single Women! Others who made vaudeville's top rung were Trixie Friganza, Irene Franklin, May Irwin, Fay Templeton, Mae West—and a hefty girl from Hartford named Sophie Abuza who after an early marriage to a man named Tuck began calling herself Sophie Tucker. When Sophie hit New York, Bayes, Tanguay, Friganza, and Franklin were her peers. But after an apprenticeship in the wintry halls of vaudeville, Sophie discovered herself in *The Ziegfeld Follies of 1909*. Here she was spotted in act one, while Nora Bayes was queen of act two. In one of the few unkind acts of a large-hearted career, Miss Bayes insisted that Sophie be fired. With this, she gave kindly advice: "Sophie, you must live well. Make a splash. It helps your prestige. People take notice of you. It makes you important." Shrewd Sophie took a calculating look at the prodigal manner in which Bayes and Tanguay tossed money around, turned to analyze Trixie Friganza. True, Trixie paid big sums for costumes and material, but offstage she lived modestly and bought annuities. Sophie chose the Friganza method. "There'll be no benefits for Soph," she decided—and she has been right. Bayes and Tanguay died broke, or nearly so. But there has never been a benefit for Soph!

Single Men! If the Single Woman was a dazzler, the Single Man was lucky. This entertainer, with great storytelling ability, sauntered out on a stage in a sack suit, perhaps holding a hat or a cigar. With a clever monologue he delighted audiences and got over $1000 a week, all of which slid comfortably into his pocket. (Indeed, on close examination, the term Single Woman may be a misnomer, for usually the gal worked with an accompanist.) Many of the great Single-Man acts are forgotten, while others strike a faint chord. Walter C. Kelly, the Virginia Judge, was an inspired dialectician who took all the parts in a hilarious Southern courtroom sketch. (Today's Grace Kelly is his niece.) Will Rogers began as a vaudeville rope twirler, rose to world fame. Fred Allen, starting as the World's Worst Juggler, began (like Rogers) to spice his act with talk. Frank Tinney worked in blackface and used the orchestra leader as an unpaid foil. When complimented on how little his act cost, Tinney registered astonishment, explaining that he spent large sums for burnt cork. "You see, I use only champagne corks," he said. Tinney lost his money, reputation, and eventually his sanity over a beautiful *Follies* girl. Charles "Chic" Sale, hilarious monologist, may have introduced the word *wisecrack* to the English language. His monologue "The Specialist" was devoted to the construction and care of outhouses, and is still available in a book. W. C. Fields was the world's greatest juggler before dipping into his comic genius. Jimmy Savo was also a juggler—"Juggles Anything from a Feather to an Automobile," his ads read. Funnymen Joe Cook and Ed Wynn scaled the dangerous gap between vaudeville and stardom in musical comedy. It was Ed Wynn who offered the classic definition, "Comedians say things funny, comics say funny things."

A popular Single Man of the Golden Age was James J. Corbett. (Sometimes he worked with a straight man.) Corbett, who turned the sports world awry by defeating beefy John L. Sullivan for the world's heavyweight championship, was known as Gentleman Jim. It was no misnomer. Wiry, graceful, dapper, and slender, he acted creditably in George Bernard Shaw's *Cashel Byron's Profession*. Long before George M. Cohan appeared on the scene, Corbett greeted everyone with a friendly, "Hi ya, kid." To this he appended a friendlier, "How's the folks?" Asked how he dared question people he didn't know about their folks, Corbett answered sensibly, "Listen, kid, *everybody* has folks." Practically every male in America thought of Gentleman Jim as a pal and often this resulted in episodes the witty fellow worked into his act. One admirer who visited his dressing room greeted Gentleman Jim so chummily that Corbett had to ask, "Say, who *are* you, anyway?" The man was taken aback. "Why, don't you remember?" he demanded. "When you beat John L. Sullivan in New Orleans, you stood on the back of the train passing through Chicago and there was a big gang of people there, must have been a couple of thousand?" "Sure, I remember," said Gentleman Jim. "How could I ever forget it?" "Well, don't you remember *me*?" the man went on. "I was the guy in the *brown derby*."

One of the great monologists was James Thornton, who sometimes appeared in a mixed act with his wife as Jim and Bonnie Thornton. As a single, Thornton strode onstage attired in a funereal Prince Albert coat, wearing heavy glasses and carrying a newspaper. Raising an admonitory finger, he roared, "One moment, please." Occasionally he varied this by saying, "I'm glad to see you all *sober*." This shook the house, for Thornton was a monumental drinker and audiences knew it. Bonnie Thornton's efforts to keep her man sober resulted in epochal stories. Once she locked him in a hotel room and vanished with the key. Jim phoned a bellboy to bring him an open pint and a straw. The bellboy stood outside while Jim used the straw to consume the pint through the keyhole. Thornton was also a man of great wisdom who utttered one vaudeville truism. In Wilkes-Barre he was approached by a member of a small-time act who said, "Mr. Thornton, you see what a riot I am here. Why can't I get a job in New York?" "Because," Thornton answered, "you are a riot in Wilkes-Barre."

Once Thornton said, "I like the idea of being drunk continuously—it eliminates hangovers." Drunk or sober, he got onstage to deliver his monologue, which began with his trip to the barber shop that morning:

> The barber put a hot towel on my face and scalded me alive. When I asked him why he put such a hot towel on my face, he explained that it was too hot to hold in his bare hands. Then a little boy about five years of age climbed on a soap box and started to shave me. He began to cut my face into jigsaw puzzles. When I objected to a boy shaving me, his father told me it was the lad's birthday and we had to let him do anything he wanted to on his birthday. All this time a dog was running around the chair howling and barking. When I asked the man why the dog was running around the chair, he told me that the dog had got a piece of ear that morning and wouldn't go away until he got another.

*   *

One day Edward F. Albee scrawled his signature across the check which constituted a week's salary to a vaudeville headliner—the kind of headliner whose drawing power was helping the Keith-Albee empire expand. When Albee finished, he threw this pen on the desk. "These damned actors have been sticking it into me for years," he snarled. "Now I'm going to stick it into them."

Albee depended on acts to fill his vaudeville theatres, just as

Erlanger needed plays for legitimate playhouses. Apparently he had been casting a speculative eye on the drama empire of Abraham Lincoln Erlanger and its operational methods. Erlanger had started with a booking office and through it had gained control of theatres. Albee had done the opposite. He acquired theatres first. But why should he not set up a booking office, bestowing on it the right to book the acts into his theatres? To Albee, this meant *exclusive* right, for acts which did not book through his office would never appear in Albee theatres, the top big-time theatres in the country. From his position of power, Albee was equipped to act as fast as he thought. Immediately, he set up the United Booking Office, which alone booked acts into his theatres. Albee's UBO took five per cent of an actor's salary, plus a five-per-cent agent's fee, for booking *into Albee theatres!*

As an attractive offshoot of the scheme, Albee also had control of salaries. Since no one except the United Booking Office could place an act in an Albee theatre, the Booking Office could also dictate how much the act got paid. Albee quickly began to cut salaries—this is what he meant by sticking it into the actors! It was said (though never quite proved) that he hired private detectives to probe the bank accounts and family responsibilities of acts he booked. Thus he was in a position to make a minimum offer—just what the actor needed to get by and no more. Actors who had been getting $1000 a week found themselves offered $700. More, they had to take it. To be cut off from the big-time Albee circuit meant a huge loss of prestige, perhaps oblivion.

So great was the anger at Albee that the White Rats union, dormant for years, again sprang to life. The White Rats purchased a small-time circuit in New York and Pennsylvania. This guaranteed members a thirty-week tour. They also bought an attractive clubhouse on West Forty-sixth Street. This, it turned out, was a dreadful mistake. Albee took over the building across the street, to station private detectives there. Just as the FBI tagged Nazi sympathizers before World War II, so Albee's men noted those entering the White Rats clubhouse.

With these names, Albee commenced an infamous blacklist. Those on it were barred forever from appearing in Albee theatres. He also drove performers to spying on other performers. Anyone who criticized Albee was reported to the main office and another name added to the blacklist. Joe Laurie, Jr., a vaudevillian himself, has said, "On the part of management there was hypocrisy and egotism. They beat down the opposition, starved the vaude actor, kidded him, made a spy of him on his fellow artists by dangling forty-week routes before his caved-in stomach. They had a blacklist that kept many a good act from the big-time bills on which they belonged."

With the White Rats clubhouse under surveillance, membership began to dwindle. Soon Albee bought the clubhouse, changing it to his own National Vaudeville Club. Membership was imperative in order to work for him. Simultaneously he conceived National Vaudeville Week, with wicker baskets passed through theatres for the benefit of indigent actors. Albee also published Souvenir Programs in which headliners were required to take expensive ads. No accounting was made of this money, nor of the coins and bills dropped into wicker baskets during Vaudeville Week. It was widely presumed that the theatre manager, after taking a modest cut, passed the rest along to Albee.

In the thin ranks opposing Albee, the show-business paper *Variety* fought hardest. Founded in 1905 by Sime Silverman, a Broadwayite who loved fair play as much as show biz, *Variety* hated Albee with a hot hatred. Its columns were open to the White Rats cause, while Silverman kept urging the actors to strike. *Variety* also used its celebrated sense of humor to needle the solemn Albee. When a billboard across the street from the UBO advertised the attraction *Are You a Crook?*, *Variety* ran a picture of this. ASKING ALBEE A QUESTION, was the headline.

This and other digs so infuriated Albee that in 1913 he tried to blacklist every actor who perused *Variety*.

Also in the opposition was a young booking agent named William Morris. Born Wilhelm Moses in Austria, he had begun his New York career by guiding Eva Tanguay to engagements paying thirty-five dollars a week. In a series of Horatio Alger moves he jumped from such humble beginnings to the high post of booker for the Proctor and Percy Williams circuits.

When these sold out to Albee, William Morris' career as Horatio Alger hero appeared over. For a time he booked special acts (Sophie Tucker was one) into Albee theatres, but with the appearance of the UBO this too finished. Morris was a man who dreamed grandiose dreams, and acted on them. He now conceived the stupendous idea of getting Klaw and Erlanger to start a vaudeville chain in competition to Albee. To the young man's mingled delight and astonishment, Erlanger showed interest. Shortly Morris found himself in command of an outfit called the United States Amusement Corporation. Klaw and Erlanger owned it, while the brothers Shubert functioned as quiet partners! Morris had been assured of unlimited funds for acts, as well as theatres in which to display them. "Vaudeville by wholesale, that's what we're going to have," he jubilated, envisioning a new dawn in the Golden Age of Vaudeville. Excitedly, he went to work putting shows together.

The initial collision between the two chains came in Philadelphia, where Morris presented a first bill at the Chestnut Street Theatre. Some $5000 worth of top talent was hurled into the fray by both sides. Morris offered a program headed by the Four Mortons, while Albee led with redoubtable Vesta Victoria. For his second show, Morris planned to spend $10,000, but at this glorious moment in his life—with dreams coming true—he began to detect a certain shiftiness in the eyes of Erlanger. Slowly it dawned on him that Klaw and Erlanger, as the United States

Amusement Corporation, had built themselves up only to be knocked down—that is, bought out. They dared compete with Albee only because they so completely understood his mania for monopoly. He would, they knew, buy opposition out at almost any price. Overtures had begun and meetings between Klaw, Erlanger, and Albee had taken place. The Syndicate insisted on one of the most peculiar deals of all time. "A million-dollar profit," was the cry. They proffered an itemized expense sheet of the short but expensive venture into vaudeville. Atop this they piled a cool million.

A million was what the Syndicate wanted. A million is what it got!

It is agreeable to report that one vaudeville performer—possibly the greatest of all—helped William Morris keep afloat. In his first euphoria at his association with Klaw and Erlanger, Morris had succeeded in luring the great Scotch entertainer Sir Harry Lauder to this country. Up to now Sir Harry had resisted blandishments from America, fearing that he might fail and do his reputation irreparable harm. Now he came, at $2500 a week, just as Morris discovered the perfidy of the United States Amusement Corporation. From the shambles, Morris redeemed two worthwhile items. One was an old contract with Annette Kellerman, whom he had discovered and promoted into fame. The other was the new one with Sir Harry Lauder. Miss Kellerman promptly informed Morris she was breaking her contract to join Albee. Sir Harry displayed a true Scotch integrity. He stayed with Morris. In gratitude, Morris upped his guarantee to $3000 a week and set about making the bookings to earn it.

The name Sir Harry Lauder is almost forgotten today, yet in his time (he died in 1950) the little man was a peerless performer. Of all those who appeared on the vaudeville boards, Sir Harry remained eternally faithful to the two-a-day. Where other top entertainers like Nora Bayes and Will Rogers alternated between vaudeville and musical comedy or movies, Sir Harry Lauder stuck to vaudeville, detouring only to make a few pioneering films. More than any headliner, Sir Harry was a master of the magical trick of appearing the happiest person in the theatre. He did not do this by loud laughs or thigh-slapping jollity. Rather, he achieved it by conspiratorial winks, cozy chuckles, and you-know-how-it-is laughs. Rakishly wearing a tam-o'-shanter, Scotch kilts, and carrying a gnarled walking stick, the little man sang "R-r-roamin' in the Gloamin'," "A Wee Doch an' Doris," and other burry tunes. There was much chitchat in a Lauder performance. He told stories on his Scotch neighbors, on drink, on himself, on his "wee wifie," and on the institution of marriage. With this, he may well be the most satisfying act show business has ever seen. After his first appearance in this country (phonograph records also spread his fame), Morris had a how-itzer of talent that Albee was utterly unable to match. People wanted to see—*had* to see—Sir Harry Lauder, and no theatre manager could disregard the clamor.

With Sir Harry, Morris had power. He booked the Scotsman on a tour of fifteen cities, playing fifty shows in twenty-six days at fifty cents to two dollars—and made $65,000 at the box office. While Lauder was busy cleaning up, Morris learned that Albee had neglected to renew his option on the Boston Music Hall. Morris grabbed it. With further Lauder profits he remodeled the neglected American Theatre at Forty-second and Eighth Avenue, in New York. Here he offered mammoth shows of twenty-two acts. Next, he managed to capture theatres in Brooklyn and Chicago, both strong centers of vaudeville. The UBO blacklisted any act who worked for Morris, but by using acts already on the blacklist he survived.

In one year he made a profit of $125,000 from the American Theatre alone. Sir Harry, in the meantime, had returned for another triumphal tour (in the end, he made as many farewells as Bernhardt). In what seemed a final lucky break, Morris was joined by Marcus Loew, owner (with David Warfield as silent partner) of some twenty small-time theatres and nickelodeons. Loew had just absorbed the information that 2,000,000 Americans daily attended motion-picture theatres and he had visions of combining vaudeville and movies in single programs. With Marcus Loew on his side, William Morris seemed impregnable. Yet at this dramatic point illness struck him down. He sold his vaudeville enterprises to Loew, retaining only the personal management of Sir Harry Lauder. With recovery, Morris took on the guidance of other special talents, founding the talent agency which today bears his name.

Theatres! In the stormy Belasco trial of years before, Abraham Lincoln Erlanger had been asked, "Are the operations of the Syndicate, as far as you know, confined to first-class attractions?" "No," Erlanger's guttural voice answered, "they are confined to first-class buildings." Erlanger's inability to see the drama as anything but real-estate packaging was to prove his undoing. Where others in the field were capable of discovering talent and taking chances on it, Erlanger cared only for box-office receipts to be sunk into what he called first-class buildings. He disregarded stars who slipped and turned a deaf ear to the arguments that a faltering play might catch on after a weak start. All he cared about was profits. As with Albee in the vaudeville field, dislike of Erlanger's sandpaper personality turned to hatred on the part of most actors. They preferred the Shuberts, who, despite their off-again on-again relationship with the Trust, had earned the reputation of being more human and flexible. Klaw and Erlanger were still powerful, but no longer all-powerful. Even with their ruthless tactics they had fought a losing battle with flesh-and-blood actors and a public which had become more discriminating in its tastes.

Ironically, theatres also caused the undoing of E. F. Albee. For while fighting rival entrepreneurs, persecuting performers, and trying to control American vaudeville, he had become fascinated by the construction of theatres. Albee was not merely interested in building. He went further, to become obsessed by theatre design and decoration. Rarely satisfied, he tore up plans and hauled down finished construction to achieve the soaring lobbies he loved. He traveled abroad to purchase oil paintings and antiques costing thousands of dollars. He personally designed marble staircases, lobby fountains, and upholstered love seats. When finally completed, an Albee theatre was likely to resemble a cathedral or a Pasha's dream palace. (Some still do!) Albee fussed over marble, fabrics, and velvet ropes for standees. He was a pioneer in air conditioning and devoted fanatical attention to fixtures in men's and ladies' retiring rooms. In one Albee theatre, startled employees found a red carpet on the cellar floor.

Altogether E. F. Albee, with his icy personality and business callousness, showed amazing skill and taste in decorating on a mighty scale. His was not the effete kind of décor which became popular in later years. He decorated in red-blooded style. Had he been alive in the Renaissance, Albee's name might have come down to us as a creator of the palaces for the doges. Yet this consuming passion for decoration slowed him down. As years passed he became totally preoccupied with the creation of theatres, and the UBO and existing theatres suffered.

Albee held out until the twenties. Erlanger began to lose his power in the teens. Both made a mighty effort to achieve goals that may or may not have been possible to reach. But possible or not, both failed.

10: PRODUCERS

On the morning of May 2, 1915, Charles Frohman stepped out of the lobby of the Hotel Knickerbocker and into a waiting taxicab. A second cab, chugging behind, was stacked with his luggage, for Frohman was about to embark on a trip to Europe.

In previous years, Mr. Theatre seemed to do this as often as the average man bought a cigar. Over the last eighteen months, however, he had not. World War I had forced him to confine most of his production activity to the United States. But now James M. Barrie had requested him to cross the ocean for a visit. To Frohman, Barrie's wish was a command. Friends—among them John Drew—advised him not to make the trip, since the submarine warfare which up to now appeared largely a threat had begun to loom as an actuality. Frohman was about to board the *Lusitania*, and this morning a newspaper notice sponsored by the German embassy had warned the ship's passengers that they were traveling at their own risk. Frohman must have seen this or been told about it, but he was sailing anyway.

In other ways the trip would be a strain, for at fifty-five Frohman suffered from severe rheumatism. In addition, the gastric condition exacerbated by his voracious consumption of sweets had worsened. Yet even in bad health the production activities of Mr. Theatre continued unabated. Over the last season he had presented no less than eighteen plays, including Maude Adams in *The Legend of Leonora;* Ethel Barrymore and John Drew in *A Scrap of Paper; The Girl from Utah* (music by Jerome Kern) with Julia Sanderson, Donald Brian, and Joseph Cawthorn; and *The Outcast,* with Elsie Ferguson. For the coming season he had scheduled *Grumpy,* with Cyril Maude, and a revival of *Peter Pan,* with Maude Adams. Nor had painful illness robbed Frohman of his courtesy and steady optimism, or the sense of humor which fed on a laugh a day. He had remained young (or a young middle-age) in heart and mind. Abed in his suite at the Knickerbocker, he enjoyed listening to the phonograph, and his favorite record, played over and over, was "Alexander's Ragtime Band."

Frohman's departure on the *Lusitania* was not without overtones. Edward Sheldon (by now author of *Romance,* the top money-making play of his career) had planned to travel with him, but at the last moment decided not to. John Drew, failing to persuade Frohman to stay in this country, gave a shrug of tailored shoulders and sent what seemed a witty wire: IF YOU GET BLOWN UP BY A SUBMARINE I'LL NEVER FORGIVE YOU. Lastly, as the *Lusitania* (with Frohman aboard) steamed through the Narrows, Minnie Maddern Fiske stood watching. At this moment the plucky little woman was at the low point of her career. Weary from the battle with the Syndicate, accepting at last a split in her marriage, she was living in near-penury on Staten Island, with little to do but watch the ships go by. Charles Frohman's influence on her career had been a peculiar one. At first he had helped. Then, as a founder of the Syndicate he had begun to harm. By his silence as a Syndicate member, he had given tacit support to Abe Erlanger as he hounded Mrs. Fiske over the country. Mrs. Fiske may have been aware that Frohman was on the *Lusitania* and she too must have known of the advertisement in the morning paper. What could have been her thoughts as the ship steamed out to sea?

Aboard with Frohman were the playwright Charles Klein and the actress Rita Jolivet. The producer joined them when he made his infrequent appearances on deck. With them, he sat through the ship's concert as the *Lusitania* approached Ireland, and at two-thirty the following afternoon stood alone on deck quietly smoking a cigar. Suddenly the *Lusitania* shuddered, and passengers heard a tremendous roar. A torpedo from a German submarine had hit, voices shouted—and it was true. Frohman, who seldom dared face his own opening nights, did not seem frightened by this. He studied the end of his cigar and said, "I didn't think they would do it." Half an hour later he was assisting Miss Jolivet into a life preserver. There were not enough to go around and women and children got the ones available. As the ship began to list a heavy wave moved toward it. Watching this lethal wall of water approach, Frohman quoted Barrie, "Why fear death? It is the most beautiful adventure in life." He was about to repeat this when the wave struck. . . .

Frohman's death was a shattering blow to Broadway, for Mr. Theatre had seemed as indestructible as his own Empire. "In the eyes of the theatre world the loss of the *Lusitania* is the loss of Charles Frohman," an obituary declared. Frohman's body was recovered and carried to New York, where funeral services were held at Temple Emanu-El. Playwright Augustus Thomas delivered the eulogy at this. In Los Angeles, Maude Adams spoke at simultaneous services. In San Francisco, John Drew officiated. In Tacoma, it was Billie Burke. In Providence, Julia Sanderson. Then Broadway turned to wonder, *Who will take his place?*

If Frohman knew how to die, he may also have known when. For despite the eighteen productions of the previous year, his impressive theatrical stature had begun to shrink. The dramatized novels and skillfully constructed imports of his prime had been elbowed aside by the theatregoing public in favor of more robust products of the American theatre. Oddly, most of the vigor to be found in these domestic efforts had been borrowed from abroad. Shaw, Ibsen, and the Irish Players—whose appearance in 1911 caused riots here as in Dublin—gave new freedom to the talents of home playwrights. But if Ireland, England, and Norway helped unfetter the American drama, the meaty foreign dramas that did it were not the polite plays habitually imported by Charles Frohman.

There was, it seemed, no lofty niche remaining for an urbane, cosmopolitan Mr. Theatre, producer of plays in quantity. George M. Cohan, in his thirties now, mouth crinkling downward, head cocked to one side, an eyelid perpetually lowered in a wise-guy wink, was busy establishing the advent of a new day. He looked at the world as if tossing it his cocky, "Hiya, kid." In return the world opened wide, welcoming arms. Cohan was the Yankee Doodle Dandy of Broadway. He wrote plays. He wrote songs. He produced plays with Sam H. Harris. He rewrote, adapted, doctored, directed, and financed plays written by others. He acted in his own works. He was a Yankee Doodle Boy of talent-plus-personality whose motto in the theatre as on the Broadway sidewalk was "Always leave 'em laughing when you say good-by."

George M. Cohan was, in the slang of the time, flip, speedy, a crackerjack guy. Success had mellowed him slightly. Gone were a few of the rough edges of his brash, I'm-a-great-little-guy youth, but he still behaved as if aware that one day a statue in his honor would stand on Broadway. At the same time he was (like most geniuses) full of paradoxes. The hiya-kid manner made him appear diamond-hard, yet he was deeply sentimental. On the surface the most confident of men, he was subject to fits of Irish gloom. He drove himself hard, making top money from his plays, songs, and productions. At the same time, he seemed ashamed of prosperity and became known as the softest touch on

Broadway, a fellow who traveled with pockets stuffed with bills to hand without question to panhandlers, out-of-work actors, and fellow producers in a financial bind. "My whole background was rough and tumble, as you know," he wrote to his friend George Middleton, "but I never got *hard-boiled* as they call it. Always tried—did the best I could with the Equipment allotted me."

The Equipment was considerable. Cohan also lived in the Hotel Knickerbocker, at the corner of Forty-second Street and Broadway, in a suite containing a grand piano on which he one-fingered song hits. A few steps away was the office of Cohan and Harris, where he functioned as a play producer. Several strides from this was the George M. Cohan Theatre, where he performed in his own plays but never (until *Ah, Wilderness* in 1933) the plays of others. He was a whirlwind of brisk, extroverted energy, rushing to Boston or Chicago for a tryout, or to the Polo Grounds for a baseball game. When playwright Channing Pollock, a man of mature years, confided that he had never seen a ball game, George M. was at a loss of words. "Why, that's un-American," he finally blurted.

George M. still wrote song hits, but had put song-and-dance days behind. In 1911 he did *Get-Rich-Quick Wallingford,* proving that he could write fast-and-furious non-musical comedy. Cohan always boasted that his plays were clean and wholesome. Patriotism was as important as religion in his life, and where other playwrights might slip in a risqué line, George M. inserted tributes to the American flag. Ironically, the breezy pace of his plays gave others the means to write suggestive, door-slamming sex-farces like *Getting Gertie's Garter.* But while others broadened areas of sex, Cohan stayed clean with successes like *Seven Keys to Baldpate,* perhaps the trickiest of all trick-ending plays. At the same time he produced a series of Cohan Revues, in which others starred. He might supervise the tryout of a Cohan-Harris production in Boston, then rush to New York to rehearse the third act of one of his own plays. Rehearsing, in the Cohan lexicon, meant writing as he rehearsed.

On the stage, George M. seemed to play himself, strutting rather than walking, delivering lines out of the side of his mouth, cocking an inquiring eyebrow at other actors, and generally behaving as he did off the boards. Yet, like John Drew, he was a consummate actor despite these individual mannerisms. "He is an actor who can hold an audience tense without acting," said the English producer Charles M. Cochran. The fledgling drama critic Heywood Broun began his career auspiciously by declaring that a performance by an actor named Steyne was "the worst in the contemporary theatre." Steyne sued for damages, and while the suit pended, Broun judged another play in which the actor appeared. "He was not up to his usual standard," Broun opined. But for George M. Cohan, Broun had only praise. After one opening he wrote:

> Somebody should create a foundation which would endow all stage aspirants with tickets for the new Cohan play. They will not find a more likely master. And I would particularly request the aspirants to note the way in which Cohan listens. He is all attention when the other person in the scene is speaking. You forget that he not only wrote the play, but produced it. He seems eager not to miss a line of the dialogue, and it is all surprising to him, as if this were the first time the lines had ever been said.

Cohan had a finger in every Broadway pie. Actors called him a brother actor. Producers thought him a producer. Playwrights embraced him as an author. Tin Pan Alley called him its own. Soon he would be forced to step forward to identify himself precisely—and this would become an unhappy moment in his life. But now he was Mr. Broadway, the Yankee Doodle Dandy, born on the Fourth of July. He was also a gingery personality, a fast talker and wisecracker who loved practical jokes and

theatre talk—the last preferably about himself. He also liked to
drink and after a wet night strutted cockily into the Lambs.
"How d'you feel, Georgie?" a friend asked. "Oh, I'm all right,
kid," Cohan flipped back. "I got up this morning and drank my
bath."

Cohan liked to be seen in the best places, especially the Plaza
Hotel and the Knickerbocker Bar, decorated with the famous
King Cole mural by Maxfield Parrish. At the same time he cared
little about food. "One of the lightest eaters I know of is George
M. Cohan," writes George Rector. "He could fly like an angel
on the diet of a sparrow." Yet Cohan always knew precisely
what kind of food he was eating. On one lunch menu he saw
"Corned Beef Hash, $1.75." He ordered it, adding, "Bring me
only half a portion." "Aren't you hungry today, Mr. Cohan?"
the solicitous headwaiter inquired. "I'm hungry enough, kid,"
Cohan replied, "but no waiter alive could carry a dollar and
seventy-five cents' worth of corned beef hash." In theatres
where he played, Cohan was the absolute boss. Once an actor
named George Parsons forgot this, undertaking to tell members
of the cast how to improve their performances. Cohan heard of
it, flew into a rage, and fired the actor. This failed to cool his
Hibernian ire and he summoned his cast and office staff to a
meeting at which he delivered a stinging attack on the dis-
charged man. "Not one of you is ever to have anything to do
with George Parsons," he concluded. "He never works for
Cohan and Harris again—that is, *unless we need him.*"

The mantle of Charles Frohman could have tumbled over the
clerically garbed shoulders of David Belasco. For that incredible
man, who had begun his theatre career arm in arm with Frohman, was destined to live far beyond him. The Bishop of Broadway had all but outlasted one set of contemporaries and started

on another group. Before his death (at seventy-five, in 1931) he would be competing strenuously with a third.

Probably in his own mind Belasco was, and always had been, Mr. Theatre. But to less biased observers certain matters kept this high accolade from him. With all his dramatic triumphs, Belasco's finest production was always himself. The best acting in any Belasco show was done before the curtain rose—at rehearsals, by Belasco. With uncanny stratagems he sparked the talents of the actors who addressed him reverently as Mr. Dave, Mr. B., D.B., Governor, Master, or Maestro, depending on their degree of intimacy.

His actors usually rewarded the Master by fine performances, but with playwrights his record was not as good. Many who occupied seats in his theatres wondered how a man so theatre-wise could pick such inferior plays. The answer may be Belasco's pounding ego—in everything he must be supreme. The author of a good play might compete with his own glory. Most of all in life, Belasco enjoyed taking a poor script and reworking it so much that he had to be acknowledged co-author. As Jane Cowl said, "His passion was for finding poor plays and doing them beautifully." In one script he changed the Midwest heroine to a Cherokee Indian, and the locale to an Indian reservation. In part this was done so that exotic Lenore Ulric might appear as a lightly garbed Indian maiden, but it also allowed D.B. to demonstrate his prodigious talents as a rewriter. At the box office such violent revising may have worked, but it hardly added up to art.

To Belasco, a rehearsal meant assembling a group of actors and playing on their emotions like a virtuoso at a giant console. Rehearsals also meant an opportunity to devise the stunts and realistic stage effects for which he was famous. His two most notable accomplishments in this field were Mrs. Leslie Carter's swing on the bell-clapper in *The Heart of Maryland* and the drops of blood in *The Girl of the Golden West* which fell on the sheriff's white handkerchief to reveal the presence of wounded Dick Johnson in the loft above. Belasco was also a fiend for realism. When a mob was needed, he employed a mob. When an actor was supposed to eat, he ate. In *The Return of Peter Grimm* an actor unhappily munched his way through a meal at each performance. By the same token, the tulips in Peter Grimm's garden were real tulips.

A play called *The Governor's Lady* required a scene in a Child's restaurant. An enraptured Mr. Dave set about duplicating this in stupendous detail: steam table, coat racks, marble-top tables, plate-glass window bearing the inverted legend CHILD'S. Members of the cast seated at tables ate the wheat cakes prepared onstage. For *The Women*, he enthusiastically constructed the lobby of a Washington hotel, with a switchboard and phone booths. Offstage an elevator could be heard operating, while through a window the audience viewed the Capitol dome. Other producers were content to indicate such backgrounds, rather than spell them out in such amazing detail. This made an interviewer ask Belasco the reason for his insistence on unflinching realism. The Master responded: "When I set a scene representing a Child's restaurant, how can I expect to hold the attention of my audience unless I show them a scene that looks real? They see it, recognize it, accept it, and then, if the actors do their part, the audience forgets that it isn't looking into a real place."

Belasco's bag of tricks was bottomless. In *The Boomerang*, he faced a script containing a twenty-five-minute stretch of dialogue spoken by characters sitting prosaically in a living room. He brightened it by using lighting to enhance the moods of the characters. The stage was dim at the beginning, with only the face of the speaker illuminated. As another spoke, he got up to push a button which turned on the chandelier. Another character turned this off and switched on floor lamps. In all, Belasco loved lighting, employing it as a composer would use music as symphonic accompaniment to a poem. His electric switchboard at the Belasco Theatre was the largest in the country. With lights themselves he experimented endlessly, covering with colored silks to achieve far-away effects. The same attention was given to costume. He believed: "Every particle of color used on the stage, every ray of light cast upon its scenes, must be carefully calculated to symbolize mood, interpret meaning, and direct and strengthen emotional appeal."

At rehearsals Belasco was gray-haired and soft-voiced, benevolent in his clerical garb, and patient in working to get proper effects. He functioned best after midnight, causing a devoted staff to call him a human owl. When actors who had been rehearsing through one day wearied in the early hours of the next, the Master had a number of psychological tricks calculated to arouse sluggish talent. One required a two-dollar watch. Apparently in a fury at a recalcitrant cast, he would draw the watch from his pocket, hurl it angrily on the stage. Then he recoiled in horror at what he had done. Falling to his knees he moaned, "My mother's watch, her last gift to me! Oh, Mother, dear Mother, darling, dearest Mother!" Carefully gathering the broken bits he cupped them in hands pressed to his chest. Lifting his fine head to his Maker, he crooned, "I am so evil, such an evil, tired old man, so tired, so evil, so old." Then, turning to the cast, he would plead, "Can't you do a little bit better for me, please?"

They always could.

Belasco firmly believed that by smashing things he could inspire actors to greater heights. Mary Pickford forced her way in to see D.B. when she reached the tender age of thirteen. Earnestly she informed him, "I think I'm at the crossroads of my life. I've got to make good between now and the time I'm twenty."

Impressed by such precocious determination, Belasco hired her for *The Warrens of Virginia*. Miss Pickford vividly recalls the night the Governor stopped rehearsal to advance upon a glass jar supposedly full of molasses. He tasted the contents and emitted a roar, at which a cringing stage manager confessed that the jar held maple syrup. This drove Mr. Dave to a fury, for when a Belasco script read jar-of-molasses it had to be molasses. Seizing the offending jar, he dashed it to the stage, though under his feet lay an expensive Oriental rug. He began jumping on the jar, grinding its contents deeper into the rug. Like others present, little Mary was both fascinated and stimulated by this performance. "To me David Belasco is like the King of England, Julius Caesar, and Napoleon all rolled into one," she thought.

Sometimes Belasco's tantrums were real. More often they were shock-therapy, effective in early-morning hours. Belasco was skilled in other ways of rousing talent. When an actor gave a particularly bad performance in rehearsal, D.B. dismissed the rest of the cast to throw an arm around the offender's shoulders. "I want to thank you for that performance," he said, in mellow tones. "The climax of your scene was one of the loveliest moments I have ever witnessed in the theatre. The way you listened! Your concentration was superb! The way emotion took hold of you and horror and disgust appeared on your face and mounted in your body, the way you swept upstage and back again, speaking your lines so vehemently, with such intensity! It was a great moment!" From then on, it *was* a great moment. As the distinguished English actor H. Reeves-Smith rehearsed a role, Belasco was heard to murmur something, as if pondering aloud. Then to himself a little louder he said, "No, no, perhaps the way he is interpreting is better." Reeves-Smith was intrigued. "Let me try it your way, Governor," he suggested. Belasco tugged the silver forelock. "Forget I said anything, my dear fellow," he urged. Reeves-Smith's eagerness increased.

"Let me try it, at least, D.B.," he begged. Belasco reluctantly assented, and of course his interpretation remained.

Belasco seldom left the theatre on Forty-fourth Street which bore his name. He worked in an ornate office crammed with memories of his productions, among them an authentic sedan chair. A spotlight shone down on him from above, and some who came to worship at the shrine recall him sitting on a raised dais. George Arliss, offered a part in *The Darling of the Gods*, returned to see Belasco in his office a day after the offer. An obsequious member of the staff immediately led him to the Presence. Arliss writes: "Although some twenty-four hours had elapsed since my former visit, it was obvious that Mr. Belasco had never moved since I left him. He had waited patiently and silently, perhaps without food or water, for my return. . . . That, at any rate, was the impression I gained."

From this picturesque office a door led into a lavish bedroom, dominated by a mighty four-poster. One bedroom wall was painted to resemble a bay window, and from the soft depths of the bed Belasco was able to push buttons which lighted the window, creating sunrise or sunset. Numerous ingenues were offered the opportunity to rehearse in this bedroom, for the lechery of the Bishop of Broadway increased with age. "I have never felt over twenty-five and I shall never see a woman looking older than twenty-one," he confided late in life.

Belasco not only kissed but told, and girls who succumbed to his blandishments soon found that all Broadway knew. One aspiring actress on whom he cast a liquid eye was radiant young Jeanne Eagels. He invited her to dinner (his office included a small kitchen). At meal's end he mentioned that the nearby bedroom was his seduction chamber and that tonight he wished to use it rapidly, since some male business associates were scheduled to arrive. Miss Eagels had no intention of being seduced, and tartly said so. At this, Belasco excused himself, to disappear into the bedroom. The shrewd girl applied eye to keyhole and saw the Master vigorously rumpling his sheets. When the business associates arrived he obviously planned to indicate the bed and claim another conquest. The indignant girl flung open the door and ordered the Master to straighten the bed. Then the two sat tight-lipped until the guests arrived, at which lovely Jeanne flounced off.

Belasco's professional and amorous activity brought him great satisfaction, together with rich dividends in money and fame. But it did not commensurately enrich the theatre. As his biographer Craig Timberlake has pointed out in the book *The Bishop of Broadway*, Belasco offered only one classic in his long career. This was the *Merchant of Venice* with David Warfield, a $250,000 failure. His most important production over fifty years of self-centered activity was *The Easiest Way*, which, though a milestone, was a dubious work of art. For the rest, his plays are all but forgotten. Who recalls *The Return of Peter Grimm, Seven Chances, The Lady in Blue, The Very Minute, A Good Little Devil, The Boomerang, The Man Inside?* Or *Marie-Odile*, the story of a nun raped by a German soldier, which one critic branded as "lacking in cumulative force, in human appeal, in every essential of dramatic quality."

The Governor did much better in the department of talent development. "There must be heart, heart, heart," he rallied actors who worked under him. "Soul is only a glow. The definite thing is the heart, the capacity to feel. Intelligence is secondary, but it is desirable." On this basis he nurtured a dazzling array of talents, among them Warfield, Blanche Bates, Frances Starr, Ina Claire, Lionel Atwill, Jane Cowl, and Lenore Ulric. Yet all actors did not respond to him. Katharine Cornell, who as a beginner appeared in *Tiger Cats*, says, "He didn't understand me and I didn't understand him."

In the end, Belasco's eternal ego and the theatrical stunts he adored vitiated the genius he possessed. The Master presented 115 plays on Broadway and the best one sympathetic biographer can say of them is: "They were skillfully and vividly staged, influenced fashion, introduced catchwords, and were important in the topical history of the times."

White-haired, white-collared Mr. Dave, seated in splendor in his cluttered office with the door to his seduction chamber close at hand, might or might not be pleased to agree with this.

Around such titans as Cohan and Belasco swirled a group of producers whose personalities increased the switch in climate from Theatre to Broadway. In the more prominent of them were to be found the rugged character traits of the buccaneer or, in some cases, the svelte skills of the faro dealer. Where a top producer of the Theatre might rise from the ranks of actors or advance men, his Broadway counterpart often came from outside the profession. From the number who reached Broadway after managing prizefighters, it can almost be said that some actually fought their way to the top.

This, however, is not to disparage the theatrical know-how of such types. The playwright George Broadhurst said that the successful producer must feel as instinctively about theatre craftsmanship as does a playwright. The only difference is that the producer cannot write. The new group of producers—they came from Harvard as well as from sweaty ringside dressing rooms—had this instinct. At the same time, they were inclined to see the drama less as artistry than as an exciting gamble. Such producers acted on hunches, played angles. They were the men who would dominate the theatre in the Roaring Twenties. . . .

Conspicuous among such producers was William A. Brady. He was middle-aged, cigar-chewing, beetle-browed, and profanely colorful. Like Belasco, Bill Brady hailed from San Fran-

cisco where he started as a boy peanut-vendor in playhouses.
Next he became a producer of small-time shows. After this, he
detoured to the management of prizefighters, where he capped
his career with the fabulous success story of Gentleman Jim Corbett, who slew the mighty John L. Sullivan. Brady's adventures
in the teeming world of sports gave him an endless fund of hearty
anecdotes. When in later years he wrote his autobiography, he
devoted nine-tenths of the book to these exciting years, with
the remainder devoted to theatre days.

Colorful, vigor-stuffed Bill Brady was the husband of the
star Grace George, who was small, talented, and fiery. Husband
and wife were outstandingly Irish in temperament, and when
Miss George appeared in Brady productions (as she often did)
sparks flew. According to Guthrie McClintic, who acted as
stage manager for Brady-George plays, "No two people I ever
knew battled more in the theatre than Grace George and her
husband."

At rehearsals Brady was living tribute to the Broadhurst dic-
tum that a good producer can do everything but write. He sat
in the darkened auditorium, slouch hat down over eyes, chewing
a cigar, mumbling to himself. The noise of the mumbling easily
reached the stage, where actors tried not to be disconcerted. All
at once the listening man would detect a flaw in an actor's reading, or spy one in a stage movement. The mumbles mounted to
shouts, a type of direction which in McClintic's words was
"electric—it was right; it was embarrassing that it should be—but
it was: the whole stage would light up."

William A. Brady carried through as a man of multifarious
talents by being one of the few producers in history who liked
to act. When a performer in a Brady production fell ill, requiring
the boss to substitute, he was a happy man indeed. Brady was an
excellent judge of acting in others, but himself dreadful. His
voice, so terrifying at rehearsals, only sounded loud from the

stage. To express sorrow he beat his barrel chest. Offstage, Brady was a man who found tact impossible and had great trouble in masking his true emotions. At one point in his career he joined with two other producers, all supposedly working for mutual gain. Called upon to speak at a theatrical dinner, Brady rose to pay graceful tribute to his two partners, saying that together they were The Three Musketeers of Broadway. Then his true feelings burst forth and he wound up thunderously, "One for all and all for William A. Brady!"

Up to this point, Brady had scored with two tremendous successes—*Way Down East,* early in his career, and *The Man Who Came Back,* by Jules Eckert Goodman, in 1916. He presented numerous other plays which were great successes, and, with the considerable sums earned from these hits, he built a theatre called the Playhouse on West Forty-eighth Street. Even the fearless Brady wondered if people would travel so far north to see a play. They would. Brady's first production at the Playhouse was *Bought and Paid For,* a play by George Broadhurst, in which a millionaire marries a telephone hello-girl. It was a hit, and others began to think of building theatres above Forty-fifth Street.

Brady's well-honed gambling instincts paid off with the Playhouse and its George Broadhurst play. But with another script the rugged man's take-it-or-leave-it attitude led to a tragedy of errors. This came with Bayard Veiller's *Within the Law,* already turned down by five producers before it was offered to Brady by Selwyn and Company, play agents. The heroine of *Within the Law*—as we have seen—was a lovely shopgirl sent to jail for alleged stealing. Brady visualized this part for fiery Grace George, who scornfully rejected it. Maybe this robbed her husband of his enthusiasm, for next he handed the script to Broadhurst (his pet playwright) for revision. He cast dignified Emily Stevens as the heroine and provided *Within the Law* with a perfunctory Chicago opening. Play-agent Arch Selwyn and his partner Crosby Gaige were enraged at this, and allowed themselves the luxury of telling Brady off at the end of the first performance. Instead of knocking the two young men down and stamping on them, as Brady admirers might expect, the burly producer was gently amused. "If you boys think you are so goddam smart," he said, "why don't you produce it yourselves? I'll give it back to you for what it has cost me so far."

Up to now Selwyn and Gaige had operated happily as play agents. Now they took a giant step toward becoming play producers. "How much is that?" they wanted to know.

"About ten thousand bucks," Brady answered.

In a series of lightning moves the young men raised the money. They summoned Veiller to eradicate the Broadhurst changes and with Jane Cowl as the wronged shopgirl *Within the Law* opened to become a landmark of suspense melodrama and a top money-grosser. The gentlemanly Crosby Gaige found it easy to resist mentioning this to Bill Brady. Arch Selwyn could not. "Got any more plays to sell, Mr. Brady?" he asked when next they met. Once more Brady displayed astonishing control. "Young man," he boomed, "it will give me a great deal of pleasure if you will get the hell out of my sight."

Brady was a much-admired man. "He had more charm than was right for any one person to have," Guthrie McClintic has written. The prolific playwright Owen Davis adds: "Of all the men I have ever known, Mr. Brady remains the most fabulous figure. . . . He is in a class by himself."

This last is truly remarkable because for years Owen Davis worked in association with Al H. Woods, a man considered by a large segment of the Broadway populace to be more colorful than Brady. Woods was dubbed Saint Al by Percy Hammond, the drama critic whose daily reviews were called venom from contented rattlesnakes. Yet Al Woods was hardly the type to be anticipated in Heaven above. He addressed everyone as "Sweetheart"—as Cohan and Corbett called the world "Kid." He could hit a brass spittoon across any uncrowded room. He was tall, with a large, untidy, Beethoven-type head. One of his eyes was disconcertingly walled. A large cigar was perpetually clamped between the teeth of a wide mouth, and from around it poured a stream of flavorsome, profanity-embellished talk.

Woods spent large amounts of money on his attire, specializing in expensive silk shirts in a day when these were a rarity. Yet as soon as he donned them, suits and shirts looked as if he had passed a sleepless night in them. The rumpled, pithy man had a likable (to many, a lovable) side. He was practically uneducated, a fact which failed completely to give him an inferiority complex. "He was vain, in a humorous way," a friend says. Woods was warmhearted and cynical. Some say he was not altogether to be trusted. But he had a neat flair for the theatre, and this alone seemed enough to render him an unusually happy man. Broadway treasured him for it.

Woods was born in Budapest and brought to New York's East Side at age three. From the moment he learned what took place inside a playhouse he by-passed education to hang around the magic precincts. His favorite theatre was Miner's Bowery and from this he came to believe that all entertainment was vaudeville or the lurid melodrama of the day. He was a young man when *The Bowery After Dark* struck him as a good title for a melodrama. He went to a printer, who helped him concoct a poster of a beautiful girl chased through a Bowery night by a predatory thug. With this lurid scene and the title, he visited Theodore Kremer, a fast-writing play craftsman of the day. "Write me a play to fit the title and match the poster," he instructed. Such orders were commonplace to Kremer, who sat

down and did the play while Woods ranged the East Side raising $1500 to put it on. *The Bowery After Dark* ran for two
prosperous years, netting $75,000.

Al Woods' producer's progress can be best charted by the
titles of his plays. After the success of *The Bowery After Dark*,
he cast around for new melodramas. Discovering an ideal play-
wright in Owen Davis, a young New Englander just out of
Harvard, he began presenting them at assembly-line speed. It
is hard to know whether to laugh or sob over the names of some
—*Nellie, the Beautiful Cloak Model; Bertha, the Beautiful Sewing Machine Girl; Edna, the Beautiful Typewriter Girl; Why
Girls Go Wrong; The Fatal Wedding* (with Mary Miles Minter);
*Queen of the White Slaves; Secret Service Sam; Chinatown
Charlie; Convict 999.* Woods acted as his own advance man on the
Road for these productions, and gained a solid foundation in
theatre ways. Outside New York his plays sometimes had financial vicissitudes and during one of these Al won a wife. Stranded
in the Midwest, he stepped into a pawnshop to raise traveling
money on a diamond. Behind the awesome wicket stood the
pawnbroker's daughter—Rose, the Beautiful Pawnshop Girl.
She recognized Woods as part of a touring troupe and, after con-
fiding that she had $500 in savings, indicated an urge to enter
show business. Still, she insisted on taking any such drastic step
as an honest woman. Woods took the hint and married her. With
the $500 he transported his company to the next town. The mar-
riage turned out to be long and compatible.

In time the public wearied of Woods' melodramas—pioneer
films like *The Great Train Robbery* seemed more tempting.
Woods tired of them as well, deftly moving onward to the
second stage of his career. Now his name became associated with
naughty bedroom farces. Again titles best tell the story—*Up in
Mabel's Room; Getting Gertie's Garter; Modest Suzanne; His
Bridal Night* (with the Dolly Sisters). Splitting from Owen

Davis (who went on to win a Pulitzer Prize), Woods began to depend on the talents of Avery Hopwood, whose naughty-farce formula relied on mistaken identity plus much bedroom door slamming, quick glimpses of several girls in lingerie, and a plot that seemed salacious until the final curtain, when all resolved into complete innocence. Nevertheless, Woods was criticized for producing such salty plays. A man with a shrewd publicity sense as well as a breezy humor, he solemnly announced an Avery Hopwood adaptation of *Othello*, to be called *Up in Desdemona's Room*. With this, someone said, Woods was going from bed to worse.

Together with bedroom farces, Woods also enriched himself by managing the career of the female impersonator Julian Eltinge. Indeed, Saint Al may have been the man behind the phony barroom brawl which was the cornerstone of Eltinge's rapt acceptance by the public. As managed by Woods, Eltinge not only headlined in vaudeville but starred in Broadway revues. He even attained the pinnacle of Broadway fame—a theatre on West Forty-second Street built in his name. On the top floor of the Eltinge Theatre, Al Woods established an office which contained so many mementos of melodrama days that it was likened to the reception room of a honky-tonk. An important feature of the decor was a life-size figure of a blackamoor smoking a cigar.

Woods employed numerous relatives on his staff and these, together with hordes of importunate actors and playwrights, made a scene of daily confusion. In the midst of it all Woods functioned with complete calm. Those who entered were greeted through a screen of Havana smoke by a friendly, "Hello, sweetheart." On Woods' desk towered a pile of playscripts, and sometimes he flipped through the pages of one of these. Most of them came from unknown authors and here Al claimed guidance by a special intuition. "I'll always take a chance on an

unknown if they smell just right," he would explain mysteriously.

When an established playwright read to him, Woods leaned far
back in his chair, with feet crossed atop the desk, shutting off
sight of his face. Only billowing cigar smoke attested his presence. Woods purchased an unusual number of the scripts read or
submitted to him, and once took a play called *Between the Sheets*
on its suggestive title alone. Most of the plays he bought never saw
the bright lights of Broadway. For Woods himself was exceedingly clever at devising tricky plots. His favorite method of production was to give one of his plots to a playwright he trusted, then
produce the result. When the playwright reappeared to read
the play for approval, Woods often refused to listen. "Why do
I have to hear it?" he would ask. "I got to produce the goddam
thing anyway." Occasionally an author grew irate with Saint Al
over an unproduced play or some other matter. One angry
writer diplomatically handed Woods a gift cigar before launch-
ing into a tirade over injuries done. Woods lit-up and after a
few puffs broke in to inquire, "Did you give me this cigar?" The
playwright admitted he had. "Then whatever I done to you,
sweetheart, we're even," Woods announced.

When producing a play, Woods hired director and actors and
sat back to await results. "He did not direct, he produced," one
associate has recalled. Even so, he had a participant's full enjoyment at rehearsals. "I sit in that dark theatre," he told an interviewer, "and I feel as if I had written the play, was performing
the principal roles, and writing the rosiest reviews. I see hundreds of thousands of people clamoring for seats and I stand in
the lobby thrilled to the hat by the rumpus I've caused."

The producer of *Getting Gertie's Garter* was capable of efforts that smacked of art (in the twenties he imported France's
Sacha Guitry and Yvonne Printemps). He offered plays starring
beautiful Elsie Ferguson, formidable Mrs. Patrick Campbell, and

jaunty Douglas Fairbanks. One Woods success was *The Yellow Ticket*, with Florence Reed, Theodore Roberts, and a John Barrymore who a few years before made Broadway history by forgetting his first opening night in favor of an evening's tippling. Now a dashing, mustachioed leading man, Jack Barrymore was still full of high jinks. In *The Yellow Ticket* he became annoyed at the sharp manner in which Theodore Roberts poked his chest during an argument scene. One night Barrymore took off his hat and hung it on Roberts' index finger. *The Yellow Ticket* was a lurid Woods effort, the ticket being the one which identified a prostitute in Russia. In it, Florence Reed emotionally laments the need to carry such identification. One night Barrymore handed her a strip of Interborough Subway tickets.

It was a serious John Barrymore who showed up in the Eltinge Theatre office one afternoon to say, "Al, I've got a play. Other producers have turned it down. I want to do it with Lionel, and we want you to take a chance without reading it." "Can't you tell me something about it?" Woods asked plaintively. "Well," said Barrymore, "in one scene Lionel calls me a bastard and I hit him over the head and knock him cold." This was enough for Woods. "You're on, sweetheart," he said, "I'll do it." The play was *Peter Ibbetson*, a sensitive drama which did much to erase Woods' stigma of bedroom farce. It also brought Al into contact with Edward Sheldon, who revised *Peter Ibbetson* for this country. To the amazement of Broadway, the uncouth Woods and the elegant Sheldon made a superb working combine. "Me for mass, Ned for class," Woods explained.

With *Peter Ibbetson*, Woods became something of a legend. It was said that he slept with the electric lights on and that the rich appointments of his bedroom included gold spittoons. Woods distrusted the routine operations of banks and kept his profits in cash in a safe-deposit box. Sums in the box varied from $100,000 to $1,000,000, depending on the extent of Saint Al's prosperity. Proudly he escorted friends to the vault to display the crisp thousand-dollar bills comprising his hoard. The only other key to the vault was kept by his wife Rose. Al was abroad during the dire days in 1929 when the stock market toppled. In New York a family friend persuaded Rose Woods to use the contents of the box to buy falling stocks on margin. When Woods returned he was broke. He remained nearly that way for the rest of his life.

Yet until this miserable moment Al was gloriously solvent. After World War I he seemed to go abroad as often as had Charles Frohman. Woods carried a passport in his pocket at all times, and made reservations on every outgoing liner on the chance that he might suddenly feel like a trip overseas. He loved diamonds and at Christmas proffered a help-yourself basket of these and other gems to his office staff. He particularly favored a diamond stickpin bright as a beacon. One dark night he found himself facing two burly men larcenously attracted to this stone. "Hey, fellas," Woods whined. "Wanta buy a big diamond for a couple of bucks? I got nowhere to sleep." The men quickly lost interest.

Peter Ibbetson was a giant moneymaker, in part because handsome John Barrymore shaved off his mustache for it. When he stepped onstage on the opening night, women in the audience gasped. While *Peter Ibbetson* prospered in New York, Woods operated twenty simultaneous road shows of other plays, paying an annual $200,000 in railroad fares. He made further money from a dramatization of the *Potash and Perlmutter* dialect stories, starring Alexander Carr and Sam Bernard. Friendly enemies onstage, Carr and Bernard became bitter foes off. This was largely because of Carr's aggressiveness, and when the play ended, gentle Sam Bernard made a pilgrimage to his mother's grave. Standing beside it, he vowed that never again would he appear on a stage with Alexander Carr. When Woods announced production of a second *Potash and Perlmutter*, he was reminded of Sam Bernard's vow. Al was unmoved. "Never mind, sweetheart," he said. "I'll fix that. I'll persuade him it was his mother-in-law's grave he swore on."

It is a tribute to Al Woods' peculiar charm that he did this.

When Woods scoured the East Side for money to produce *The Bowery After Dark*, he met a slim, ingratiating youngster named Sam H. Harris. He, too, was the son of immigrants, and his tenement home lay a block from the Oliver Street neighborhood of Al Smith. Harris, also stage-struck, steered Woods to a well-heeled nephew of political leader Big Tim Sullivan. Thus *The Bowery After Dark* and subsequent melodramas were presented by the firm of Sullivan, Harris, and Woods, which listed the partners in reverse order of importance. Sam Harris was a sports enthusiast. In a gym he observed a whirlwind fighter named Terry McGovern. Harris became his manager, guiding him along the championship route and starring him in *Bertha, the Beautiful Sewing Machine Girl*.

In time, the firm of Sullivan, Harris, and Woods dissolved. On the day George M. Cohan cast around for a business-minded partner for *Little Johnny Jones*, he became the one to shake the hand of Sam Harris. Among other things, a mutual interest in baseball drew these two together. They tested potential partnership by attending a game at the Polo Grounds. The afternoon turned out well (presumably the New York team won) and the firm of Cohan and Harris was born. "A wise little guy," Cohan informed Broadway of his new partner. "Never rubs anybody the wrong way, but if you think you can put anything over on him, why, kid, you're a sucker."

Cohan and Harris saw no worth in *Peg o' My Heart*. They rejected *Within the Law* (Sam liked it, George M. did not) and other hits. It made little difference. With Cohan's all-around versatility and Harris' pleasant astuteness the firm could not help but prosper. Cohan's *Seven Keys to Baldpate*, dramatized from the Earl Derr Biggers novel, was a top hit. They also did *The Fortune Hunter* (with John Barrymore), *Officer 666*, *It Pays to Advertise*, and (as coproducers) *On Trial*, the melodrama which for the first time used flashbacks on a stage. Cohan's *Get-Rich-Quick Wallingford* (with Victor Moore and Fay Templeton) was another smash hit, presented at the George M. Cohan Theatre. Harris, the business mind of the pair, was especially pleased at operating a theatre and told interviewer John Peter Toohey: "This *Wallingford* engagement has proved to me that the great thing is to have your own theatre. I'm sold on the idea one thousand per cent. You can make your own terms and plan to open when you want to and not depend on any booking office."

Cohan and Harris began acquiring other theatres, in Chicago as well as New York. However, Sam Harris' euphoria soon vanished. Next he was telling another interviewer what the Syndicate had learned: "I've found it better not to own theatres. When you own them you don't wait until you have a good play—you put on a play to keep the place open."

George C. Tyler was the producer who brought the Irish Players to this country, for a rowdy opening of Synge's *Playboy of the Western World*. The flavorsome speech of the Irish actors (led by J. M. Kerrigan) and the shock-impact of the iconoclastic play brought stimulus to American drama. Tyler also imported Mrs. Patrick Campbell and Eleanora Duse. He was born in Chillicothe, Ohio, and in a long career produced many hit plays, including *The Garden of Allah* and *Alias Jimmy Valentine*.

Yet Tyler was never content to produce. He was a theatre carpenter who liked to match the right playwright with a germ of a plot he (Tyler) had come across. He heard that Israel Zangwill was impressed by a newspaper story about an English slavey who inherited a million dollars. CAN YOU DELIVER PLAY ON IT IN A MONTH? he cabled Zangwill. So *Merely Mary Ann* was born. He next encountered George Arliss at a moment when the cryptic English actor seemed blocked in a distinguished career. Arliss had come here in support of Mrs. Campbell, remained to act for Belasco in *The Darling of the Gods,* toured with Mrs. Fiske in strenuous repertory, and won stardom in Molnar's *The Devil.* After that the monocled man had difficulty in finding another role. Tyler understood perfectly. When the two met he said, "If you've got any good ideas maybe we could get a play written for you."

Arliss recollects that he used up thirty-five minutes suggesting ideas to which Tyler grunted dissent. Finally Arliss stood up to leave, as an afterthought murmuring, "Of course, I once had the impression that a play written round Disraeli would be interesting." No grunt came from Tyler. Instead he said reverently, "That's a damned good idea." Tyler journeyed to London, where he interested the playwright Louis N. Parker in it. After suitable labor pains, Parker completed a script which was first tested in Chicago. When finally *Disraeli* opened in New York, it was smooth as silk. Because the opening was so flawless, legend has it that *Disraeli* was one of those rare plays perfect from the beginning. Yet the record shows it played through a full season in Chicago, and during that time much tinkering and switching went on. Like other perfect plays, the silken *Disraeli* became silken only after hard work.

For all his genius at matching authors and ideas, George Tyler's intuition shone even brighter in discovering actors. He became the mentor of a child actress named Helen Hayes, following her inauspicious debut in the Lew Fields musical *Old Dutch.* After watching Lynn Fontanne in rehearsal, he ordered her part expanded. He performed similar prodigies with Laurette Taylor and Dustin Farnum of early years, and Glenn Hunter, Alfred Lunt, and Jeanne Eagels of later. Where other producers seemed to be gambling with money, Tyler (who may have loved money as well) always gave the impression of gambling on talent. This fact was recognized by Nat Goodwin, who had been plucked by Tyler from a career-tailspin to play the role of Fagin in *Oliver Twist*. Goodwin urges: "If there are any laurel wreaths in your neighborhood, dear reader, buy one and bestow it on the brow of George C. Tyler."

On the smiling surface it appears that good fortune—or Lady Luck—played a substantial part in the prosperity of Crosby Gaige, the young man who joined with Arch Selwyn to remove *Within the Law* from William A. Brady's grasp.

Gaige was born in Skunk Hollow, in the Erie Canal region of New York state. He discovered himself theatre-struck at Columbia, after joining with a classmate named Roi Cooper Megrue to write the Varsity Show. This brought contact with Elizabeth Marbury, Broadway's pioneer play agent. After graduation Megrue went to work for Miss Marbury, while Gaige joined the office of Alice Kauser, who had mastered the trade under Miss Marbury. To add to the confusion, Arch Selwyn had once worked for Miss Kauser (Gaige had taken his place). Next he tempted Gaige into the fold of Selwyn and Company, Play Brokers, who specialized in melodramas like *Nellie, the Beautiful Cloak Model*.

A stroke of good fortune that befell Gaige changed all this. Leafing through a morning paper in 1905, he noted that the famed English playwright, Henry Arthur Jones, was to arrive in New York that day. On a hunch Gaige sped to the Cunard pier. He had no difficulty in locating Jones, who was known to affect a red spade beard. Stepping forward with an offer of assistance, Gaige found himself rebuffed. "I have come over to

confer with Charles Frohman," said Jones coolly. "I'm sure someone from the Frohman office is here to meet me." But no one
was, and after an interval Jones allowed Gaige to escort him to
a hotel. Here the two sat down to a luncheon of caviar and ruddy
duck which may have put Gaige on the road to becoming the
noted epicure he was in later years. By meal's end (the dessert
was strawberries, the wine Chambertin '96), Henry Arthur
Jones had become a client of Selwyn and Company. A short
time later Gaige married and Jones presented the young couple
with a European honeymoon as a wedding gift. In those days
playwrights could afford such pro-consular gestures.

Gaige worked as a play agent until the huge success of *Within
the Law*. After it, he and Selwyn were producers, offering plays
by Roi Cooper Megrue, Avery Hopwood, Margaret Mayo, and
Selwyn himself. The two had a long succession of hits, and for
one opening night Gaige dispatched sets of sterling-silver tickets
made by Tiffany to each newspaper critic.

Yet luck did not always beam on Crosby Gaige. He once read
a script called *According to the Evidence*, by Elmer Reitzenstein,
a young man who identified himself as a law clerk in a downtown
office. It was a courtroom melodrama, which flashed amazingly
back into the past for illustration of its testimony. Gaige de-
voured it, and dispatched an urgent note to the author. Gaige was
a methodical man who liked to arrive at work early and eat lunch
with the rest of the world. So he was out when young Reitzenstein came uptown on his own lunch hour. The author turned
to the office of Arthur Hopkins, who had also expressed interest
in the script. Hopkins kept producers' hours, sleeping late and
arriving at his office shortly before noon. He was freshly en-
sconced behind his desk when the playwright appeared. Hopkins took the play and went to Cohan and Harris for assistance
in production.

The play was retitled *On Trial*, and the playwright's name

shaved to Elmer Rice. It made over $500,000 for its producers, and a solid reputation for Rice. To Crosby Gaige it became one of life's great disappointments. Yet he was partly assuaged when *Why Marry?* by Jesse Lynch Williams won the first Pulitzer Prize. Gaige was its producer, Roi Cooper Megrue the director, and in it, playing his last role on any stage (he died soon after), was the estimable actor Nat Goodwin.

Along with these robust figures went the so-called gentlemen-producers. Outstanding among them was Winthrop Ames. New England-born, Harvard-bred, Ames was tall, fastidious, formal, aloof—and somehow warm and kindly. His physical person as well as his productions carried the stamp of quality, and with varying degrees of approval he was called the first gentleman among producers. Because of his superlative taste Ames was chosen to manage the New Theatre, where the vastness of stage and scenery contributed to a fiasco. He vowed that once his New Theatre tenure ended he would build his own theatre, the smallest possible. He did so in 1909, and his Little Theatre on Forty-fourth Street opened with Galsworthy's *The Pigeon.* Ames' new theatre seated only 299 people, but it was a miniature jewel and the admiration it won opened up the blocks west of Broadway to theatres, as Brady's Playhouse did for northern Broadway regions. The Little Theatre office was a courtly place, for the staff had orders to be polite to all aspiring actors and playwrights. Among numerous other productions, Winthrop Ames offered an impeccable *Affairs of Anatol,* with John Barrymore and five leading ladies, two of them Marguerite Clark and Doris Keane; *The Green Goddess,* with George Arliss; and probably the finest Gilbert and Sullivan ever seen in America.

Only slightly less gentlemanly than Ames were Charles Hopkins, a graduate of Yale, and Arthur Hopkins who (like George

Tyler) was born in Ohio. The two were not related by blood,
but in taste and high artistic integrity might be brothers. Arthur
Hopkins began a distinguished career with a bit of treacle called
Poor Little Rich Girl. After his success with *On Trial,* he built
the Plymouth Theatre, where he offered Alla Nazimova in *The
Wild Duck,* then began nurturing the remarkable talents of John
Barrymore. He presented the vibrant actor in Tolstoy's *Redemption, The Jest, Richard III,* and, finally, *Hamlet.* Quite properly,
it is Arthur Hopkins who best put into words the reason why
Barrymore, finest actor of his generation, failed to achieve his
full potential. "He was that rarest of phenomena," writes Hopkins, "the actor who hates to act. He loved to create [a role] but
once that had been accomplished he was like an artist who could
not bear to look again upon a finished painting, or a writer who
was nauseated by a glimpse of some past creation. . . . He did
not want the slavery that continuous service in the theatre
demands."

Despite the activities of its gentlemen-producers, Broadway
remained a turbulent place. The gambler often appeared more
at home than the man of superior taste.

There is the story of a producer named Walter Hast, who
picked up the discarded pieces of a Crosby Gaige production
(just as Gaige and Selwyn had picked up *Within the Law* from
Brady). Where Gaige had put Jane Cowl into his *Within the
Law,* Walter Hast substituted a vivid, supercharged redhead
named Francine Larrimore. He also renamed the play *Scandal.*
Having done this much, he was far from optimistic—instinct
told him he had a flop on his hands. It was a moment for cleverness, and he set about selling one hundred per cent of the play
before its opening night. He did this so easily that he found
another group of investors and sold a second hundred per cent.
After this, he sold a third.

Scandal, with Francine Larrimore, opened to rave reviews, which placed Hast in one of the oddest predicaments ever known to man. If he made $10,000 the first week (as he did) he would have to pay out $30,000 to backers. The unhappy man stalled by spending large amounts for newspaper advertising and billboard space. This only drew more people to the box office. Finally, he assembled his multitude of backers and made a tearful confession. The startled group agreed to adjust shares drastically downward, and charitably kept Hast on as production manager.

Broadway was amused—but hardly more. Things like that were happening all the time!

11: *OVER THERE!*

On the night when Frances Starr as Laura Murdock spoke the shocking final lines of *The Easiest Way*, the restaurant known as Rector's suffered a body blow. "I'm going out to Rector's to make a hit, and to hell with the rest" was an unmistakable (if misleading) suggestion that girls of no virtue used the lobster palace as a happy hunting ground.

As a result, the brand-new Rector's Hotel practically suffered a boycott and one night George Rector stood forlornly contemplating the ornate emptiness of his lobby. As if on stage-cue, George M. Cohan strutted in to inquire the cause of Rector's woe. Rector told his sad story and Cohan, who had a home-suite in the nearby Hotel Knickerbocker, said out of the side of his mouth, "I'm going to live in your hotel. Rector's has always been a great little place. You're a great little guy and so am I. I'm going to live here by the year."

The patronage of Mr. Broadway attracted other Rector habitués and sons of habitués, but not enough. For five years George Rector bravely held off bankruptcy, but during this time his enterprise slowly fell to its knees—the theatre folk to whom he had catered so royally for more than a decade having doomed it. Finally Rector sadly appraised the situation and decided, "Like the bulldog that tackled the marble statue, we have bitten off more than we can chew." Rector's closed its doors. For the first time the Great White Way was without the Supreme Court of Triviality where the swan-necked beauty had dipped perfume on the lump of sugar and happily munched it. Gone forever was the lobster palace of tender memory where anything might happen, a happy state of affairs immortalized in the boy-to-girl verse which ended:

> And we motored down to Rector's
> Where all was gay and bright;
> And by the way, dear empress,
> Who took you home that night?

True Broadwayites were desolated—but not for long. For this there was a reason. The dance craze had hit the Great White Way, and Broadway had begun cavorting madly to music that was a mixture of Negro ragtime and hints of jazz-to-come. No longer did Diamond Jim Brady (who would die in 1917) sit down before his massive meals. Jim had lost his pretty Edna McCauley, and buxom Lillian Russell had also left his side to marry someone else. Now Diamond Jim toured Great White Way night spots in the company of six young girls who surrounded him like tugs around an ocean liner. Through the night he danced with this bevy of beauties, never seeming to tire or visibly wear down. So Rector's with its sedate gypsy orchestra had become an anachronism. The gay places were Casino de Paree, Maxim's, Moulin Rouge, Bustanoby's, and Reisenweber's. This last boasted no less than four active floors. On the first was a dining room; on the second a 400 Club (soon known as the Sophie Tucker Room); on the third a Paradise Room; and on top a Hawaiian Room, where a girl named Doralina danced scandalously barelegged in a grass skirt.

The Great White Way could not claim full credit for the new dance mania. The original impetus stemmed from San Francisco's Barbary Coast by way of a cute trick named Blossom Seeley, who came east to dance in *The Hen Pecks,* a musical produced by Lew Fields. In it Blossom sang the song "Toddlin' the Todolo." While singing, she did a Barbary Coast dance step which did just that—toddled—to the ragtime tune. Up to now it had been difficult to dance to the fast beat of the ragtime popularized by Negroes such as Rosamond and James Weldon Johnson, and boosted (in 1911) to the jazz echelon by Irving Berlin's "Alexander's Ragtime Band." The familiar two-step and waltz were too slow for ragtime jazz. The speedy one-step was better, but dull. The cakewalk, done by Negroes on the variety stage, was difficult. But toddlin', as Blossom Seeley did it, was easy—and fun.

Also prominent in *The Hen Pecks* was the stringy, insouciant dancer-comedian Vernon Castle. (Women adored Vernon, one fervent admirer being the child Helen Hayes, a cast member.) English-born, loose-limbed, and blithely debonair, Vernon had recently shattered feminine hearts by marrying Irene Foote, a flower of New Rochelle society. He had got Irene a small part in *The Hen Pecks* and nightly the two stood in the wings watching Blossom Seeley do her ragtime toddle.

The scene shifts to Paris, where Vernon and Irene sit broke and disconsolate in the middle of a delayed honeymoon. Irene's mother writes from home that, thanks to Blossom Seeley and the svelte dance team of Maurice and Florence Walton, New York has gone frantic over a dance known as the Texas Tommy, the Bunny Hug, the Turkey Trot, the Grizzly Bear—call it what you will. One merely grabs a partner and toddles around the floor, seesawing arms and shoulders in time with the music. Irene and Vernon look at one another, struck by a simultaneous inspiration. Why not dance themselves out of poverty by introducing the Turkey Trot to Paris? . . .

The rest—in a stupendous sort of way—is history. The Castles first danced in Paris, sitting elegantly at a ringside table, rising on cue to sway around the floor to the music of "Alexander's Ragtime Band." Their fame reached America and they were called home. Here the lucky couple made a glorious discovery— their youthful good looks perfectly fitted the new dance craze. (Maurice, of Maurice and Florence, was a sleek fellow, reputed to have broken a wife's neck doing an adagio.) The entire country whirled ecstatically into step behind the handsome Castles as they whisked into the Grizzly Bear, Lame Duck, Half-in-Half, Innovation, and Castle Walk, not to mention a jazzed-up tango, maxixe, and waltz. They danced to "Too Much Mustard" and "Snookie Oookums" at breakfast dances, lunch dances, tea dances, supper dances, and after-midnight dances. Once they did a jazz tango down the aisle at a fashionable wedding. Play agent Elizabeth Marbury, sensing opportunity, took the pair under her capacious wing, opening an elegant East Side establishment called Castle House for afternoon dances. Here Vernon charged one dollar a minute to instruct dowagers in the intricacies of the dance. Soon he asked (and easily got) one hundred dollars an hour. For after-theatre, the Castles opened a Great White Way supper club called Sans Souci, followed by the more elegant Castles-in-the-Air. A host of imitators popped up, but none seemed to have the tremendous style of the Castles. "We were young, clean, and married," Irene explains. All America believed there never had been a man as graceful as lanky Vernon, while Irene was light as vapor and ravishing to look upon. Most important, perhaps, was the fact that the Castles themselves loved every moment of it. "We had a great sense of bubbling joy as we danced," Mrs. Castle says.

The Castles danced so often that their need for new steps and music became desperate. For music they turned to the Negro bandleader James Reese Europe, who had already advanced the cause of ragtime-jazz by presenting two concerts of Europe's

Society Band at Carnegie Hall. The Castles were anxious to extend the boundaries of dancing. Jim Europe, tall and scholarly looking, wished to do the same for syncopated jazz—or jass, as it was sometimes called. "A sort of partnership was formed between the Castles and Jim Europe," reported *The Outlook*. There was little difference between the Bunny Hug, the Turkey Trot, the Grizzly Bear, and other steps. Sometimes even Irene Castle was unsure which dance Vernon was leading her through. But to the delight of the Castles, Jim Europe's syncopated music made each dance seem different.

On Sunday afternoons, Jim Europe and an associate named Ford Dabney traveled to the Castles' home in Manhasset. There the four rehearsed for the week to come. Vernon Castle, whose balance was superb, liked to move fast, carrying Irene into intricate steps at dazzling speed. Jim Europe kept urging him to slow down, *dance* more. One Sunday, Europe refused to play anything but slow music which stressed the back, or *after*, beat heard in the delayed handclapping to Negro jubilee songs. In an effort to match this slowness Vernon found himself rising up on the beat, *holding* the step. So the Fox Trot was born, and with the rhythmic, simple dance the Castles' popularity soared higher.

Everybody's doin' it, doin' it, doin' it, chortled Irving Berlin's latest tune. It was true. The jubilant Castles pirouetted on the crest of a cross-country wave. *Castle House, The Castle Rock, Castles-in-the Air, Mr. and Mrs. Vernon Castle* . . . Irene bobbed her hair and girls across the country stampeded to do likewise. She discarded corsets and that instrument of torture vanished from the American scene. She tossed out petticoats and shortened her skirts. Irene, Vernon, and Jim Europe's Band toured the country in a Whirlwind Dance Contest. THE CASTLES ARE COMING! HOORAY! HOORAY! banners shouted. They went into two-a-day vaudeville, to spend most of a large salary buying the animals they saw abused. Inevitably, Broadway beckoned and the Castles signed to appear in *Watch Your Step*, the first musical to have a score by up-and-coming Irving Berlin.

Watch Your Step was one of those rare shows which from the beginning seems destined for smash success. The fame of the glorious young Castles, the jazz music by Berlin, the blackface-comedy art of Frank Tinney—all these combined to make it sure-fire. "From the beginning *Watch Your Step* was a sure thing and everybody connected with the show knew it," Irene Castle writes. Yet it did contain a surprise. Irene made her first entrance between two rows of chorus boys who musically asked (in the manner of *Florodora's* kind-sirs) how to do the Fox Trot. "You have to watch your step," dainty Irene replied in a voice that sounded like a foghorn. That such an ethereal creature could have a bassoon voice was a stunning shock to the first-night and later audiences. Irene's voice continued shattering throughout the show—it was no trick effect. Yet she danced as divinely as ever, and with Vernon introduced The Syncopated Walk. Most of her admirers easily forgot her voice in favor of her Fox Trot.

Watch Your Step racked up another musical hit for Charles Dillingham, the onetime assistant to Charles Frohman. As a young man Dillingham had attained a contemporary youth's dream by being a cowboy. In middle-age, the word to apply to him was *boulevardier*. An outstanding dresser who always sported a carnation, Dillingham was known as the whitest man on Broadway, where he was cherished for his jollity, quick wit, and practical jokes. Nothing seemed to dent his chuckling amiability. Once he dispatched a new leading lady to an Arnold Daly company playing a Dillingham show in Chicago. Came a frantic wire from Daly, LEADING LADY TERRIBLE. WHY DID YOU SEND ME THIS AWFUL GIRL? Dillingham replied, SHE HAD NEVER SEEN THE STOCK-YARDS.

As every producer must, Dillingham guessed wrong and rejected a play that turned out a hit. After the ovation of the first night, he went backstage, fell to hands and knees, and crawled to the star's dressing room, where he apologized for his poor judgment. Actors enjoyed dealing with Good-Time-Charlie Dillingham because of his jovial kidding and the cosmopolitan bonhomie he radiated. But once outside his Globe Theatre office, laughter died down. The realization struck that Charlie had got the terms he wanted, while the actor had not.

A Dillingham musical was replete with lively tunes and clean comedy of the type supplied by Montgomery and Stone, and later by wholesome Fred Stone alone. Another Dillingham star was tam-o'-shantered Elsie Janis, who looked so hoydenish that Charles Frohman once bought her a play called *The Hoyden* on title alone. Pert and fetchingly all-American, Elsie Janis was Broadway's Sweetheart. She was also respected as a hard worker who since the turn of the century had starred in a succession of hits like *The Vanderbilt Cup, The Slim Princess, The Lady of the Slipper, Miss Information,* and *The Century Girl.*

But whatever the artistic gifts of Elsie Janis, she remains unique for possessing the most terrifying mother Broadway (and perhaps Hollywood) has ever known. The furious skill with which Ma Janis drove contracts for Elsie aroused awe on the part of managers. Ma Janis had decided early that her talented daughter must become a show-business headliner. While Elsie appeared onstage, Ma stood in the wings, tapping time with an iron foot when Elsie sang, calling "Tell 'em another, tell 'em another," when the hoyden gave out with stories. Elsie was an uncanny mimic who at age ten imitated Anna Held so well that she may rate half-credit for popularizing such Held numbers as "The Maiden with the Dreamy Eyes." But no matter where Elsie went, the long shadow of Ma fell over her. As Elsie grew older, shapelier, and pretty, she displayed a deplorable tendency toward falling in love. Ma Janis would not allow this and became adept at killing her daughter's romances, one a crush on Maurice Chevalier.

Through it all Elsie continued to adore Ma, which further endeared her to the sentimental theatrical profession. Elsie was a girl of simple tastes, but Ma preferred a lusher life. She liked automobiles, expensive surroundings, and Nora-Bayes-size suites in hotels. Ma's whims and caprices never ceased. Fred Allen records his pride and joy when assigned a first-floor vaudeville dressing room next to Elsie Janis in Seattle. His happiness was short-lived, however. Ma soon appeared in the doorway to inform him that she and Elsie had so many friends in town that his room was needed for reception purposes. The obliging Fred moved upstairs, and in thanks Ma offered him a bag of cherries.

The public's desire for musical entertainment went far beyond Dillingham shows to a summit inhabited exclusively by Florenz Ziegfeld, whose *Follies* had achieved spectacular heights of lavish, extravagant splendor. Ziegfeld's slogan for his revues— the *Follies* were never plot-musicals—was "Glorifying the American Girl." In line with this, he stocked his shows with a resident group of superlative beauties, among them such famous faces as Dolores, Olive Thomas, Jessica Reed, Vera Maxwell, Lillian Lorraine, Peggy Hopkins Joyce, and Kay Laurell. The Ziegfeld Girl was tall, stately, and long-legged, with the trimmest of ankles. She was busty and full-hipped with a radiant smile, shiny teeth, and an indefinable magnetism which caused Ziegfeld to pick her from a group of beauties who looked exactly like her. In stunning gowns against wondrous backgrounds, the Follies Girls paraded haughtily across the stage or posed immovable in magnificent Ben Ali Haggin tableaux. Occasionally (for fleeting seconds) one or all the Follies Girls appeared with bosoms artistically bare.

While his girls populated the stage, Ziggy—as favored beauties were allowed to call him—was a happy man. The hawk-faced, nasal-voiced producer loved luxury, and when feasting eyes on the beauty, opulence, and richness of his girl-scenes he was thoroughly in his element. But when comedians were onstage Ziegfeld fidgeted. He had to admit that comedy was necessary as counterpoint to the lushness of the *Follies*, but he was not a humorous man, and needed others to guide him toward comic talent. The quality of the guidance (by Gene Buck, especially) is demonstrated by the fact that *Follies* comedians included Will Rogers, W. C. Fields, Ed Wynn, Eddie Cantor, Bert Williams, Fannie Brice, and Leon Errol. Even so, Flo Ziegfeld never felt at ease with funny people, considering them fill-in acts while his glorious girls changed from one lovely gown to a lovelier one. He once infuriated W. C. Fields by sitting mute through a carefully prepared comedy routine. At its conclusion Ziggy summoned an assistant. "How long does it take the girls to dress here?" he asked. "Seven minutes," he was told. "Hold your sketch to seven minutes," he told Fields.

Yet Ziegfeld had a lovable side—radiant Billie Burke adored her husband until the day he died. But to the Great White Way he was a cool, inscrutable figure, difficult to fathom. Ziegfeld seemed to work best surrounded by total confusion, while each mixed-up moment ate up vast amounts of money. The real wonder of the *Follies* was not that the revues were so good, but that they ever opened. To Channing Pollock and Rennold Wolf, who undertook to write *The Follies of 1915*, Ziegfeld first sent one hundred pounds of loose paper on which he had jotted notes and suggestions for the show. As the collaborators perused this, there were constant interruptions by telephone as Ziegfeld passed along new ideas. The extravagant producer also sent telegrams, some of which ran to several thousand words.

Having at last completed twenty sketches, Pollock and Wolf

journeyed to the New Amsterdam Roof, where *Follies* dances and songs were in strident rehearsal. Here they discovered that designer Joseph Urban had created twenty stage sets which bore no relation to their written material. It was easier (Ziegfeld decided) to write new sketches than to build new sets, so the collaborators labored again. Leon Errol and Bert Williams were the comedians needing material, but now Annette Kellerman was signed for the show. She had to have words to utter before high-diving into a $25,000 Roman pool designed by Urban. Soon Miss Kellerman was out of the show and in her place Ziegfeld hired demure Ina Claire, who had scored in *The Quaker Girl*. (The $25,000 pool was easily adapted into a locale for undraped Ziegfeld beauties to loll.) Leon Errol and Bert Williams were still in the cast, but now the producer hired W. C. Fields and Ed Wynn. (It was in this *Follies* that onstage Fields conked Wynn with a billiard cue for interfering with his act.)

With each cast change, the writers made changes too. "We wrote a library and produced a pamphlet," Pollock states. But no one at a Ziegfeld rehearsal ever felt abused. All worked surrounded by the same magnificent confusion. Only Ziegfeld seemed to know what the final show would be like. Usually the dress rehearsal ran hours long, and with it Ziegfeld rose to full majesty. "Mr. Icewater," Mae Murray called him then. Under his cold, inspired guidance, the *Follies* was cut to achieve a flawless opening night.

The *Ziegfeld Follies* were lavish and super-costly, perhaps the most expensive productions (comparatively) ever to grace the Great White Way. A far simpler—and to many better—form of entertainment was to be discovered at the tiny Princess Theatre on Thirty-ninth Street. Busy Elizabeth Marbury was the one who got the idea of using this theatre for midget musicals. Teaming with producer F. Ray Comstock, she picked as composer Jerome Kern, who had just established himself with *The Girl from*

Utah and its haunting "They Didn't Believe Me." For book and lyrics she hired Guy Bolton and P. G. Wodehouse, the latter drama critic on the magazine *Vanity Fair*. These three—certainly the most civilized trio ever to amble the theatre district—wrote the so-called Princess Shows, small, witty, informal, and altogether memorable.

The first Princess success was *Very Good, Eddie*. In it were Ernest Truex, Jack Hazzard, Alice Dovey, and Oscar Shaw. This was the first American musical to weave a sophisticated plot through songs and comedy—or to hang songs and comedy on a believable plot-line. With *Oh Boy!*, the second Princess hit, Ray Comstock took abrupt control and announced plans to steal Florenz Ziegfeld's two most splendid Follies Girls.

The two he picked were Marion Davies and Justine Johnstone. In response to overtures from Comstock the *Follies* queens arrived in chauffeur-driven limousines, one (Marion's) a Pierce-Arrow, the other a French Delage. Both agreed with the glib Comstock that speaking a few lines in *Oh Boy!* would make them dramatic actresses. Eagerly they signed contracts. On the tryout tour the girls dwelt at company expense in splendor matching the mink-and-limousine life of New York. At the Hollenden Hotel in Cleveland—Bolton and Wodehouse recall—they took a suite comprising reception room, large sitting room, small sitting room, dining room, two bedrooms, two baths, clothes-pressing room, maid's room, and maid's bathroom. On the Road such expense caused alarm, but all was forgiven in New York. *Oh Boy!* ran for nearly 500 performances, while four other companies toured the country. *Oh, Lady, Lady!*, the last Princess hit, received still another honor. While playing at the little Princess, it was performed by a second company at the larger Casino Theatre, just down the street.

In this bubbling, dance-mad, musical-comedy Great White

Way, a new Rector's was inevitable. George Rector, having lost his old place, presently joined with two money-bags partners to open a shiny new one at Broadway and Forty-eighth Street. Those who loved the old Rector's pulled back in horror at the new. So, in a sense, did Rector. Analyzing the Broadway which his father had discovered as a little lane of ham and eggs, George Rector decided that noise rather than nourishment was what the new generation craved. Accordingly, he opened a restaurant which emphasized music and dancing, while practically by-passing food. At a cover charge of one dollar a head (unheard of in the old Rector's) he nightly jammed-in 1500 people. Four orchestras (one Ted Lewis) played in rapid relay. Rector was a witty man who cherished few illusions. "They played like mechanics repairing a locomotive," he recalls of his busy musicians. To brazen music, couples madly Fox-Trotted and Bunny-Hugged. "The diners would drop knives and napkins the minute the orchestra broke loose, to stampede for the postage-stamp floor," Rector remembers. "The couples were jammed back to back, elbow to elbow, and cheek to neck. It looked like an elephant dancing on a butcher's block."

Rector's not only pioneered in offering dancing to the dollar-a-head multitudes. For the restless society dowager, the restaurant conceived the nattily named Thé Dansant. At four in the afternoon, an unescorted lady might enter Rector's for tea. No sooner was she seated than a young man appeared to bend over her hand, asking if she cared to dance. At Rector's the young man who did this most gracefully was a glossy Italian named Rudolph Valentino.

All of which made George Rector sad. But he did most of his weeping en route to the bank. In its first year, the Forty-eighth-Street Rector's earned back its initial investment of $200,000 and piled $100,000 on top of it. In the following years, the take-home profit was even greater.

In 1915 the talked-about dramatic successes were Jane Cowl in *Common Clay*, John Barrymore in *Kick In*, Marie Dressler in *A Mix-Up*, and Ina Claire in *Lady Luxury*. In 1916, Patricia Collinge appeared in *Pollyanna*, Ethel Barrymore in *Our Mrs. McChesney*, Otis Skinner in *Mr. Antonio*, and Mrs. Fiske (hitting the comeback trail) in *Erstwhile Susan*. In 1917, Jane Cowl made the town weep in the war play *Lilac Time*, while Laurette Taylor starred in *Out There*, Grant Mitchell in *A Tailor-Made Man*, John Barrymore in *Peter Ibbetson*, George Arliss in *Hamilton*, and Lenore Ulric in *Tiger Rose*.

To some these seemed trivial, machine-made plays which evaded reality. In other words, plays which did not show life as it was. After seeing all the Broadway productions she could, a Chicago girl named Susan Glaspell summed up her feelings: "The plays . . . were patterned. They didn't ask much of *you*, these plays. Having paid for your seat, the thing was all done for you, and your mind came out where it went in, only tireder. What was this Broadway, which could make a thing as interesting as life . . . dull?"

In Greenwich Village, where Miss Glaspell lived, others had identical thoughts. Both the Neighborhood Playhouse and Washington Square Players had begun to give plays which made audiences respond with thought and feeling. Indeed, the Washington Square Players would soon turn into the history-making Theatre Guild. But a more important development had come when young Eugene O'Neill, son of actor James O'Neill of *Monte Cristo* fame, began rising from a life of self-destructive dissipation to contemplate the career of playwright. O'Neill carried his first plays to Provincetown, on the tip of Cape Cod. There George Cram Cook (Susan Glaspell's husband) read them. With tremendous enthusiasm, Cook started making O'Neill the revolutionizing force which brought realism to

Broadway, doing for the American stage what Ibsen and Shaw had done for the world theatre. . . .

But if Broadway's plays lacked true drama, there was far too much of that commodity in the Greek tragedy which now befell one of the theatre's favorites. For the Fates, which so often turn on the fortunate, had struck down Edward Sheldon. At the age of thirty, the Wonder Boy of *Salvation Nell* and *The Nigger* had behind him four outstanding hits out of six major efforts. He was currently the author of *Romance,* which seemed destined to go on forever, making the lucky Sheldon appear more lucky. He had remained the same, still looking so boyish that a stage doorman at *Romance* barred him as too young to enter backstage regions. He had abandoned hope of marrying the radiant Doris Keane, the luminous star of his play. But Ned Sheldon remained as handsome, ebullient, sought-after, and respected as before.

One day he felt a stiffness in his knees. Slowly, it spread to other parts of his body. Sheldon was a wealthy man with a summer home on Lake Como. He was able to travel to any part of this country or Europe for any special medical treatment the era offered. Yet the creeping paralysis would not stop. It was diagnosed as a progressive arthritis which crippled rather than killed. Nothing more could be done, and shortly Sheldon lay completely bedridden in his Gramercy Square apartment.

There has never been an invalid like Ned Sheldon. His boyish face seemed unmarked by the intense pain he suffered. His voice remained resonant, his mind clear. He begged theatrical visitors to make him laugh. Trying to seem as little as possible like an invalid, he designed wrap-around suits which could easily be changed. In the morning he donned a boyish turtle-neck sweater. By dinner, he was in a formal tuxedo. "He looks like a young man lying down for a moment," thought actress Louise Closser

Hale after a visit. Others saw more tragedy. "He was rosy of face as ever, lying like a living corpse in his catafalque," a friend recalls. "He had all the old warmth and friendliness, but I have never gotten over the horror of seeing him so dreadfully man-handled by destiny."

Theatre people flocked to his apartment. An unending succession of stage celebrities asked his advice on personal matters, consulted him on scripts (he collaborated on several), or acted out troublesome scenes. To them all he was friendly, cheerful, helpful. Some found him an inspiration, others a saint. Looking as buoyant and alive as when he first enchanted Minnie Maddern Fiske, stricken Ned Sheldon had found the life-pattern he must endure for the next thirty years.

Sheldon's terrible tragedy was reflected in the outer world as the United States took the steps which led to World War I. With the emotionalism for which it is famous, the theatre (together with vaudeville and the now established movie industry) responded to the country's call.

From the beginning the profession displayed sympathy and warmth of heart. As German armies marched into Belgium, Mrs. August Belmont (the former actress Eleanor Robson) persuaded Winthrop Ames to join her in a mammoth Belgian Relief Benefit at the newly built Strand Theatre. King Albert of Belgium was one sponsor, and to his side rallied the kings and queens of Broadway to make an evening which was a recapitulation of the American stage since 1900. Henry Miller appeared as Sydney Carton in a scene from *A Tale of Two Cities*, Blanche Bates in a bit from *Madame Butterfly* (the original Belasco stage production). Others were Frances Starr in *The Rose of the Rancho;* William Gillette as *Sherlock Holmes;* William H. Crane as *David Harum;* Marie Doro in *The Morals of Marcus;* Francis Wilson in *Ermanie;* Nazimova as *Hedda Gabler;* Jane Cowl in

Within the Law; Holbrook Blinn as the Sheriff in *Salomy Jane;*
Ethel Barrymore in *Captain Jinks of the Horse Marines;* Mrs.
Patrick Campbell as *Melisande;* and Ellen Terry in the Mercy
speech from *The Merchant of Venice.* When Frances Alda sang
the Belgian National Anthem she was accompanied by the entire
Metropolitan Opera orchestra. In honor of the evening, Irving
Berlin composed a song: "I Hear the Voice of Belgium."

War seemed remote indeed as these great stars re-created the
peak performances of their careers. But it came closer with the
death of Charles Frohman in 1915, and closer still when Vernon
Castle departed *Watch Your Step* to return to England, where
he joined the Air Force. (In 1918 he was killed in Texas while
training American aviators.) The stately magnificence of Mrs.
Belmont's benefit was matched by the emotion of the night
Charles Dillingham engaged the Hippodrome for a farewell to
the Vernon Castles. The gossamer couple danced to the stern
pumpings of John Philip Sousa's Band, with Irene wearing a
Flying Corps insignia and an aviator's cap tilted over an eye.
The giant crowd clapped, cheered, wept, and stamped feet, saying good-by forever to Mr. and Mrs. Vernon Castle.

Julia Marlowe and E. H. Sothern were living in England
when war broke out in 1914. They returned to this country with
a special awareness of a world touched with fire. Miss Marlowe
immediately undertook a one-woman tour of this country for the
benefit of the British Red Cross. In addition to her beloved
Shakespeare, she recited "The Battle Hymn of the Republic"
and "In Flanders Fields." Sothern took to the Road with a revival of *If I Were King*, with receipts for Britain. Meanwhile
the country sang "Tipperary" and "Keep the Home Fires Burn-
ing," both imports from England. At the same time, President
Wilson proclaimed the nation too proud to fight, and Americans
were content to favor songs that agreed with him. Three favorites were "I Didn't Raise My Boy To Be a Soldier," "Don't

Take My Darling Boy Away," and "We're With You, Mr. Wilson." The last caused riots when sung across the border in combatant Canada.

But with America's involvement in the war, Tin Pan Alley burst loose. "The one-key composers of Tin Pan Alley turned their pianos into drums," states Edward B. Marks, in his book *They All Sang.* "A great many other parts of the war machine fell down lamentably—the Service of Supply, the shipyards, the airplane manufacturers. But Tin Pan Alley did a swell job."

The swellest of jobs was done by Mr. Broadway. On the day in April 1917 when America declared war, George M. Cohan donned the mantle of Tin-Pan-Alleyite to tap out a simple ditty with the clarity of a bugle call. He named it "Over There" and quickly added a lyric which matched the tune's simplicity. Even the Yankee Doodle Dandy, who still thought everything he did was the greatest ever, felt that here he had excelled himself. Apparently he did not think of introducing "Over There" himself. It was a great little tune, perhaps the best little tune ever. Who, then, was worthy of the honor of singing it first? The name that ricocheted back at him was Nora Bayes, Empress of the Two-a-Day. Cohan personally took the song to her at the Thirty-ninth Street Theatre, where she was appearing in a show of her own. Nora Bayes rendered "Over There" that night and after a few bars the audience rose to cheer. World War I had found its favorite song!

With "Over There" as a stimulus, the rest of Tin Pan Alley went to work. Al Jolson had already popularized "Sister Susie's Sewing Shirts for Soldiers" in his Winter Garden performances. Now the departure of the first American troops was saluted by "Good-by Broadway, Hello France." Song-title mothers, who had been used to back up Wilson's too-proud-to-fight, found their position reversed. "I'm Proud To Be the Mother of a Soldier," and "America Needs You Like a Mother, Would You

Turn Your Mother Down?" were hot-off-the-press hits. Patriotism was stimulated by "Liberty Bell, It's Time to Ring Again." Slackers were warned away from soldiers' girls by "Don't Try To Steal the Sweetheart of a Soldier."

With the landing of troops in France came the plaintive "Rose of No Man's Land." As America began to take the war in stride, the humor songs began—"They're All Out of Step But Jim," "I Don't Want To Get Well, I'm in Love with a Beautiful Nurse," and the all-too-true "How You Gonna Keep 'Em Down on the Farm After They've Seen Paree?" Defiance of the enemy was expressed in a song favored by vaudeville's Single Women, "If He Fights Like He Makes Love, Good-by Germany!" Optimism shone through "Just Like Washington Crossed the Delaware, Pershing Will Cross the Rhine," "Keep Your Head Down, Fritzie Boy," and "When Yankee Doodle Learns to Parlez-Vous Français."

The better songs—all of inestimable value to the war effort—were of top quality and remain stimulating still. A country heated to a fever pitch of patriotism sang, whistled, or listened (on phonograph records) to "Pack Up Your Troubles in Your Old Kit Bag," "There's a Long, Long Trail A-Winding," "Hinky Dinky Parlay-Voo," "Mademoiselle from Armentieres," "Madelon," "Beautiful K-K-K-Katy," "Good Morning, Mr. Zip-Zip-Zip," "Smiles," "Where Do We Go from Here, Boys?" and "Till We Meet Again."

Across the ocean Elsie Janis sang these and other songs to troops just behind the front. For the Sweetheart of Broadway had quickly become the Sweetheart of the AEF. In her velvet tam-o'-shanter, Elsie stood on platforms before entire regiments, dancing, singing, turning handsprings, and leading leather-lunged doughboys through "God Save Kaiser Bill!" Also abroad was E. H. Sothern, dispatched by the YMCA in the dual capacity of entertainer and observer of troop morale. In the first capacity Sothern appeared before hushed soldiers giving Hamlet's Soliloquy and Macbeth's Dagger speech. As a surveyor of morale, he reported home that Lieutenant Jim Europe's Band was a superb morale booster. Returning to the United States, Sothern joined with Winthrop Ames and George M. Cohan to establish the Over There League, which sent entertainment overseas in the manner of the later USO.

Top actors and actresses sold Liberty Bonds from the steps of the New York Public Library and other strategic spots across the country. Julia Marlowe added a spoken rendition of "The Star-Spangled Banner" to her repertory and began making Liberty Bond speeches. In less than half an hour actress Elsie Ferguson sold $85,000 worth of Liberty Bonds in New York City. The Red Cross also needed money and for it a tour of top stars was organized. Sixteen went along, among them Mrs. Fiske, Laurette Taylor, George M. Cohan, James K. Hackett, and De Wolf Hopper. The Red Cross Tour covered seventeen cities and gave twenty-three performances in a span of three weeks. Each star gave his talents free and paid his own expenses, together with those of maids or secretaries. Managers co-operated by making no charge for theatres and hotels refused to bill the troupe. In all, this star-studded Red Cross Tour raised the tidy sum of $685,632.

Less spectacular shows were presented at the so-called Liberty theatres built in troop encampments. In these hastily erected structures touring companies performed hot-off-Broadway hits like *Turn to the Right, Cheating Cheaters*, and *Kick In*. One spot which had no need for outside entertainment was Camp Upton, at Yaphank, Long Island. Here Private (later Sergeant) Irving Berlin was stationed. With difficulty he persuaded Major-General J. Franklin Bell to permit a show named *Yip, Yip Yaphank* to be put together for the benefit of the camp treasury. General Bell had a vague awareness of the importance of the unprepossessing private who stood at attention before him. He still seemed unsure when *Yip, Yip Yaphank* was transported to the huge Century Theatre on Central Park West. In one sketch Berlin, a night-owl in civilian life, was aroused by the morning bugle call. Tottering to reluctant feet, he plaintively warbled, *"Oh! How I hate to get up in the morning!"* Later, on K.P. he piped, *"I scrub dishes against my wishes to make this wide world safe for democracy."* Amid the enthusiastic cheers at the end of the performance, General Bell rose proudly to his feet. "I have heard that Berlin is among the foremost songwriters of the world," he stated, "and now I believe it. . . . Berlin is as good a soldier as he is a songwriter, and as popular in Camp Upton as he is on Broadway."

On Broadway, *The Better 'Ole*, by Bruce Bairnsfeather, gave a realistic British-Tommies-eye-view of the war. In it, Charles Coburn starred as ruddy-faced, walrus-mustached Old Bill. For the most part, however, the stagnation of the contemporary theatre was underlined by the fact that the greatest conflict in world history produced only tricky spy stories. "They were dashed off by noncombatants who got their plots at the Knickerbocker Bar," says Ward Morehouse of the crop of 1917–18 war plays. Yet actors continued valiantly to support the government, appearing at Liberty Bond rallies and even at rummage sales. When Grand Central Palace was turned into a mighty bazaar, stage celebrities presided over each counter. Over one display hung the sign MRS. LANGTRY HERE! It is a sad commentary on a wicked world that the Jersey Lily's counter remained almost unpatronized while males battled for space at those of beautiful young actresses like Ivy Troutman.

If the dramatic stage did not rise to the challenge of war, the musical theatre did. In numerous musical comedies, actor-doughboys sang tuneful farewells to home-town sweethearts or poured out the longings of lonely hearts in the trenches of simulated No Man's Lands. In *The Ziegfeld Follies of 1917*, Kay Laurell posed before crossed American and French flags wearing the fatigue uniform of an embattled French poilu. Her shirt was open, obviously ripped by a rapacious Hun. This allowed a full view of one of Miss Laurell's ripe breasts. She made an exceedingly patriotic sight and it was said that the French government ordered 200,000 photographs of her as a poster for enlistment purposes. Or were Florenz Ziegfeld's press agents merely working overtime?

In 1918, the *Follies* did better. Advertisements boasted that stars of the show were Will Rogers, W. C. Fields, Eddie Cantor, Harry Kelly, Marilyn Miller, Ann Pennington, and the team of Savoy and Brennan. But the top luminary was Patriotism. On first-night seats the audience found a notice saying that Ziegfeld's chorus boys were not slackers—each had officially been exempted from the draft. The overture was a rousing rendition of "The Star-Spangled Banner." Early in the glittering show came an Irving Berlin song, "I'll Pin a Medal on the Girl I Left Behind Me," chanted by a handsome doughboy in the depths of a stage trench. Kay Laurell was featured in a tableau called "This Warring World," where she stood atop a spinning globe lightly attired as "The Spirit of the Follies." In another scene the Follies Girls promenaded as lovely aviators.

The greatest moment came with the tableau that brought down the curtain on act one. Conceived and staged by Ben Ali Haggin, the figures in this breathtaking scene run the gamut from two bedraggled French war orphans (female) to a Red Cross nurse and a dying soldier attended by rugged (but draft-exempt) chorus boys wearing Red Cross armbands. Other battle-muddy French and American soldiers are in the act of tossing grenades, throttling Huns, bayonetting Huns, dying, bandaging themselves, and charging Over the Top. High above stand the inevitable Follies Girls. Kay Laurell, bosom exposed, delineates the Spirit of France, while other girls (fully attired) hold the flags of other Allies. "Forward Allies!" the tableau was named. It evoked thundering applause.

Said President Wilson: "The theatre was one of the most potent contributing factors to American victory in the World War."

It was a tribute which the Great White Way considered fully deserved. But with the Armistice Broadway quickly reverted to its prewar norm. The big hit of 1918–19 was a Barrie fantasy without Maude Adams, who had retired in 1917. It was *Dear Brutus,* with William Gillette and a grown-up Helen Hayes, whose skill in the play caused Broadway to pay more attention to its young actresses. Helen Hayes, Katharine Cornell, Lynn Fontanne, Jeanne Eagels—these and others would change the emphasis of stardom so that the next decade would be called "The Golden Age of the Young Actress."

Another hit was *The Copperhead,* by the veteran Augustus Thomas, and starring Lionel Barrymore. A greater one was *Lightnin',* by and with Frank Bacon, an actor who for most of his sixty years had toured the Road without reaching Broadway. Other hits were John Barrymore in *Redemption,* Nazimova in *A Doll's House,* and Henry Miller and Blanche Bates in *The Famous Mrs. Fair.*

Returning doughboys noted joyously that girls' dresses were tighter, with skirts slipping upward. The dance of the day was the Shimmy Shewabble, quickly shortened to the Shimmy. The Jazz Age had dawned with "Dardanella" and "Ja-Da," and Dixieland jazz had been heard for the first time in New York at Reisenweber's on January 19, 1917, where it was played by Nick LaRocca's Dixie Land Jass Band of white musicians from New Orleans by way of Chicago. Yet Tin Pan Alley still held sway with such tunes as "Oh Johnny," "They're Wearing Them Higher in Hawaii," "Everybody Loves a Jazz Band," and "I Love You, Billy Sunday, But Oh You Saturday Night!" Soldiers marching home also learned that the Prohibition Amendment had been foisted on them. It would spoil the Great White Way, change the Broadway theatre, and end the world as the homecoming soldiers had known it.

In France, Elsie Janis still entertained returning troops. She was fully enjoying the role of Sweetheart of the AEF, but Ma Janis was restive. Elsie was in France—why not let her make a little money there? Ma visited a Paris manager and began the relentless bargaining which had whitened the hair of many Broadway managers.

She first named a salary so high that the Frenchman was appalled. "But, Madame," he protested, "you seem to think your daughter is better than our famous entertainers like Mistinguett and Yvette Guilbert."

"Of course, she's better," Ma Janis screeched. "Isn't my daughter a VIRGIN?"

12: THE STRIKE

After engaging with such spirit in the war to make the world
safe for democracy, the theatre next found itself involved in a
conflict of its own.

For the abuses from which actors suffered at the turn of the
century had never been corrected. While unions gained strength
in other fields, with protesting workers gradually winning improved treatment, the actor was still regarded as bottom man on
the theatre ladder. "Acting takes more nerve than skill," Lee
Shubert was on the record as contemptuously stating. Actors
were still expected to rehearse without pay and rehearsals (especially for musical comedies and revues) could run twelve
weeks or more. A producer could still discharge an actor at will
or whim. New abuses had sprung up. Some managers made a
policy of opening plays with top actors as stars. Once the good
reviews were in, the name-actors were fired and lesser names at
lower salaries substituted. (The public was believed to be unaware of all this.) The tribulations of wartime, inroads of movies,
loss of power on the part of the Syndicate—these factors had
combined to disrupt bookings on the Road. To achieve a solid
tour was far more difficult in 1919 than in the past. Sometimes
producers sent plays out on tours which called for layovers of
weeks between cities. During this idle time the actor was paid no

salary and was required to foot all expenses involved in living away from home.

Protest was in the air. Seated one night in Shanley's, Victor Herbert listened to the restaurant orchestra render a sprightly medley of his tunes. For this he would get absolutely nothing. As he pondered this fact the usually genial composer grew seething mad. He sued Shanley's, commencing the court fight which led to the formation of ASCAP, zealous protector of the royalties of composers and lyricists. Dramatists, too, were preparing to fight for rights. With Channing Pollock and George Middleton in the lead, playwrights were moving toward establishment of the potent Dramatists Guild.

In 1913 a group of actors had banded together in a union called Actors Equity Association. With Francis Wilson as its head, Equity joined the American Federation of Labor and started advocating half-pay for all rehearsals over four weeks. In addition, it asked full-pay for extra performances during actual runs. By 1919, Equity had 2700 members and $14,000 in its till. Opposing Equity—though this was not quite the word to use yet—stood the Producing Managers Association, or the PMA. It was the brainchild of producer John Golden and at its infrequent meetings he and colleagues from Ames to Ziegfeld discussed censorship, taxation, and ticket-selling problems. A more sensitive matter than any of these was the fierce guerrilla warfare between producers, who frequently stole stars and theatres from one another. Gatherings of the PMA were seldom harmonious. At one, as he watched the rumpus he had wrought, John Golden remarked, "These meetings have the aspect of minor riots."

On one subject, though, the producers found perfect unanimity. They completely opposed dealing with actors. To Equity's demands for half-pay at rehearsals, the PMA dictatorially answered, "Can't afford it." Equity suggested arbitration of this and other claims. The producers turned pious. To deal with a union, they intoned, would be degrading in a profession devoted to pure art. Besides, what was there to arbitrate?

Not a single producer believed that Actors Equity would dare call a strike or make real trouble, and so a hastily convened PMA meeting was jolted into stupefaction when producers F. Ray Comstock and Morris Gest reported that the union had commenced to agitate at rehearsals of the extravaganza *Chu Chin Chow*. The rehearsals had been under way for two weeks at the Century Theatre, yet none of the actors knew how long they would continue, nor did they know how much pay to expect once *Chu Chin Chow* opened. This latter fact was stressed by Equity in trying to persuade the cast to strike. But the PMA knew how to handle such situations. Comstock and Gest rushed back to make firm offers of good salaries to the actors. Equity had lost its first skirmish.

Even so, the producers had fair warning that Equity meant business. Men like Golden, Al Woods, and Sam Harris seemed inclined to deal with the actors by making enough small concessions to assure peace. (A strike, of course, would be a hugely expensive business all around.) It has been said that PMA members listened respectfully to this argument for minimum concessions, and were almost ready to agree when E. F. Albee burst in the door. Requesting permission to address the assembled group, he cited in fire-eating terms his success in demolishing the spirit of the White Rats. Any strike of actors, he swore, could be broken by the kind of tactics he had used. He then brought up another matter. In the White Rats and other struggles, top performers had stood aside, letting the smaller fry knock themselves out in actual battle. Albee himself had been dealing with vaudeville headliners even as the rank and file struggled. It was Albee's fervent contention that top stars of the legitimate theatre would behave in the same way. This rousing speech completely reversed the tenor of PMA thinking. Even David Belasco became bellicose. "We'll starve the actors out," he grated through clenched teeth.

What Equity now needed was a hero to dramatize its position. One promptly appeared in the person of Frank Bacon, the actor who for thirty years had toured the Road without achieving Broadway. Bacon specialized in quaint, folksy, philosophical characters and possessed these warm attributes himself. He lived surrounded by a wife and brood of children (one became movie director Lloyd Bacon). The pride of the family group was Aunt Em, who spent her days crocheting in a rocking chair, from time to time contributing pithy comments. Bacon had all but given up hope of a success in the theatre and had turned to playing bit parts in Hollywood. He was rescued from this form of slavery by John Golden and Winchell Smith for a road tour of *The Fortune Hunter*. When he met the producers, Bacon remarked that he had written a play called *A House Divided*. Smith asked to see it, then offered himself as collaborator. This was standard practice in Golden-Smith productions. Smith was a demon play-doctor who had already scored with improvements on Jack Hazzard's *Turn to the Right*. His skillful efforts were characterized by intellectuals as The Old Hokum Bucket, but audiences loved the cheery, sentimental plays. He changed *A House Divided* into *Lightnin'*, and made it the comfy saga of Lightnin' Bill Jones, an oldster (Bacon, of course) with a weakness for tall stories. Once he drove a herd of bees across the desert, "Without losin' a one," he ended proudly.

The story of Frank Bacon's late-life rise to Broadway stardom brought his emotional profession to the brink of tears. Thirty years on the grubby Road, now stardom in his own Broadway play! It was heart-warming, tear-jerking. Everyone was broken-up but Aunt Em, whose rocking chair was placed in Bacon's dressing room on opening night. As excitement increased during the performance, Aunt Em sat quietly crocheting, speaking not a word. Finally, after the last well-wisher had departed, Bacon asked, "Well, Auntie, what did you think of it all?" "I don't see what they're makin' all that fuss about," she answered tartly. "You ain't no different than you ever was."

Ticket-hungry hordes surged to *Lightnin'* and for the first time in his life Frank Bacon was magnificently solvent. At the end of several months he was persuaded to take a vacation, but on the first Monday of the respite he was spotted in the rear of the theatre watching the other actor do his part. He was there every night until time came to return. Yet success did nothing to change the veteran actor's underlying compassion for his fellow man, including actors. Bacon became active in the councils of Equity, and during discussions about striking a first play he spoke up. "I'll do it," he said. "I'll close *Lightnin'* tonight." When he learned this, Golden hastened to the Gaiety Theatre. Here— the night was August 7, 1919—he found Lightnin' Bill alone in his dressing room. "It's a fight for principle," Bacon told him, "and you are on the other side of the fence. Although I have always looked on you as a friend, let's shake hands now and be enemies. I'm striking."

Golden left the theatre, ruefully observing that a line had already formed at the box office to get ticket-money back. Word of the closing of *Lightnin'* spread like fire through the theatre district and the casts of fourteen other plays refused to step on the stage. One of these was *Nightie Night*, which was having its premiere that evening. Another was *The Better 'Ole*. Charles Coburn, its star, was not in favor of the strike but his supporting cast stranded him in mid-scene. In the Cohan and Harris office, Sam Harris heard that Frederic Santley, Tessa Kosta, and Mary Eaton had abandoned the musical import *A Royal Vagabond*, which had been revised for America by George M. Cohan. Harris sighed gloomily and said, "I never thought the boys would go so far."

A few blocks uptown Ed Wynn was starring in the Shuberts' *Gaieties of 1919*. He too walked out. A crowd of audience members gathered around him on the sidewalk. The excitable comedian leaped aboard a soapbox (or its equivalent) to deliver an impassioned speech in favor of the actors. He became so eloquent that the crowd (now swelled by hundreds of the curious) hefted him to its shoulders and marched down Broadway. The Shuberts, meantime, had summoned lawyers to begin a court fight to force Wynn and the rest of the cast back to work. Equity was closing only shows produced by members of the PMA; those sponsored by others could continue. Backstage at the *Follies*, Florenz Ziegfeld was working hard to persuade firebrand Eddie Cantor and others in his cast that he was no PMA member. He succeeded, and the *Follies* played that night.

The actors early made the gratifying discovery that the public was almost completely on their side. Over the years the public too had suffered at the hands of arbitrary management. Among other things, box-office men had grown increasingly rude. Theatregoers, it turned out, had been only too aware of the substitution of inferior casts for top stars in hit shows. Newspapers highlighted PMA arrogance by printing its "We'll-break-them" ukases. Public reaction to all this was stated in a *Variety* editorial: "The producers brought it on themselves, and [so] left the actors, represented by Actors Equity, with the best cause possible for a strike—a just cause."

Stimulated by such expressions of sympathy, the actors began presenting a far-flung open-air show that won more friends. Frank Bacon and his cast hired a stagecoach, drove around town waving a banner LIGHTNIN' HAS STRUCK! Pretty young actresses picketed the offices of PMA members holding placards WE ARE NOT AFTER MORE PAY BUT FAIR PLAY, and NATIONS ARBITRATE BUT PRODUCERS WON'T. Around Times Square shopkeepers put cards in windows: STRIKING ACTORS, GET YOUR CIGARETTES HERE AND PAY LATER. The actors organized a colorful parade which marched from Columbus Circle to Forty-second Street, then snaked through Times Square streets. By now chorus girls, often obliged to buy sixty-dollar dancing shoes at their own expense, had joined the fray and were agitating for Chorus Equity. A group of stunning girls invaded the financial district to proclaim the Equity cause from the running board of a Stutz Bearcat. One had a perfect answer when a heckler called out, "How can you afford to strike?" "If we can afford to rehearse for six weeks without pay," she snapped back, "we can afford to strike for six weeks without pay."

In the forefront of the parades and rallies stood the stars of the stage. For E. F. Albee had been proved almost totally wrong in predicting that the big names of the theatre would sit on their hands during the strike. John and Lionel Barrymore, Marie Dressler, Al Jolson, Eddie Foy, Chic Sale—names that customarily blazed from theatre marquees now blazed for Actors Equity. Wrote one observer: "Men and women who never seemed to have a thought for anything but their own advantage are absolutely forgetting themselves—they are working for others and for a principle and there is a look of devotion on their faces." De Wolf Hopper stated it this way: "The thought of union and collective bargaining by a profession of rampant egoists was laughable until it happened." The Lambs Club, though its members were largely stars and well-paid leading men, was a hotbed of union partisans.

The hub of the strike was Equity headquarters at 160 West Forty-fifth Street. This had become a mass of busy actors and dedicated actresses on the afternoon John Drew appeared to lend support. Work stopped as cheers, tears, and fervent handclasps welcomed this fine gentleman. To newsmen, Drew explained, "I feel that the traditions of my family and my personal predilections ally me, logically and irremediably, with the members of my profession in Actors Equity Assocition." Next, his niece Ethel Barrymore returned to town from a long vacation which had begun at the Dempsey-Willard fight in Toledo. This aloof and lovely star seemed unaware of what had transpired in her absence. As her car jammed in the crowds around Broadway, she asked, "What's happening?" When told, she exclaimed, "Oh, I ought to belong to Equity." At her side sat cousin Georgie Drew, who told her, "You damn fool, you're a life-member already."

From such vagueness emerged a militant crusader. Miss Barrymore was persuaded that her appearance at Equity headquarters would—no less than that of Uncle Jack—arouse and inspire. She walked up Forty-fifth Street and stood for a moment on the outskirts of the crowd. Then:

> someone caught sight of me and suddenly a sound went up—a great shout that seemed to come from the souls of these people who were my people. It left me trembling from head to foot with a feeling of exaltation and happiness. . . . I was practically carried along up the steps and into the house. I found myself up on a table. People were crying and kissing my hands and even the hem of my dress. . . . I had a moment's feeling of being Joan of Arc. It was all terribly moving and exciting. All I said was, "I'm with you, whatever it is. . . ."

Not all Broadway stars were arrayed on the side of the strike. To some rugged individuals among them, the word *union* was anathema. The knowledge that by joining Equity they also joined the American Federation of Labor with its membership of stagehands, plumbers, and other laboring types added gall to an already sour potion. William Collier was one who felt this way. "I don't want a lot of stagehands calling me Willie," he griped. Collier's stand was so unpopular at the Lambs that he took refuge in his summer home at St. James, Long Island. There he was

joined by an actor named Rapley Holmes. In New York, other
Lambs wondered about Holmes, and decided to send him a
questioning wire. ARE YOU WITH US OR AGAINST US? they asked.
YES, Holmes replied cryptically.

E. H. Sothern also took an opposing stand. This important actor
seemed genuinely to believe that the strike would kill the theatre.
Using his considerable influence, he called a mass meeting at
which he urged those present to abandon the fight. Beside him
on the platform as he spoke were Charles Coburn, Janet Beecher,
and the Belasco stars David Warfield, Frances Starr, and Lenore
Ulric. More amazing, perhaps, was the presence of Mrs. Minnie
Maddern Fiske. For the lady whose heart cried out to all dumb
animals was refusing to assist her fellow actors in their moment
of need. There may have been reasons for this. Mrs. Fiske was
in the forefront of those moved to terror by the word *union*.
"Acting is an art, not a trade," she declared with asperity. She
also believed that an actor's strength came from complete independence, and cited David Garrick, Edmund Kean, and Edwin
Booth to prove that thespians had always suffered alone. There
was possibly another motive to Mrs. Fiske's seeming apostasy.
She was the wife of a producer, who was also her personal
manager. Some thought her appearance with the non-union
actors reflected lingering love for Harrison Grey Fiske.

But the opposition of Mrs. Fiske and others dwindled almost
to nothingness beside the violent stand taken by Mr. Broadway.
From the time of *The Governor's Son*, nearly twenty years before, George M. Cohan had abominated unions. He now professed
to be convinced that the actors were being misled and even
victimized by Equity, into whose every move he read sinister
meaning. Surrounding himself with a cast of fifth-rate non-
Equity actors, he himself stepped into the lead of his musical *A
Royal Vagabond*. He urged other producers to pull the same

trick of substituting non-union casts, and some did. Though he was performing nightly, the man who at the age of forty had spent forty years on the stage declared that he was not an actor. Stepping forward as a member of PMA, he gloatingly said, "The actors overlooked one important thing when they called the strike—that's me."

Inevitably he became the spearhead of opposition to Equity, and in one angry speech swore that if Equity won the strike he would move his activities to London. In another he threatened to become an elevator operator, which caused one Equity partisan to post a sign:

WANTED

ELEVATOR OPERATOR

GEORGE M. COHAN

PREFERRED

The violence of the Yankee Doodle Boy's stand made him lose friends at the Lambs and the Friars, where he was the revered Abbot. In a fury he resigned from both. To make a touching scene, a delegation of Friars—newspapers said 400—solemnly marched down Broadway to beg him to rejoin and (by implication) mellow his attitude toward Equity. He met them at the stage door of *A Royal Vagabond* and said, "I know what you are going to say, so don't say it. I'm through forever with the Friars and the Lambs." To a newspaper reporter who pointed out merit in the actors' cause, the Song and Dance Man snarled, "I don't care, I won't deal with them—well—because I won't." He made several efforts to win Equity members over to his side, and after hearing one of his near-hysterical pleas, Ethel Barrymore said, "He's like a bad little boy who has lost his temper."

When the actors opposing Equity banded into the Actors FidelityAssociation (Fidoes, other actors scornfully called them), Cohan became president. At its initial meeting, he conveniently became an actor again. "I come to you not as a manager, but an actor," he commenced. Next he waved a check for $100,000 as a donation to the Fido cause. It was a Cohan and Harris check, a fact which annoyed Sam Harris and opened the schism which soon ended a partnership of seventeen years. Cohan pledged his entire personal fortune to the Fidoes, hinting that this first $100,000 was merely a drop in a bottomless bucket. Introducing his supporters on the platform, he dubbed Janet Beecher "the purest woman on the American stage." Hearing this, the sardonic Lionel Barrymore inquired, "What does that mean? It sounds like the freshest egg in New Jersey."

The actors' strike ran a month, during which time the Equity membership grew to 14,000. One day 600 new applications came in. Forty Broadway shows were shut down, with sixteen more prevented from opening. The strike spread to Boston, Chicago, and other Road cities. One New York casualty was the *Follies,* for Florenz Ziegfeld was finally unmasked as a PMA member in good standing. On the night this became apparent, an indignant Eddie Cantor stepped forward. "My conscience will not allow me to play," he declared. "My place is to stand by the actors and see that justice is done." He walked out of the theatre, followed by Van and Schenck, Eddie Dowling, Ray and Johnny Dooley, and (surprisingly) a number of regal *Follies* beauties. Except for the parades, speeches, and crowds, the Great White Way was strangely dark without the bright-lights illumination of theatres. On Sixth Avenue the vast Hippodrome was shuttered with its marquee reading:

NOTHING DOING

TWICE DAILY

AT THIS THEATRE

UNTIL FURTHER NOTICE

To provide money for the expensive strike—the AFL gave some assistance—Equity produced three weeks of monster bene-

fits at the Lexington Avenue Opera House. ("We must give
more monstrous ones," urged Willie Collier, on hearing this announcement.) They proved to be exciting. At the first, W. C.
Fields was master of ceremonies. Ethel Barrymore appeared in
a scene from the *Lady of Camellias*, with brother Lionel and
Conway Tearle (at later performances she was Juliet to Tearle's
Romeo). Midway through the second part of the program,
Fields announced that Ed Wynn had been enjoined by the
Shuberts from appearing on the stage. Thereupon a spotlight
swung to Wynn, who rose from his aisle seat to do everything
he would have done in his act. In superlative show-business
tradition, an almost-unknown scored the hit of the night. Surrounded by the greatest names of the profession, burlesque-
trained James Barton brought down the house with his eccentric
dancing and smart patter. "Thanks for the use of the hall," he
shouted, exiting.

Altogether, the benefits raised $30,000 for Equity coffers.
More money came from an Equity Ball at the Astor, where John
Drew and Ethel Barrymore led the Grand March. Hastening
from Hollywood, Mary Pickford and Douglas Fairbanks, together with other screen luminaries, took boxes at the ball and
from these pledged another $20,000.

Meantime, what of the producers?

From the beginning some members of the PMA felt that the
managers' stand was too rigid. Charles Dillingham enraged his
fellow PMA-ers by paying his departing casts a full week's wage
and personally handing out the envelopes as well. Out of his own
pocket Al Woods bought raincoats for chorus girls who picketed
his office on a suddenly stormy day. At turbulent PMA meetings Woods tried to smooth the waters by handing out cigars
with the words, "Here, smoke yourself to death, sweetheart."
Still, a tight core of opposition remained. When one prominent

citizen offered to mediate, a diehard rose to state, "This man cannot represent me. No man can represent me. I will fight to the bitter end for the principle involved." As he finished another producer rose to say, "I hope anybody who votes for the motion drops dead on the spot." "Not *this* spot," quipped Good-Time-Charlie Dillingham, jumping nimbly from where he stood.

A sense of defeat began to pervade the defiant group. The whole town seemed to be against them. Taxi drivers reviled PMA members who used their cabs. Newspaper editorials called them theatrical robber barons. The strike was costing all parties a total of $500,000 a week, and in the end would amount to an over-all $2,000,000. Yet a few producers flatly refused to recognize an actors' union. As passions bubbled, David Belasco, who was back to normal, made this characteristic appeal:

> Abhorring each other, how can we think we are going to succeed? We cannot. Ours is a profession of intense and sympathetic temperamentality, less tangible than a dream; highly strung and emotional, the dearest and best and most bohemian-like people in the world, all of whom would give his or her life-blood to any just cause. Why not do the same for each other?

John Golden noted that a near-majority of PMA members had come to favor compromise. But what to do, when the diehards still remained strong? Golden consulted a Tammany politician who advised him to call a sudden meeting of those in favor of sitting down with Equity. To this, he could forget to invite the opposition. Golden did this and by shouted approval of his group sent a telegram to playwright Augustus Thomas, asking him to serve as mediator. FOR GOD'S SAKE, GET IN HERE AND HELP US BACK-PEDAL, the wire read. But the diehards heard of this and stalled for another week.

Then, on September 6, the battling groups finally got together. The actors were led by Frank Gillmore, who had risen from the ranks of actors to become a shrewd mastermind of the strike. With him were Francis Wilson, Ethel Barrymore, and Lillian Russell. For the producers were Al Woods, William A. Brady, Arthur Hopkins, and John Golden. It was, according to Golden, more like a love feast than the settlement of a bitter strike. "We were all so happy to see each other," he elucidates. Both sides had brought expensive batteries of lawyers, but for once the legal profession was unable to get a word in. The producers gave in on every point. Where actors had asked half-pay after four weeks of rehearsal, the managers unexpectedly offered full-pay. "The producers call it a compromise, and perhaps it is," an Equity man said after the meeting broke up at three a.m. But it was no compromise—it was surrender.

In Great Neck, Long Island, where many actors had homes, Ed Wynn was informed by telephone that the strike was over. He leaped out of bed, got dressed, and jumped into his car. Then he raced the roads like a latter-day Paul Revere, jubilantly honking his horn and shouting under the windows of friends, "We've won! Isn't it wonderful? We've won!"

Only the tarnished Yankee Doodle Dandy continued resentful. Not for many years would George M. Cohan again be called Mr. Broadway, and then the words would be halfhearted. Cohan was a bitter man and continued to nurse his grievance until the day of his death. He never operated an elevator, nor did he move his producing activities to London. Soon he was acting and writing as profitably as ever. He had vowed that he would not join Actors Equity, and he never did. But with a combination of irony and magnanimity Equity allowed him to function without becoming a member. He was the only actor in the United States allowed on a stage without an Equity card.

Looking around after the turmoil of the strike, the actors
found that the Great White Way had all but reverted to the
little lane of ham and eggs.

For Prohibition had arrived in the Land of the Free, and it
brought sadness to the Great White Way. The Volstead Act
marked the end of an era. No more would cabaret patrons dress
to the nines, drink champagne and other wines while dancing the
Bunny Hug and Fox Trot. Prohibition was certain to end all this,
for Broadwayites needed wine to sustain nights of prancing,
dancing fun. Realizing that an era was over, some cabaret owners
had already shut up their premises. Rector's was one of these
—it turned into the Café de Paree. Jack Dunston, proprietor of
the famous Jack's, let his guests revel until four a.m. one night.
Then he locked the door of his place and tossed away the key.

Prohibition became law in the summer of 1919, but at that
time the government had no means of enforcing it. So Americans
continued blissfully to drink. Beginning on January 17, 1920,
however, the sum of $5,000,000 was allocated to put teeth
in the law. With this, the government hired 1500 revenue agents
at a salary of $2000 a year. It was believed that this number of
agents was sufficient to make certain that the law was strictly
obeyed. Further, Washington believed that agents so well paid
would be absolutely incorruptible.

So January 17 loomed as the moment of truth. From then on—
it was widely believed—no one in the United States would again
be able to purchase a drink. It made the night of the 16th one of
misery along the Great White Way. In bars along the side
streets, drinkers began lining up in the early afternoon. Newspaper accounts the next day reported that these tipplers drank
slowly and unemotionally. Many complained that the stowed-
away liquor had no effect. It seemed impossible, in such sober-
ing circumstances, to get drunk or even mildly exhilarated.
Glasses were lifted to lips with reverent care and the liquor was

held in mouths longer than usual, so that the sweet taste might fully be savored. Men walked around their favorite bars, picking out souvenirs to take home. Some took beer mugs, others swinging doors, barstools, saloon art, or door handles.

The law ordered bars to close at midnight, but the big cabarets like Reisenweber's, Café de Paree, Churchill's, and Pre-Catalan were bold enough to serve to the usual closing hour of four a.m. With the arrival of after-theatre crowds, these cabarets and cafés were jammed. Said the *New York Herald*:

> Oh, how New York's Great Glittering Way did feast and drink! Broadway was agleam with the spirit of the last night of the bubbling glass! All evening long, all night long, they laughed and drank to old John Barleycorn. They bade farewell in a royal manner, nor thought of the morrow and its black despair.

At the Knickerbocker Bar and other celebrity haunts, Enrico Caruso, John Barrymore, De Wolf Hopper, Gentleman Jim Corbett, and Bill Fallon (The Great Mouthpiece) made merry with wives or lady friends. From time to time around the Great White Way spotlights swung to tenors who rendered a special lament provided by Tin Pan Alley for the occasion:

> Where are you going to wet your whistle
> When the whole darn town goes dry?
> Where will you go after seeing the show
> To make the weary hours fly?

In cabarets, a melancholy motif was featured. Privileged guests were summoned to Reisenweber's by elegant black-bordered invitations to "Last rites and ceremonies attending the departure of our spirited friend, John Barleycorn." Waiters were dressed in black and at midnight the orchestra played the "Funeral March" and "Good-by Forever." At Churchill's, Maxim's, Delmonico's, Luchow's, the Everglades, Pabst's, Shanley's, Moulin

Rouge, and other spots waiters garbed as pallbearers shuffled around holding up a coffin.

At the Majestic, comedian Dan Healy dressed like the Rollin Kirby cartoon figure of Prohibition. Tall and gaunt, he wore the somber get-up of stovepipe hat, long dark coat, and baggy pants. In one pocket bulged a pint bottle and, like the Kirby cartoon, his nose was suspiciously red and bulbous. At the Café de Paree, two gold slippers were passed from table to table, filled with champagne, and emptied by celebrants. A great argument then arose over whose dainty feet the soggy slippers should be placed upon. Finally chosen was a showgirl named Violet McMillan.

It was hard to be festive in the midst of gloomy reminders, yet people tried. The city's panhandlers had never had it so good. "Give a guy a quarter for a last drink," they begged all over town, and a multitude of quarters were forthcoming. The McAlpin, Claridge, and Waldorf-Astoria hotels opened wide and began offering free champagne. At the four-sided men's bar of the Waldorf a tippling tenor suddenly began to sing. First he rendered "Sweet Ad-o--line," then "Auld Lang Syne." When he finished there wasn't a dry eye in the place.

So the Great White Way was no longer as gay, and would never again sparkle with the inimitable spirit of the old Rector's and Diamond Jim Brady. Broadway's night life would shortly be paced by speakeasies and the gangster murders of a street-turned-vicious. The theatre would reflect this. The young actresses whose era it became charmed audiences as nymphomaniacs like Iris March (Katharine Cornell) in *The Green Hat* or outright prostitutes like Sadie Thompson (Jeanne Eagels) in *Rain*. Eugene O'Neill's first full-length play, *Beyond the Horizon*, had already moved uptown from the Provincetown Theatre in Greenwich Village. With this, the old-time playwrights fell back and a new type moved forward.

On this shifting Broadway, *Lightnin'* reached the end of a triumphant two-year run. Frank Bacon was still Lightnin' Bill and he planned to take his play to Chicago, first stop on a nation-wide tour of the Road he knew so well. Said John Golden to himself, as he posted notice for the closing of the play, "This calls for something special." He visited Actors Equity offices and talked to Frank Gillmore, who had become executive secre-tary of the union. The two went to the Lambs to find De Wolf Hopper.

The result was the most emotional closing Broadway has ever known. The afternoon the company was to entrain, ceremonies were held on the stage of the Gaiety Theatre. President Hard-ing sent his Postmaster General, Will H. Hays. Mayor Hylan of New York City made an appearance (late). The poet Bliss Carman recited a specially written "Lightnin' Ode." Golden, Gillmore, and assorted actors and actresses rose to pay heartfelt tribute to Frank Bacon. Packed into the Gaiety were as many members of the profession as could fit in. Others waited on the sidewalk outside. All were members of Actors Equity, grate-ful to Bacon for being the first to strike his play in the hot sum-mer of 1919.

Came the moment to start for Chicago, and the *Lightnin'* troupe assembled on the street before the Gaiety. A brass band began to play, then another—four in all. Word passed down Broadway that the *Lightnin'* cast would parade as far downtown as Thirty-fourth Street and turn west to Penn Station. Crowds began to assemble on the line for march. It was five p.m. and office workers leaving jobs cheered as Bacon, wiping sentimental tears from his eyes, led the company in its farewell march down Broadway.

New Yorkers were aware of Frank Bacon's part in the actors'

strike, and most of those who watched the parade had seen his play. It was a rapidly changing world, with Eugene O'Neill uptown and movie cathedrals like the Strand, Rialto, and Rivoli built especially for the products of Hollywood. Some of those who watched Frank Bacon walk down Broadway may have recognized with a twinge that he symbolized a departing era. An actor who passed most of his life on the Road, then scored unexpectedly on Broadway! He was a type the world was not likely to see again.

At the same time Bacon, for all his folksiness, was an actor who knew his craft, a redoubtable performer. As he marched down Broadway, tears welling in his eyes, those who watched may have thought back on the great actors of years just passed. They were notable figures and, as an obituary of Minnie Maddern Fiske would later say:

"Each, in his way, acted with a passion."

BIBLIOGRAPHY

INDEX

BIBLIOGRAPHY

In addition to contemporary newspapers and magazines, and interviews with those who remember the era the author is indebted to the following books for source material:

Adams, Samuel Hopkins. *A. Woollcott, His Life and His World.* New York: Reynal & Hitchcock, 1945.

Allen, Fred. *Much Ado About Me.* Boston: Little Brown & Co., 1956.

Ardmore, Jane. *The Self Enchanted: Mae Murray, Image of an Era.* New York: McGraw-Hill Book Co., 1959.

Arliss, George. *Up the Years from Bloomsbury.* Boston: Little Brown & Co., 1927.

Barnes, Eric Woollencott. *The Man Who Lived Twice, the Biography of Edward Sheldon.* New York: Charles Scribner's Sons, 1956.

Barrymore, Ethel. *Memories, an Autobiography.* New York: Harper & Bros., 1955.

Beer, Thomas. *The Mauve Decade.* New York: Alfred A. Knopf, 1926.

Belasco, David (edited by Louis V. Defoe). *The Theatre Through Its Stage Door.* New York: Harper & Bros., 1919.

Bell, Archie. *The Clyde Fitch I Knew.* New York: Broadway Publishing Co., 1909.

Blum, Daniel. *A Pictorial History of the American Theatre, 1860–1960.* New York and Philadelphia: Chilton Company, 1950.

Brady, William A. *Showman.* New York: E. P. Dutton & Co., 1937.

Burke, Billie (with Cameron Shipp). *With a Feather on My Nose.* New York: Appleton-Century-Crofts, 1949.

Castle, Irene (as told to Bob and Wanda Duncan). *Castles in the Air.* New York: Doubleday & Co., 1958.

Cobb, Irvin S. *Exit Laughing, an Autobiography.* Indianapolis and New York: Bobbs-Merrill Co., 1941.

Cohan, George M. *Twenty Years on Broadway.* New York: Harper & Bros., 1925.

Courtenay, Marguerite. *Laurette, the Intimate Biography of Laurette Taylor.* New York: Rinehart & Co., 1955.

Davies, Acton. *Maude Adams.* New York: F. A. Stokes, 1901.

Davis, Owen. *I'd Like To Do It Again.* New York: Farrar & Rinehart, 1931.

———. *My First Fifty Years in the Theatre.* Boston: Walter H. Baker Co., 1950.

Downey, Fairfax. *Richard Harding Davis, His Day.* New York: Charles Scribner's Sons, 1933.

Drew, John. *My Years on the Stage.* New York: E. P. Dutton & Co., 1922.

Eaton, Walter Prichard. *At the New Theater and Others, 1908–1910.* Boston: Small Maynard & Co., 1910.

Farnsworth, Marjorie. *The Ziegfeld Follies.* New York: G. P. Putnam's Sons, 1956.

Fowler, Gene. *Good Night, Sweet Prince.* New York: Viking Press, 1944.

Frohman, Daniel. *Memoirs of a Manager.* Garden City, N.Y.: Doubleday Page & Co., 1911.

Gaige, Crosby. *Footlights and Highlights*. New York: E. P. Dutton & Co., 1948.

Golden, John (with Viola Brothers Shore). *Stage Struck*. New York: Samuel French, 1930.

Goodwin, Nat C. *Nat Goodwin's Book*. Boston: Richard G. Badger the Gorham Press, 1914.

Green, Abel (editor). *The Spice of Variety*. New York: Henry Holt & Co., 1952.

———— and Laurie, Joe, Jr. *Show Biz, from Vaude to Video*. New York: Henry Holt & Co., 1951.

Hammond, Percy. *But—Is It Art?* Garden City, N.Y.: Doubleday Page & Co., 1927.

Harding, Alfred. *Revolt of the Actors*. New York: William Morrow & Co., 1929.

Hopper, De Wolf (with W. W. Stout). *Once a Clown, Always a Clown*. Boston: Little Brown & Co., 1927.

Hopper, Hedda. *From Under My Hat*. New York: Doubleday & Co., 1952.

Isman, Felix. *Weber and Fields*. New York: Boni & Liveright, 1924.

Izard, Forrest. *Heroines of the Modern Stage*. New York: Sturgis & Walton, 1915.

Johnson, James Weldon. *Along This Way*. New York: Viking Press, 1933.

Johnston, Alva. *Legendary Mizners*. New York: Farrar Straus & Young, 1953.

Kaye, Joseph. *Victor Herbert*. New York: G. Howard Watt, 1931.

Keaton, Buster (with Charles Samuels). *My Wonderful World of Slapstick*. New York: Doubleday & Co., 1960.

Kirkland, Alexander (editor). *Rector's Naughty 90's Cookbook*. New York: Doubleday & Co., 1949.

Laurie, Joe, Jr. *Vaudeville*. New York: Henry Holt & Co., 1953.

Livingstone, Belle (with Cleveland Amory). *Belle Out of Order*. New York: Henry Holt & Co., 1959.

Loraine, Winifred. *Head Wind, the Story of Robert Loraine*. New York: William Morrow & Co., 1938.

Marbury, Elizabeth. *My Crystal Ball*. New York: Boni & Liveright, 1927.

Marcosson, Isaac F., and Frohman, Daniel. *Charles Frohman, Manager and Man*. New York: Harper & Bros., 1916.

Marks, Edward B. (as told to A. J. Liebling). *They All Sang*. New York: Viking Press, 1934.

McCarthy, James Remington. *Peacock Alley, the Romance of the Waldorf-Astoria*. New York: Harper & Bros., 1931.

McClintic, Guthrie. *Me and Kit*. Boston: Little Brown & Co., 1955.

Middleton, George. *These Things Are Mine*. New York: The Macmillan Co., 1947.

Morehouse, Ward. *Matinee Today, Fifty Years of Our Theatre*. New York: McGraw-Hill Book Co., 1949.

Morell, Parker. *Diamond Jim, the Life and Times of James Buchanan Brady*. New York: Simon & Schuster, 1934.

―――. *Lillian Russell, the Era of Plush*. New York: Random House, 1940.

Morris, Lloyd. *Incredible New York*. New York: Random House, 1951.

―――. *Not So Long Ago*. New York: Random House, 1949.

―――. *Postscript to Yesterday*. New York: Random House, 1947.

Moses, Montrose J., and Gerson, Virginia. *Clyde Fitch and His Letters*. Boston: Little Brown & Co., 1924.

Nathan, George Jean. *Since Ibsen*. New York: Alfred A. Knopf, 1933.

————. *The Theatre, The Drama, The Girls*. New York: Alfred A. Knopf, 1921.

Oppenheimer, George (editor). *The Passionate Playgoer*. New York: Viking Press, 1958.

Patterson, Ada. *Maude Adams, a Biography*. New York: Meyer Bros. & Co., 1907.

Pickford, Mary. *Sunshine and Shadow*. New York: Doubleday & Co., 1955.

Pollock, Channing. *Harvest of My Years*. Indianapolis and New York: Bobbs-Merrill Co., 1943.

Rector, George. *The Girl from Rector's*. Garden City, N.Y.: Doubleday Page & Co., 1927.

Robbins, Phyllis. *Maude Adams, an Intimate Portrait*. New York: G. P. Putnam's Sons, 1956.

Rogers, W. G., and Weston, Mildred. *Carnival Crossroads, the Story of Times Square*. New York: Doubleday & Co., 1960.

Russell, Charles Edward. *Julia Marlowe, Her Life and Art*. New York: D. Appleton Co., 1927.

Schriftgeisser, Karl. *Oscar of the Waldorf*. New York: E. P. Dutton & Co., 1943.

Skinner, Otis. *Footlights and Spotlights*. Indianapolis and New York: Bobbs-Merrill Co., 1924.

Smith, Harry B. *First Nights and First Editions*. Boston: Little Brown & Co., 1931.

Sothern, E. H. (edited by Fairfax Downey). *Julia Marlowe's Story*. New York: Rinehart & Co., 1957.

Sullivan, Mark. *Our Times, the Turn of the Century*. New York: Charles Scribner's Sons, 1926.

Taylor, Robert Lewis. *W. C. Fields, His Follies and Fortunes*. New York: Doubleday & Co., 1949.

Thomas, Augustus. *The Print of My Remembrance*. New York: Charles Scribner's Sons, 1922.

Timberlake, Craig. *The Bishop of Broadway, David Belasco, His Life and Work*. New York: Library Publishers, 1954.

Tucker, Sophie. *Some of These Days*. Privately Printed, 1945.

Veiller, Bayard. *The Fun I've Had!* New York: Reynal & Hitchcock, 1941.

Winter, William. *The Life of David Belasco*. 2 vols. New York: Moffat Yard & Co., 1918.

Wodehouse, P. G., and Bolton, Guy. *Bring On the Girls!* New York: Simon & Schuster, 1953.

Wynn, Keenan (as told to James Brough). *Ed Wynn's Son*. New York: Doubleday & Co., 1959.

The Saturday Evening Post, Theatre Magazine, and Anniversary issues of *Stage*.

INDEX